The **Teen** Whisperer

COLLINS LIVING

An Imprint of HarperCollins*Publishers*

The **Teen Whisperer**

How to Break Through the

Silence and Secrecy of Teenage Life

Mike Linderman

with Gary Brozek

This book is designed to give information on various conditions, treatments, and procedures for your personal knowledge and to help you be a more informed parent where the mental health of your teen is concerned. It is not intended to be complete or exhaustive, nor is it a substitute for the advice of your physician or other health care professional. You should seek professional advice and/or treatment promptly for any specific problem your teen may have.

All efforts have been made to ensure the accuracy of the information contained in this book as of the date published. The authors and the publisher expressly disclaim responsibility for any adverse effects arising from the use or application of the information contained herein.

Names and identifying characteristics of the individuals discussed have been changed to protect their privacy, and in some cases composites have been created to facilitate the discussion and aid in providing advice.

A hardcover edition of this book was published in 2007 by Collins, an imprint of HarperCollins Publishers. THE TEEN WHISPERER. Copyright © 2007 by Mike Linderman. All rights reserved. Printed in the United States of America. No part of this book may be used or reproduced in any manner whatsoever without written permission except in the case of brief quotations embodied in critical articles and reviews. For information, address HarperCollins Publishers, 10 East 53rd Street, New York, NY 10022.

HarperCollins books may be purchased for educational, business, or sales promotional use. For information, please write: Special Markets Department, HarperCollins Publishers, 10 East 53rd Street, New York, NY 10022.

FIRST PAPERBACK EDITION PUBLISHED 2008

Designed by Sunil Manchikanti

The Library of Congress has cataloged the hardcover edition as follows:

Linderman, Mike.
    The teen whisperer : how to break through the silence and secrecy of teenage life / Mike Linderman, with Gary Brozek. – 1st ed.
        p. cm.
    Includes index.
    ISBN 978-0-06-123865-9
        1. Parent and teenager.   2. Adolescent psychology.   I. Brozek, Gary.   II. Title.

HQ799.15.L55 2007
649'.154—dc22   2007019232

ISBN 978-0-06-137374-9 (pbk.)

08 09 10 11 12 WBC/RRD 10 9 8 7 6 5 4 3 2 1

For my dad,
BRUCE LINDERMAN, 1942–2006,
I miss you.

For JANNA, ALICIA, CODY, and JESSY,
Thanks, guys, for sticking with me
through the tough times and for being
the greatest family a guy could ask for.

Acknowledgments

If I've learned one thing over the years, it's that no project of any kind is possible without contributions from many corners. I've been blessed to have had significant input and support from many people. Among them, I want to thank the following:

Kristen McGuiness: For helping me formulate the foundation of this book and teaching the basics to a "greenhorn" in the business.

Claire Fontaine: For your friendship, for your honesty, and for sharing your story and creating the opportunity for me to tell mine.

Mia Fontaine: For your attitude and orneriness; you were an amazing teen and have become an even more amazing young woman.

Matt Harper: I could not have asked for a better editor. I'm grateful for the hours you spent on the phone walking me through the process. Your patience, brilliance, and sense of humor made the entire process a wonderful experience.

Stacey Glick: You're a wonderfully supportive agent. Thanks for your tireless efforts on my behalf and for always being there to reassure me.

Judith Regan: For believing in who I am and what I do enough to initiate this project.

Michelle Dominguez: You are a publicist extraordinaire. Thank you for going the extra mile to put the word out.

Thanks to the rest of the staff at HarperCollins for always supporting this project.

Cameron and Chaffin and the rest of the staff past and present at Spring Creek Lodge Academy: This is the place where it all started. Thank you for believing in me and taking a chance on a local boy right out of graduate school.

Mom and Dad: Bruce and Nancy Linderman, the parents who built the foundation of what has become my approach with kids. You raised two amazing kids . . . and then me. Two out of three ain't bad.

Steve and Stacy: As siblings you knocked me around, picked me up, and shared the lessons of our parents and grandparents.

Alicia, Cody, and Jessy: Thanks for your support and patience through this project and the past year in general. You are three special kids. I have been blessed to have children like you. I am proud of you and I love you.

Janna: For putting up with the late nights, the groggy mornings, the cranky moods, and the really long hours . . . and the bad days too! I have loved you since I was fifteen years old, and I love you still.

Gary Brozek: Without your tireless efforts, this book would never have gotten off the ground. I am deeply indebted to you. You brought my words and stories to a format that we can share with the world. You are the consummate professional.

The kids I have worked with over the past decade: You have touched my heart, recharged my soul, and made me the therapist I am today.

Contents

Part IV Developing the Right Approach

How to Use This Book

No two kids and issues are ever going to be the same. The approach I've taken in this book reflects that reality. Eventually, I'll tell you how I learned the importance of being adaptable and flexible. The same is true with how you choose to read this book.

I've broken the book down into four separate sections. Part I serves as an introduction to me, my philosophy, and how it was shaped by my experiences in working with kids. The method I've devised is also based on some theory—a school of thought called reality therapy.

Part II expands on that theory by incorporating a discussion of your teen's five primary needs. I firmly believe that most of the teens we find in crisis or who are acting out inappropriately are doing so because those needs aren't being met. I discuss each of those five needs so you can better understand some of the "why" behind your teen's sometimes mysterious actions. At the end of each chapter in Part II, there are quick guides to recognizing the signs of these unmet needs. Use them as a checklist to help evaluate what your child is experiencing.

Part III discusses the types of acting-out behaviors that can result from unmet needs, helping you understand why your teen is making the self-destructive choices that result in harmful or dangerous behavior.

Finally, Part IV is where you combine all this knowledge with an understanding of teen communication to put together an approach that will help you lift your teen out of a dangerous pattern of acting out behavior.

You can certainly read the book from start to finish, and I encourage you to do that. But it may be that you are not as interested in the background information and are looking for more immediate solutions to a crisis situation that you've already identified. If that's the case, then by using either the table of contents or the book's index you can find solutions in Part IV that deal with some of the typical acting out behaviors teens engage in—drinking, violence, eating disorders, and others. While I think it's important for you to understand some of the thinking that underpins my philosophy, that information, depending upon where you are in the process with your child, may or may not be the most pertinent information in the book.

Think of it this way. When I was a firefighter, I had to study a lot about fuels and the effect the environment can have on a fire. When I arrived on scene and a building was already engulfed in flames, I didn't have the luxury to study how the fire started, why it was spreading, and other things like that. I had to put it out. I had to assess whether lives were at risk. By doing that initial evaluation, I could then determine my course of action. That's what you need to do as a parent. Are you seeing and smelling smoke? Is the situation already aflame? Or are you just thinking about and planning for and anticipating problems in the future? Depending on where you are, you need to use this book differently. It's a tool, and it's effective only when used properly.

I will repeat this point over and over again in Parts II and III, but you need to understand this from the get-go. If you believe that your teen is a threat to himself or herself, to you, or to someone else, you must act immediately. Throughout Part III, I offer you lists of warning signs you can use to determine what level of potential threat you're dealing with.

Most of you are probably not at the immediate crisis stage, so you still have some flexibility in using this book as a resource. Ideally, you'd read all my words of wisdom as I've laid them out here, but I know that in the real world, that's not always the most effective solution. Maybe there's a lesson to be learned here about flexibility and adaptability.

The Teen Whisperer

Part I

Meet the Teen Whisperer

1

You Can Call Me Mr. Mike

You can call me Mr. Mike. Just about every teen or parent I've worked with has. Once you get to know me better, you'll understand that I don't stand on ceremony much. I demand respect (and get it) because I earn it. I don't have a fancy pedigree from Ivy League schools, nor do I have a trail of abbreviations dangling off my last name like an anchor to keep my overinflated ego from floating off into the clouds.

I live in Trout Creek, Montana, a town of fewer than a thousand souls, and folks here more than likely remember me as a chubby little runny-nosed kid who left home at eighteen to go to school and serve in the military. They might mention that a couple of years later, I returned to town and took up work in the lumber mill while hanging my shingle in private practice for a while. And if you really prod them enough, they'll start talking about my football days and remember that like my father before me, I take pride in my community, head up the local school board, coach various ball teams, and have raised up three kids as solid citizens. Around here, nobody cares what degrees I've earned; they just know that I've got a way with kids.

Not that I'm the kind of guy who's competitive and keeps score or anything, but I do have a pretty good track record of success. I can't tell you that every kid I've ever worked with has been turned around

100%. That's not a realistic expectation. Since I'm always encouraging the kids I work with to deal more effectively with reality, I have to place the same demand on myself. I can remember only two kids whom I've had to refer to other therapists because I just couldn't make a really strong connection with them, or they simply refused outright to cooperate with me. That stuff happens, and I'm at a loss to explain why, other than to chalk it up to the nearly infinite variables that go into human relationships. I haven't lost a lot of sleep thinking about those two losses, though I do tend to be very hard on myself. I've got far too many other places to focus my time and energies on. Took me a while to learn that, but it was a very valuable lesson—not something I could have gotten out of any lecture or reading assignment from my days at the University of Montana, Park College, or Montana State Northern.

I'm not a theory kind of guy. I learned lessons about raising kids and getting those who are off track back into the fold the hard way—through more than 25,000 hours of clinical work with teens and young adults. I've done a lot of different things in my life—worked in that lumber mill, served as a firefighter in the U.S. Air Force, ran a forklift, even clerked at a convenience store to help pay for my undergraduate education. But nothing has been as difficult, exhausting, rewarding, and completely fulfilling as the work I did for ten years as the clinical director at the Spring Creek Lodge Academy in Thompson Falls, Montana. Now that I'm back in private practice, working with at-risk kids in this setting, I can see how influential my years at that alternative school have been. I know I'll carry those lessons over into whatever next steps I take next in my career.

Spring Creek Lodge is a year-round boarding school, a place where kids who haven't found success in traditional schools (and often in other alternative educational settings) can find a quiet place away from the negative environments and peer groups that contributed to some of their academic and social problems.

Along with any academic deficiencies they may have to make up for, the students there are often placed in that setting by their parents because of addiction (drugs and alcohol), difficulty with anger management, sexual and emotional abuse, and a host of other issues. I dare say I've not seen it all here, but I've seen a fair bit of the spectrum of troubles that teens encounter in making that most difficult transition from child to adult.

Maybe because I was born and raised in this area, I think this locale has had a lot to do with my success. Like most rural communities, Trout Creek has undergone changes in the forty-odd years my family has been here since moving from Puyallup, Washington, in the mid-1960s. My parents wanted to escape the big-city influences that were encroaching on just about every place of any size during that tumultuous decade, and rural Montana and a 180-acre parcel of ranch and forest land backing up a mountainside between the Bitterroot and Cabinet Ranges seemed about ideal. Of course, nothing is ever completely perfect, but Trout Creek has remained my home, the place where my wife, Janna, and I have raised our three kids. I don't ever remember anybody using the term "family values" around here or mentioning that it takes a village to raise up kids right. We didn't talk it; we lived it. Same thing went on in Spring Creek—everybody was everybody's business.

YOUNG PEOPLE TODAY

I'm accustomed to telling it like it is, so let's get some things out of way. It may strike you as a bit odd that a man who lives in rural America—a guy who was raised on a hobby ranch and broke his first horse at thirteen under his grandfather's watchful eye—has anything at all to say about today's young people. It may seem strange that a stereotypical farm boy, who grew up mending fences and pulling calves with his tough-as-dirt father, feels that he has what it takes to relate to America's youth. I'll admit that I carried a pocketknife to school every day, not a cell phone or iPod. Instant messaging meant my mother stepping out onto the porch to holler at us to come in from the barn, field, or woods for our supper, not something sent electronically over a high-speed data line or bounced off a cellular relay tower. Belly shirts were something that we wore under our shoulder pads during late-summer football practice, not a fashion trend designed to show off a pierced navel and a tattooed wedge of flesh above a pair of low, low, low-rise jeans.

I understand the reality of where and when I grew up is a bit different from where most of you are raising your children. I also understand that the complexities our teens face—what they're exposed to from the media, from their parents, and from their peers—differ greatly from what I encountered. The question comes up all the time about whether or not teens are different today from the teens of earlier days. I'd have to say that they are.

Despite these differences, and despite the fact that many of the things I grew up with are no longer prevalent today, much of my experience and my success with troubled teenagers has come from my unconventional background. For most of these kids, their experiences and mine are a world and a lifetime apart. I'm not trying to pretend that I know what they're going through, and they don't ever assume that I should. When they come into my office, they do so because they realize that my advice is not the kind most therapists are going to give them. A lot of what I've learned about helping kids has come through my experiences in working with young people, but it's also come from what I've learned living a life. What I have to say is different because where I've been is different.

"Only Two Games Out"

Rather than tell you why you should believe some of things I say, let me show you. That's how I'm used to dealing with issues of trust. I've always found it best to ground every discussion in the here and now. Shortly before leaving Spring Creek, I sat in my office. As was my custom, I began the day at my desk, my feet up on its cluttered surface (I love my job but am not a big fan of paperwork), and I scanned the opposite wall. On it hung dozens of pictures my kids had sent me, and each face told a story. Most of them were success stories—but remember, I'm awfully hard on myself, so what I tend to recall most often is the handful of times when I failed to help a kid find his or her way through the dense undergrowth of adolescence and early adulthood.

Before I could get too involved in my memories, the door swung open and in stepped Lauren, her blunt-cut chestnut hair curtaining her cheeks. She pushed her hair to the side to reveal a spade-shaped face dominated by a pair of large doe eyes.

"Hey, Mr. Mike. Only two games out."

Lauren was from a small college town in Ohio, about fifty miles from Cleveland. In my first meetings with any of the kids I work with, I let them set the tone, trying to get them to tell me a bit about themselves. In Lauren's case, I quickly learned that her devotion to the Cleveland Indians baseball team was almost as intense as mine is to the Seattle Mariners. She and her dad used to watch all the games together when she was younger, but that was a lifetime of heartache ago for both of them.

We talk about the potential playoff matchups, and what the schedule told us about the last weeks of September. She reminded me that the Mariners would be only playing out the string. There was a practiced kind of teasing quality to her voice. In this context, it was mostly harmless, but I knew that like a lot of the kids I had dealt with in the ten years I'd been at that school, she was a master manipulator.

"And how about it, Mr. Mike. Travis Hafner for MVP?"

"Anything's possible, kiddo. You know that."

She saw through my effort to transition from small talk to the real issues, and she gave me a sarcastic smile. "That's why I always reach for the stars." She rolled her eyes.

I swung my feet off the desk and tugged at my tie and scratched my neck. All these years, and I was still not really comfortable wearing the dang thing.

"Any of those stars you're reaching for making it into the classroom?"

"Everything's sweet there, if that's what you're asking."

I didn't respond. I rolled my chair out from behind the desk and crept closer to her.

Lauren had been holding my gaze, but now her eyes found the window and then wandered over the faces on the wall, which she surely could have memorized after nearly eighteen months in the program. Until this week, she was within a month or two of earning her way out of the program and returning to her parents, or to whatever next steps awaited her.

"I've been doing my work. Some of it. A lot of this stuff is just so bogus. I feel like I've been studying the Constitution my whole life. I want to amend the damn thing to outlaw the study of it." She looked at me, her eyes expectant, hoping I'd reward her wit with a laugh. When I didn't, she pressed on, spinning a more intricate web of half-truths and blaming. When she began her usual litany of the teachers at her old high school back in Ohio and their campaign of conspiracy to get rid of her, I held up my hand. Lauren knew better than that. The past was not prologue in my office. The past was prohibited in most instances. We had to deal with the here and now.

"What was working for you before this week?"

She whipped her head from side to side and ended up staring at the ceiling, her teeth gritted, her lips pulled across them in a tight grimace. "Staying on task. Of course that was what was working, but what about when the task never ends? What if you just don't give a shit anymore about doing the same freaking things all the time? I want this to end. I want this to be over."

I slid closer to her. My proximity made Lauren look at me. She held my gaze, though both of us knew that what she was telling me was a bunch of bull. Spring Creek operates under a strict system of points and levels. Do the right things in the classroom and in your interactions with peers and staff, and you pile up points that move you up levels and closer to going home and "graduating." Mess up, and you lose points—what we mostly refer to as being "consequented." Rewards and consequences.

You're going to hear a lot more about those concepts. Get consequented enough times and you drop a level or even levels. Each level entitles you to certain privileges. Drop a level, and you lose those privileges and earn the right to begin the Sisyphean task of rolling that rock back up the hill until you get to the top and stay there. I didn't have to explain any of this to Lauren. She was one of our veteran rock rollers.

With my eyes still locked on Lauren's, I kept my voice as steady and as neutral as possible and told her, "You know, kiddo. This is going to be hard for you to hear. But you've got to understand this. You are eighteen years old, and you have so little integrity." I saw her flinch at that word, but I pressed on. "You come into this office and you tell me everything's fine. I know that you know that I know that you dropped a level. I know that you were consequented for passing notes to a boy. I know that when Ms. Allen confronted you about it, you made up some piss-poor excuse and then ranted and raved at her for being the one who caught you doing something you so clearly know is a violation. You're this close"—I held up my fingers with just a sliver of daylight showing between them—"to getting out of here. You tell every one of us all the time that you want nothing more than to get done with this program and this place. Soon as you get close to the finish line, you bolt off the course. You may not have enough re-spect for yourself to come in here and lie, but you better have more re-spect for me than to do it. All anyone around here has ever done is root for you and support you. Blaming them just doesn't cut it with me. You're the one in the batter's box. All we can do is put you there so you can get a hit. Don't blame us when you strike out."

The contrast between the Lauren after my little speech and the one who had walked in there earlier was stark. She seemed to have shrunk, to have folded in on herself. Her arms crossed defiantly across her chest, her gaze narrowed, her brow furrowed, she seemed to be drilling herself through her seat and down through the floor. I saw the tendons in her jaw pulsing. Lauren had been a part of my anger management group for nearly a year. Believe it or not, her re-sponse was a definite improvement over her past fits of hurling ob-jects and having blood-curdling fits of yelling and swearing.

Deciding that our session was over, Lauren stood. I could see the ef-fort it was taking her to remain in control. From her posture and from the "fuck you" that I could see straining against the hard thin line of her lips strung like barbed wire across her face. I could tell that she was really pissed off. My heart went out to her, but I was equally unhappy about these developments as she was—maybe even more so.

"I'll see you tomorrow. We can talk more about all this then."

My words were met with silence and Lauren's defiant strut as she exited the building, pushing the sleeves of her sweater up and punching the air.

Every Kid Has a Story

Most every kid who sees me as a therapist has a tale of woe I need to connect to their present situation. Lauren came to us after failing most of her classes in her junior year at the local public high school she attended. During her early sessions with me, she stated that her problem was a kind of reverse prejudice. She was labeled a talented and gifted kid early on. Her parents were both professors, one in English and the other in comparative literature, at the small liberal arts school in town. She did eight years of private school, first at a Montessori school and then a private academy as a day student. She earned top grades, but when it came time to move into the private high school, she balked at the idea, saying that she hated the elitist nature of private schools.

Her parents pressed her for a reason for her decision to go to the public school, but Lauren was tight-lipped and insisted she had just had enough. No real reason. Just wanted a change. They suspected that something was going on, but they didn't match up their summer travels to do research with Lauren's staying at home with her grandparents as a possible cause of some problems. Mom and Dad were both working on books—she a novel and he a textbook—and the early days of their shared interest in Native American culture, in movies, and in Lauren's budding field hockey career waned and then ended.

Lauren excelled in the classroom at first, but as the year progressed her initial attempts to audition for parts in the school's drama productions proved disastrous. She resigned herself to working on the makeup and props crews, and the behind-the-scenes anonymity of those roles bled into the rest of her social life as well. All her friends from her private school days seemed to abandon her. Her parents chalked up her withdrawal, and the hours she spent holed up in her room, as a typical adolescent phase. They expressed some concern over her choice to go Goth, and they tolerated the dark clothes and what they felt was macabre makeup—which to them seemed better suited to a production of *Dracula* than to normal social outings. However, they drew the line at piercings and tattoos. As long as Lauren's grades remained good, her parents remained alert but unconcerned. What they didn't realize was that a young woman with Lauren's brainpower was going to do well academically as much from habit as from a real desire to achieve. What they also didn't realize was that their daughter was screaming for their attention.

The only way she was going to get it was by escalating her escapades. The first time the campus police called to let them know that their daughter had been found drunk in a men's dormitory stairwell, Lauren's parents dismissed it as youthful indiscretion. Their daughter's contrition nearly shamed them for being so hard on her when they grounded her for two weekends. By the time Lauren was a junior, she was a regular fixture at on-campus and off-campus parties at the college, she had had multiple sex partners, and her grade point average had fallen from a sterling 4.0 to an awful 2.5. Her parents tried private counseling to determine the source of her deep unhappiness, but that proved unsuccessful because of Lauren's ability to manipulate both them and her therapist.

They thought a change in environment would do her good, and re-enrolled her in private school two months into her junior year. That experiment lasted only three weeks. Lauren took an old field hockey stick to school and did more than $25,000 in damage to the school's audiovisual supply room. This time she showed no contrition. The school's administrators were willing to give her a second chance, but on the morning after the attack, Lauren's mother accompanied her daughter to her locker and discovered a cache of alcohol and several vials of Ritalin and Percocet. The die was cast.

The first time I met Lauren, sullen wouldn't even begin to describe her. Only when I finally got her to understand that she was the expert on her own life and psyche and that I wasn't there—as she so aptly put it—as a "Band-Aid man" did we establish some kind of common ground. In time, she slowly revealed the kind of pressures put on her as a faculty kid and the unrelenting forces that demanded she fit in with her peer group. Always slightly overweight and with an athletic build, she suffered from some serious body image issues, and the popular piranha among her classmates had fed on that weakness, eventually driving her to public school.

Cast adrift, and with parents who thought that riding it out and tolerating her expressions of individuality constituted the best practice, she hooked up with the wrong set of kids and made incredibly poor choices. Because Lauren never told her parents about her painful experiences at the private school, they had no way of knowing that in her mind, they were part of the vast conspiracy that was allied against her. Taking out a series of DVD players, VCRs, and television sets in the audiovisual supply room let everyone know for the first time how truly angry she was. Once unleashed, that anger proved awfully hard to put back in the bottle.

Revisiting Lauren

By the time my day was nearly over, I'd run the mental videotape of our session over and over again in my mind. Ultimately, I decided I'd done the right thing and said what needed to be said. This was a young woman who would sabotage any success she might ever have, not realizing that all the payback she was giving out to everyone else was really just hurting her in the long run. After being in this program so long, she knew that the consequences of her rules violations meant additional time at Spring Creek. I wanted her to know that there were consequences associated with that as well. I couldn't go along with her plan and not call her on her increasingly obvious self-destructive pattern and lack of values. I also knew that once I said something, it was out there, and there was no taking it back. It's a whole lot easier to let the cat out of the bag than to put it back in. Most important, though, I'd also spoken the truth.

With my lunch box in hand and a couple of file folders tucked under my arm, I made my way toward my pickup. Late afternoons in the Montana summer are some of my favorite times of year, and on that day the sun filtered through the trees just as a soft breeze started to fan me. I was about to get into my truck when I saw Lauren sitting under a lodgepole pine, her face turned upward. She wasn't basking in the sun but recovering from a crying jag. I set my things down, walked over to her, and sat. At first she didn't acknowledge my presence and kept breaking off pieces of bark and flicking them. I wasn't about to back off on what I'd said earlier, but I also knew that she needed some gesture from me to let her know that even though I was greatly disappointed in her, I hadn't stopped caring about her. I spoke some words to that effect.

She nodded and choked out a barely audible "I know."

This wasn't acting on her part. I could tell she was genuinely upset and moved. Her lips quivered into a smile. "It's just that what you said hurt. It reminded me of what my dad kept telling me after a while. That I was never going to be anything in life but what I was—a screw-up."

"Hey, listen, I've screwed up bunches of times. Just because you screw up doesn't mean you are a screw-up. You just made a choice that didn't work for you. I know it doesn't feel like that right now, but it's so. It's possible for me to not like what you did, but that doesn't mean I don't like you. Everybody here wants to see you do well. We've seen you do well, and you know yourself that you feel better when you follow your heart and succeed."

Lauren's stuttering post-crying breathing had calmed. She smiled a bit when I reminded her of the good choices she'd made. We talked for a few minutes longer, and she assured me that she'd be back in my office for her next appointment. That's what I love about working with kids. In the course of an hour, we've run the emotional gamut together. No matter how bad things seem to get sometimes, there's always hope.

I checked my watch. It was almost 4:30, and I had to get somewhere. Lauren noticed and asked, "Got a ball game?"

"I sure do."

"Don't want to be late for that, coach. Hope you do a number on them."

I thanked her and headed back to the truck. Lauren waved as I pulled out of the parking lot, and I saw her get up off the ground and brush herself off and head back toward the dormitories. That's what we hope for a lot of the time. Just to see them make an effort.

MANAGING FROM THE DUGOUT

The American Legion field is nearly halfway across the county, and it took me fifty minutes to get there. I thought about how much my approach to Lauren and other kids like her had changed. I hadn't always been able to talk to my counselees the way I had with Lauren. I'd had to take my lumps more than a time or two—both before and after I earned the privilege of being the clinical director at Spring Creek. Now it seemed a natural fit for me. After all, I'd been up and down a few levels myself, and had to deal with some consequences myself.

After high school, I attended Montana State University in Bozeman for a semester and then finished out the year at the University of Montana. It was a tough year financially. My parents couldn't provide much financial assistance, and because there were a couple of really lean years when we didn't file a tax return, I couldn't apply for financial aid. Janna and I were together already, and as much as we were able to support each other emotionally, the simple truth was that we couldn't make a go of my being a full-time student while working at a minimum wage job at a convenience store.

I faced a hard choice but made the right one. I stopped going to school and came back to Trout Creek. I took a job at a lumber mill and spent my days stacking boards. For a guy with a strong inclination to be around people and talk with them, this wasn't an ideal situation, but I had to do what I had to do. When the mill burned down, I was out of a job. I did some construction work with my father but saw no real future for me there. I faced another tough decision. If I was ever going to get a college education, I was going to have to take some drastic measures.

For me, that meant having to join the U.S. Air Force. In hindsight, that was the best decision I'd ever made. During my first semester in college several years earlier, I had fallen in love with the study of psychology, and through various Air Force programs I was able to get an undergraduate degree in social psychology. I also traveled a good bit, spent some significant time in Egypt during the Gulf War, endured a few missile attacks and some terrorists threats, and seven years later earned my honorable discharge.

Throughout my time in the military, I learned a whole lot more than the firefighting skills I was putting to use in my base assignment. I learned to get along with a variety of people with diverse backgrounds, I understood the importance of keeping cool under pressure, and I experienced what it means to be adaptable. I also took advantage of every possible opportunity to take college courses— graduate and undergraduate—while in the military. When I got out of the Air Force, I wanted to put those skills and my education to good use and give back to the community that had raised me. So, seven years later, after I got discharged, Janna, the kids, and I (all three had been born by then) headed back to Trout Creek.

When I returned, I had all of my graduate work completed but was still short half of the three thousand hours of practicum required by the state of Montana. The bookwork was pretty easy for me, and I hung out my shingle as an intern while I was still getting my state certifications. Getting clients in a small town like Trout Creek wasn't easy, and I wasn't making nearly enough from my counseling work to survive on, so I had a regular day job running a forklift and saw clients in the evenings. That is, I saw clients when they decided to keep their appointments. They didn't do that regularly, and they paid me even less regularly. Many of the reasons for their sporadic attendance were financial, but in a small town like Trout Creek, a real stigma was attached to seeking psychological counseling.

My transition from all my book learning to practical applications of that knowledge in the real world was bit bumpy, and I learned pretty quickly that I was going to have to fly by the seat of my pants. I also learned that my aggressive "let's get 'er done" nature wasn't my best asset away from the football field or the job site. I was sometimes so eager to get my clients to see the answer that I was constantly giving it to them instead of letting them come to the realization themselves.

I was blunt and I was direct, but I was also a lot less effective than I wanted to be. It was a tough position to be in, and often my direct communications with my clients resulted, unfortunately, in hostility and resentment toward me. The more I practiced, the more I found myself scratching my head about how I could best handle working with patients—especially teenagers. My straight-talking attitude wasn't just frustrating my patients; it was frustrating me as well.

An Approach That Works

It was not until the administration at Spring Creek Lodge Academy asked me to do some part-time counseling there that I really began to see what methods were effective with kids and why they were effective. At the time, Spring Creek was nothing like the size it is today. Back when I first started going there to see maybe three kids out of the total enrollment of thirty, I couldn't imagine that it would be what it is today, with an enrollment of three hundred, a staff of eight therapists (social workers), and a national reputation for excellence. When I first started, I had no office on the campus. I met with my counselees wherever I could. I wasn't handed a mission statement and wasn't told what to do with the kids. I could shape my approach to them as I saw fit.

I spent a good bit of time on campus just observing the kids as they interacted with one another. One of the school's primary concerns is that its students act as peer-advisors with one another. The first time I saw one of the kids give direct feedback to another I was shocked. She couldn't have been more than seventeen, she was a mere wisp of a girl at barely five feet one or two and eighty pounds, and she was talking to a hulking kid easily a foot taller and a hundred pounds heavier. She looked him in the eye and said, "My experience with you is that you come across as all hard and uncaring, and that's just a bunch of crap. It is your way of hiding your insecurities. We all know it is a bunch of b.s. because all you want is for people to care about you."

I was waiting for some kind of volcanic response, but none came. At first he just stared hard at her, his face a rock. Then he looked down at the ground and nodded—barely perceptible nods at first, and then longer and wider arcs. Finally he mumbled, "Thank you."

What puzzled me at first was why her direct approach with him worked and the direct approaches that I had tried in my private practice did not. I quickly realized that the way I had been thinking about communication had a lot to do with it. Spring Creek was an environment that encouraged honest communication on a daily basis. The kids were in a situation where most of them had been through individual or group counseling (or both) before, and now they were immersed in a culture that expected and encouraged that kind of self-assessment and peer assessment. By the time I showed up, those thirty or so kids were fairly practiced in the art and felt comfortable (most of them at least) talking to one another in that way and thinking that way.

In addition, it occurred to me that the young woman I observed giving feedback to the other student was doing so from a position of equality. They were peers, and she clearly had earned his respect and trust. A part of that may have been attributable to the fact that he could have just easily unloaded on her, and the more time I spent at Spring Creek the more I witnessed that. "Unloaded" is probably not the right word. When I first observed kids talking so honestly with one another, it sure appeared to me that they were unloading on one another, but the more times I saw them interacting that way, the more natural, honest, and purely intentioned it seemed. I filed that lesson away. The staff made sure that giving feedback was appropriate, useful, and not motivated by revenge, resentment, or anger. The kids weren't getting even with one another; they were giving something that was, in the long run if not immediately, welcomed and purposeful.

Even though I had not been given specific instructions on what to say to these kids and how to say it, I was learning how I could modify and refine my therapeutic approach to dovetail with theirs. I remembered the words of wisdom my grandfather had given me when I was thirteen or fourteen years old. He said, "You've got to treat horses a lot like people you love. Give them a little bit of sugar but a whole lot of love." I saw at Spring Creek how that principle could be put to better use. Even though I was with those kids only a few hours a week at most, they were under adult care twenty-four hours a day. Notice I didn't say "supervision." They were under the care of adults and received the kind of attention that their behavior merited. If they did something positive, they received positive attention. If they did something negative, they received negative attention. No matter what, they were receiving some kind of attention from an adult. I can't tell you the number of kids I've worked with over the years who felt as though they'd been left to raise themselves and were simply clamoring for attention. They needed to feel that they belonged, and when they felt as if their ties with family had been severed, they turned to other groups to get the attention they were deprived of at home.

As my caseload increased at Spring Creek, I learned more and more about what it meant to be an effective counselor. In working with young people, I didn't have the same hesitation that I did when working with adults. As a twenty-six-year-old or twenty-seven-year-old newly hatched therapist I often experienced a lot of self-doubt about my ability to assist someone who had lived longer and experienced more than I had. With kids, that self-questioning wasn't as prominent. I'd been there and done that myself, and I was also working through some of these issues with my kids at home—though certainly not to the same extent as with the more troubled young people at Spring Creek.

My days as a forklift jockey ended when I got hurt on the job, and that made me determined—and I'll admit not a little bit desperate— for something to latch on to that could keep me afloat financially and emotionally. I saw a need at Spring Creek that I could fill, and that as much as anything else prompted me to approach the administrators there with the idea of becoming a full-time member of the staff. They agreed, and the rest is history. While working at Spring Creek, I had kids under my care from just about every state in the union, from urban gang-bangers to kids from the most sheltered and prosperous suburbs. In the course of my career and in raising my own three children, I became able to combine what I've learned in the field with some of the theory I learned in my graduate and undergraduate courses to create a program that will help you deal with the issues you encounter with your own teen. I've enjoyed some great success by using these strategies and investing the time and effort necessary to make it clear to these troubled young people that their lives matter to me. Because of that, I'm heading toward the baseball diamond when a part of me wishes I could just go home and relax. That small part of me loses every time.

We've got a 6:00 start, so as soon as I get out of the truck, I walk over to the dugout, grab a glove and a bag of balls, and head to the pitcher's mound. Various football-related injuries and what seems like a million tosses in batting practice, games of catch with my kids, and ranch work have taken their toll on my shoulder. I don't want to waste any pitches on warming up, and the first few tosses either land in the dirt or rattle against the backstop, a far piece from where the first hitter stands. In time, I find my groove and lay a few good ones in there. I squint into the angling sunlight, and a drop of sweat stings my eyes. I'm happy, though. I love what I'm doing and what I've just done all day. The loose and loopy banter of the kids is like a favorite song I could play over and over.

Batting practice over, I look into the bleachers, and there are Janna and Jessy and Alicia. Cody is warming up in the bullpen as tonight's pitcher, and he waves at his mom and siblings. Since getting my degree in counseling and taking the job at Spring Creek Lodge Academy, I've done over twenty-five thousand hours of counseling with at-risk kids. I've seen and heard some things that would chill your blood and bring a tear to your eye. My oldest, Alicia, is seventeen now. I'm not real good with math, but the way I figure it, those twenty-five thousand hours can't hold a candle to seventeen years times three hundred sixty-five days times twenty-four hours a day of being a parent. I'm proud of what I do and how I'm able to help kids from families other than my own find their place in the world.

My work at Spring Creek has helped me find my place as a parent. I was lucky that I had a good place to start. My mother and father were money poor but attention rich. As a result, I never felt a lack of any kind. We had tough times, but I don't remember that they felt that way. My brother and sister and I talk about that, now that we're grown and have families of our own. We've all got more materially than our parents did, and yet it's a greater challenge to keep that family feeling going.

Like I said, I'm sometimes prone to look too hard at myself and my successes and failures. My dad always said that it ain't bragging if it's so, and that's how I feel about stating that if I've done one thing right in this world, it's raising good kids. In fact, this evening as the game begins, I'm still basking in the warm glow of the feeling that hit me last night when Alicia asked Janna and me to chaperone her junior prom. At a time in their lives when a lot of kids are doing everything they can to separate themselves from their parents, our kid wants us to be there to share in one of the biggest nights of her young life. That connection is what I want Lauren to be able to feel again, what I want all the kids I work with to feel.

In the pages that follow, I'm going to provide you with some advice on how you can either prevent that connection from being broken or restore it after it's been damaged. In the ten years that I've been working with some of the most troubled kids you can imagine, and in my life as a father for going on eighteen years, I've picked up a thing or two that I hope will come in handy for you. My work and my family have taught me a great deal, and I'm pleased to have the opportunity to pass some of that along to you. I've spent a good portion of my life working our ranch as well. Lots of fences needed mending in that time—literal and figurative ones. I'm hoping that I can help you either mend the ones you've got established or put up new ones that will stand the test of time and circumstances.

Fences serve as boundary markers, and those are good and necessary in any relationship. They can keep things in and keep things out. But a fence is pretty much useless without a gate. If you know anything at all about building fences, getting a gate to swing sturdy and true is probably the most difficult part of the whole process. Knowing when and how to let your kids pass through the boundaries that you've set up for them is probably the hardest part of being a parent. We're going to take a close look at how you can do these things so that you can rest easy knowing that you and your kids are safe.

But before we get too far into all that, I want to give you a bit of a warning or reminder. None of what I have to say in this book will be effective if it isn't used in the service of doing the right thing. You have to have the genuine desire to be of service to your child in order for any kind of program, approach, or style of parenting to work.

Having respect and determination to do what's right and make painful choices is what being a parent means. We have to instill solid values in our children. We have to teach by word and most importantly by example. To me, anyone who believes that "Do as I say and not as I do" is a viable option probably shouldn't say or do anything. In working with the troubled young people I encounter every day, I see that many of them, like Lauren, have no moral posts to ground them. It's beyond the scope of this book to discuss all the cultural influences that have so set many of our young people and so many adults adrift. I told you that I'm going to tell it like it is, and I also want you to know that my philosophy is firmly rooted in the belief that finger pointing and blaming serve no purpose. The main goal is to create a workable situation for both parties—you and your teen.

Intentions and goals are at the root of everything I do with kids. I truly believe that if you engage in any activity with pure intentions, a willingness to work hard, the humility to accept your failures, and the grit to bounce back from those setbacks, you will eventually attain your goals. If that goal is to raise a successful child or to help set right some things that have gone wrong, the program that's outlined in this book should prove helpful.

We've got some work to do, and we're burning daylight.

2

Understanding Reality Therapy

I don't have to tell you that parenting is hard work. That's one thing I've never been afraid of. We never had what you'd call a working ranch, but we always had a few milk cows, pigs, chickens, and an enormous garden that needed tending to. Growing up, I had chores assigned to me every day—from milking, to weeding, to cleaning the barn. It was get your work done and then get yourself off to school and come home and do some hunting and your homework and, of course, your evening chores. My dad was a tough guy who overcame polio and a prognosis that he would never walk. Whether it was stringing lines for the Bonneville Power Company when we got hooked up to the main grid in the mid-sixties or doing carpentry, logging, or whatever else needed to be done, by example and by word my father let me know that a very simple equation existed when it came to success:

$$Effort = Results$$

I believe that at the heart of successfully raising a child and especially in dealing with a difficult teen, the same basic formula is at work. Of course, any time you're working with human beings, you have to include a lot of other variables. And while effort is a key component of success, it is far from being the only one. Effort will get you a good distance down the road, but it won't get you the whole way. There's working hard, and there's working smart. No sense beating your head against the wall.

You already know a little bit about how my experiences helped to shape my approach to young people, but in this chapter, we're going to take a look at the other side of that equation—some of the theory I was exposed to in my course work that helped me shape my philosophy about raising good, smart, healthy kids. Though much of my success with kids has come from my personal experience, everything I've done with kids has been rooted in the theory and research from the work and ideas of many skilled therapists. To understand how I do things, you need to understand how they do things.

At a recent conference of the National Association of Therapeutic Schools, Dr. John McKinnon, who did his residency at the Yale University School of Medicine and is the cofounder and clinical director of the highly regarded Montana Academy, identified six areas of concern about today's teens:

- Concreteness: They struggle with abstract, complex thought.
- Gross self-preoccupation: They tend to be self-involved.
- Lack of empathy for others: As a result of their self-involvement they appear to have little regard for other people and their feelings.
- Magical conception of past and future: They don't see the connections among the past, present, and future.
- Puppet relationships: They view connections as an exercise in string pulling—one person manipulating another to get what they want.
- Unrefined moral reasoning: Not getting caught makes it okay; getting caught makes it wrong.

Dr. McKinnon's observations about teens and their behavior struck a real chord with me and put into sharper focus something I'd long observed in teens I worked with. In dealing with teens and in thinking about how today's teens differ from past generations, I think he did a very good job of identifying many of the things that trouble me about teens and their behavior—and what may have troubled previous generations of parents about their teens. When you look at this list, you can see that a lot of these factors result from the lack of development of the typical teen's brain. This is not to say that there's been damage to the structures of the brain, but simply the teen brain is not fully developed. Many teens, because their brains are still growing, aren't capable of the kind of higher-level reasoning, abstract thought, formulating a vision of the future, and feeling empathy for others the way adults can.

Have you ever asked your teen "What were you thinking?" and then received the response "I don't know" or a shrug of the shoulders. Most likely, they were telling you the truth. Many teens lack the skills and abilities to self-evaluate, understand the consequences of their present actions on their future well-being, and practice other hallmarks of "maturity."

None of this is an excuse, by the way. Teens need to be taught, and they are capable of learning these higher-level functions. Just because a teen's brain hasn't fully developed doesn't mean he or she isn't capable of learning to perform these higher-level cognitive functions. It's just going to take more time and effort on our part. As parents, if we emphasize values like empathy, and if we model reasoning and evaluating the long-term consequences of our actions, our kids can and will learn these concepts.

WHERE IS YOUR TEEN'S BRAIN?

It seems to me that nearly every decade for the past twenty or thirty years has been proclaimed the "Decade of the Brain." We've made amazing advances in studying how the brain works. One conclusion researchers have come to is that the brain is not as rigidly structured and formed as we once thought. In other words, the concept that the brain is like a computer and is hardwired by a certain age isn't true. The brain is infinitely more flexible and adaptable, and the truth is that we can indeed, as old dogs, learn new tricks. On the flip side, we've also learned that the centers of the brain that allow us to process higher-level thought don't become fully activated until we are out of our teens. It is true that 95% of our brain's development occurs before the age of five, but the most critical 5% doesn't develop fully until well after adolescence is over and we are into our twenties.

In particular, scientists have studied a specific region of the brain, the corpus callosum, and have come to some very interesting conclusions. They found that this area takes much longer to develop than was previously thought. Because the corpus callosum is a set of nerves that connect to all other parts of the brain in an intricately woven set of structures, this means that teenagers' brains do not have the same speed of connectivity between the areas of their brain as adults have. Scientists have also discovered that the prefrontal cortex, long considered the site of higher reasoning in humans, goes through a growth spurt from age twelve to age twenty, just as our bodies do.

In practical terms, that means that your teen's brain likely does not have all the connections and development necessary to enable sound, logical, reasoned, whole-brained decisions. To illustrate this point, as I was in the process of writing this, a teen from Indiana was arrested for driving well over one hundred miles an hour. When he was stopped by the Indiana State Police, he told the police that he had a good reason for speeding—he was late for his curfew, and his parents would punish him for being late. That sounds like something a smart-ass kid might say, but by all accounts this was a good kid who got good grades and had never been in trouble with the law before. In his underdeveloped mind, he was making a rational choice by speeding. All he could think of was that late = bad and late = punishment; therefore I must not be late; therefore the only way to not be late is to go fast. Certainly, a lot of other options would occur to you and me, but our brains are more fully developed.

That's one physiological explanation for the list that Dr. McKinnon has observed, but it offers little comfort. While it is useful and important to recognize these advances in our understanding of the teenage brain, this cannot become an excuse for inaction. Unfortunately, the "My kid's brain isn't fully developed" explanation is likely to fall on deaf ears when you're standing with your neighbor looking at his once immaculately landscaped lawn and the telltale ruts and tracks your son's or daughter's dirt bike has left in it. Though some of those higher functions might not be fully operational, we can't use the brain as an excuse for bad behavior most of the time.

Ultimately, understanding the development of teens' brains is useful, but it has little impact on your teen's day-to-day behavior. In truth, there isn't much we can do to alter brain development, and while it helps to know that it's a contributing factor to behavior, it's not something to focus too much time and attention on. As is true with all things behavioral, nurture plays a role as well, and it is in nurture that you have the power to effect change—to exert some influence on your teens and the environment in which your teen lives. The steps you take have the ability to help offset the egotism, lack of empathy, disconnection of time and consequences, poor moral reasoning, and the other developmental troubles listed by Dr. McKinnon.

I don't believe we can prescribe a single magic pill or a single approach that will eliminate all of the problems we encounter as parents of teens. I do think we have to give some thought to causes that contribute to our teens' problems. I guess it's like looking at an illness and deciding that we can't just treat the symptom but need to treat whatever underlies it.

REALITY THERAPY

Given what I've said so far, it should come as no surprise to you that someone with my background would be intrigued by, and eventually use, a counseling strategy called reality therapy. I first encountered the theories of William Glasser in an undergraduate course on adolescent development. Something about it really resonated with me, even back then, long before I started working with kids myself. Instead of trying to merely identify a particular syndrome that a patient is suffering from (about 374 of them are listed in the Diagnostic and Statistical Manual of Mental Disorders) and trying to prescribe the right psychotropic drug, Dr. Glasser instead emphasizes personal choice, personal responsibility, and personal transformation. He's a great believer in cause and effect, and so am I. I can't tell you the number of times I stood alongside my father or one of my uncles or my grandfather and stared at the guts of an automobile or tractor engine or some other device and tried to figure out why it wouldn't start or run properly. Humans aren't machines, of course, but it is important that teens understand that choices and actions produce results and that those results have consequences.

One of the guiding principles I've developed over the years is the concept of work. Whenever I talk to teens and parents, one of the questions I always ask is "And how is that working for you?" If what you or your teen is doing produces the results you want, then keep doing it. If not, then we need to figure out something you can do so that your life will work as you hope it will. I even go so far as to ask teens to identify which of their friends are "working friends"—those who help them avoid engaging in negative behaviors—and which are "acting out friends" who encourage the acting out behaviors that we'll discuss later on. As an evaluative tool, analyzing what works and what doesn't may seem like common sense, but for me and the teens I see, it's an incredibly useful tool.

Dr. Glasser's reality therapy is founded on the belief that most of our problems as humans are caused by a lack of connection, or poor connections, with other people. The goal of reality therapy is to help people reconnect with those they need in their life. Coming from a tight-knit community as I did, I thought this therapy made a lot of sense when I first learned it, since I understood how important those connections had been in my own personal growth. Not only was I surrounded by a small community of caring adults, my grandparents and an uncle lived on the same property as my family did. I felt a bond with all of them and that I was part of something larger than myself. Sadly, what I've observed in the past few years is that many young people don't experience that same kind of connection with their families or their communities.

Since first learning of Dr. Glasser's ideas, I have incorporated many of his theories and teachings into my own work with teens. What appealed to me about Dr. Glasser's work and his model for effective counseling was its emphasis on controlling what you can do and not dwelling on what you can't. Part of my training as a firefighter really helped reinforce this concept. You can't fight a fire if you're focusing on what caused it. You can't get too involved in that in the immediate moment. Later on, it will be important to consider, but focusing on the present and on the immediate is central to lessening the amount of damage. As a result, as much as possible, in working with young people, I don't dwell on the past because most of teenagers' problems have their roots in present relationships that aren't working for them. The more time you spend focusing on the past, the more the fire burns them up.

Also, Glasser's work taught me that it's important to reduce what I call the whine factor. This is something that my counseling has confirmed time and time again, since it's way too easy in counseling kids to have every session turn into a complaining session during which they lay the blame on everyone and everything except themselves. That's not productive, and that's how they've chosen to deal with their bad relationships in the past. If that griping and finger pointing were successful, they wouldn't be in my office. They've got to leave that at the door.

In addition, I believe in Glasser's concept of total behavior. Again, this is a very empowering idea in practice. In theory, total behavior consists of four parts: acting, thinking, feeling, and physiology. Glasser's work emphasizes the importance of the first two of the four. In a lot of classic therapy sessions, the role of the professional is to lead the counselee through an exploration of his or her emotions. You've probably watched scenes on television and in the movies in which the client is constantly asked, "And how did that make you feel?" While I don't discount feelings entirely, and the emotional lives of kids are important, I do ask my kids to focus on what they can do. They can act and they can think. Thoughts and actions are easier to change than feelings.

Even more difficult to change is our physiology, and we see those kinds of changes taking place only after thoughts and actions have changed. Think of it this way: You notice muscle development only after you've started to train with weights. Along with that action, your thoughts about becoming stronger and more fit play a part in your physical development, and along with that comes a change in how you feel about yourself. You aren't going to get more fit and develop muscle strength unless you do the work. Thinking and feeling stronger are the product of your actions.

CHOICE THEORY

What underpins reality therapy is another concept of Dr. Glasser's that I also have adopted as a part of my therapeutic model: choice theory. Just as I mentioned above how it is important to focus on the things we can change most easily—our thoughts and actions— choice theory states that all we ever do is behave. More important is that we behave on the basis of our choices. Most important is that our choices in life are motivated by a desire to satisfy one of our five basic needs:

- Survival
- Love and belonging
- Power
- Freedom
- Fun

In working with teens for the past twelve years and in raising my own kids, I've come to see just how closely choice theory mirrors reality. When you examine your own behavior and your kid's behaviors, you'll see that all of our choices have one or more of these five needs as a motivation. Again, because this is such an action-oriented focus on behavior and choices, it becomes particularly relevant in working with teens because it gives you and them the power to change the situation.

Glasser's model also cuts through a lot of potential confusion and uncertainty and keeps the focus where it should be—on one essential question that is a choice theory axiom: Is what I am doing getting me closer to the people I need? If the answer is no, then I have to help lead the counselee to make better choices that will produce the desired result.

As I said earlier, effort=results, and teens have to work hard to recognize that their behavior, their choices, and their desire to fulfill one of those five needs will produce either positive results or negative results. For now, we'll hold off on dealing with the question of who makes the decision about whether their behaviors and the results of those behaviors are positive or negative. Instead, I want to concentrate on each of those five needs and how they work in the lives of the teenagers I encounter.

Survival

Many of the adolescents and young adults I've worked with have had most of their basic survival needs met and have not been motivated by a simple desire for food, water, shelter, and clothing to keep alive. In a few extreme cases, I have counseled kids from environments in which their physical safety was not something they could easily take for granted. For those unfortunate few—not all of whom were raised in the inner city and faced gang-related violence—the choices they made to survive often took them outside the boundaries of what most of us would consider acceptable, often leading them to high-risk and illegal actions. The potential consequences of those actions were quite high—loss of life, loss of freedom, great physical harm. No one, especially no child, should have to face those circumstances, but thousands and thousands do.

Fortunately for the kids who have come into my office, once they've been removed from their environment and the threats have been eliminated, those really awful potential consequences are just about nonexistent. Unfortunately, those old behaviors become habitual. If a teen manages to survive any kind of abuse—physical, emotional, or sexual—the mechanisms he or she used to get through that experience are difficult to abandon, even after the threat is removed. Whether those mechanisms take the form of denial and withdrawal, physical aggression, self-mutilation, high-risk sexual behaviors, or any other form of negative acting out, they may continue long after the threat to the teenager's survival has diminished. Change is uncomfortable, and that discomfort is as much of a threat as a menacing bully or an abusive parent.

When we speak of survival, we are primarily talking about physiological needs, including sex, along with food, drink, shelter, and clothing. These physiological needs are fairly distinct—you know when you are making a choice based on thirst versus a choice based on hunger. You're not likely to confuse the two—you won't slug down a bottle of Gatorade to satisfy your hunger or wolf down a steak to slake your thirst. Our other needs are more complex. You may engage in an activity not knowing whether it will satisfy your need for belonging or fun or power or some combination of all three. There is far more overlap among these needs than there is with survival needs. While the other needs focus on psychological elements, this is the only one that focuses on the physical. At its simplest, breaking down the five primary needs into physiological and psychological makes a lot of sense in theory. As you'll see, when we enter into the realm of the psychological, things get more complicated, and the lines of distinction can be blurry at best and completely obscured at worst. For our purposes, we'll limit survival to physical survival. In reality, a teen can fail to survive in lots of ways—emotional, spiritual, social—but in the strictest sense those three fall under the heading of psychological needs.

Belonging

In Chapter One, I mentioned how I always felt that I belonged to the community I lived in as well as the family I was born into. While there were times when I felt like a bit of an outsider, most of the time I felt I had some place to go and someone to turn to for guidance and comfort. We all need that feeling, and if you are a parent of a teen, you've no doubt seen how this need can motivate your child to do things.

Fitting in is never easy, but it's something we all try to do with greater or less effort and success. While styles may have changed from the clean-cut preppy look of Levi's and button-down collar shirts of my young adulthood to the baggy low-slung boxer-short-exposing denim pants and hoodies of today, how we choose to dress is often a function of our desire to fit in and identify ourselves with a certain crowd. Our kids are exposed to so many more forms of media than you and I were, that even here in rural northwest Montana, we have kids dressing and talking as if they were living in south central Los Angeles or Cypress Hill, Brooklyn.

What parents might find surprising is that the one group their kids most want to belong to is their family. At a time when separation from their parents and establishing their individual identities is a strong need, the vast majority of the kids I work with long for the kind of connection they had with their families when they were younger. Their desire to spend more time with their mothers and fathers, to have their parents be more actively involved in their school and social lives, goes unmet, so they act out. My counselees respect me and envy my dedication to my family and support my efforts to be there at my kids' activities and at home with them 100%. The story I told you about Lauren and her understanding my need to be at my son's baseball game is one I could tell you with a hundred variations but the same ending. They all say to me, "That's okay, Mr. Mike. You go on. It's important/cool that you be there for your kids. I wish my mom and dad would take the time to be with me."

At their age, teens have the desire to individuate, but they frequently lack the strength to stand alone. I'm sure you're aware of, and frequently frustrated by, that desire and the peer pressure to fit in. I'm also pretty sure you've uttered some variation of this question: "If everyone else was jumping off a bridge, would you jump off, too?"

This idea of belonging is further complicated when coupled with the role that love plays. More so than just simple acceptance into the group, we want to be cherished, recognized, and appreciated for our uniqueness, and made to feel that we have an intimate connection with another person. Many of the students at Spring Creek claim that their parents do not love them or that they seldom hear those words from them.

If teens often seem like a bundle of contradictions, that's because they are. Even though they say that they want to be treated like adults and say they are willing to accept the consequences of being adult, they still retain the childlike need to be loved. Intellectually they understand that they are loved and that love takes many different forms, but emotionally they tend to remain in a state of denial in which it seems that the only kind of love they recognize is a completely non-judgmental, unconditional, idealized version.

As with all of these needs, when the need for belonging is unmet, the choices teens make can produce some frustrating and negative behaviors. A teen's desire for love may result in acting out in order to test the limits of the parents' devotion. Also, a teen who feels unloved may act in ways that ensures that (in the teen's mind) he or she will be seen as unlovable.

Power

According to Glasser, 95% of all discipline problems with children have their roots in a child's attempts to achieve power. From the time a child makes his or her first efforts to exert control over environment, power becomes an incredible force. But control and power are a double-edged sword. As parents we want to see our kids gain independence and take on greater responsibility. We also worry a great deal about whether or not they have the skills necessary to make good decisions. How and when to let go is a delicate dance that we all have to finesse our way through. I know firsthand from raising my own kids that it is *very* easy to get sucked into a power struggle. The most innocent discussion can veer off into a battle in which you are pitted against them and viewed as a control freak bent on dominating them.

One the first things I do in my counseling sessions is try to establish a rapport with counselees. I also let them know immediately that I am not the expert on them—they are the expert on this subject. By giving them that sense of control, I'm letting them see that we are on a more level playing field. Even though I'm an authority figure, I'm on their side, I have their best interests at heart, and I have no interest in making decisions for them. In the chapters that follow, I'll offer some specific suggestions on how to avoid power struggles, how to enable your teen to gain power and use it properly, and how to negotiate the transfer of power in an orderly fashion. We don't want any bloody coups, and the negotiations necessary to avoid them are delicate.

Freedom

Power and freedom are inextricably linked. Most often, teens want power to gain what they view as independence. That's not always the case, but very often it is. Much of what I said above applies here. One of the most difficult concepts for many teens to understand is that freedom has limits—probably more limits than any of us are comfortable with as adults. They often view adulthood as a utopian state in which we exist free of any and all constraints. This highly idealized and unrealistic view of what it means to be an adult has them operating from a very skewed perspective. What they also chafe against is the idea that with freedom comes responsibility.

While they may roll their eyes at what they consider to be clichéd ideas and formulaic responses, the truth is that these notions are borne out every day in our adult reality. What we have to realize as adults is that our kids do need the freedom to fail. It's also important that they have that idealized concept of freedom in their minds as a starting point. A necessary part of maturing is having some of our ideas tested, and our kids will never truly grow up until they've been tested, and perhaps stung by, the limits of their freedom. Sometimes we have to come to painful realizations, and as parents our very cells vibrate with the desire to protect our children from pain. How we walk the tightrope between protecting them and stifling them requires a great deal of concentration and practice. We're likely to fall off from time to time, and our teens need to know that. They also need to understand that they are going to walk that same tightrope and that the net is there for them and for us.

Fun

Glasser talks about the need for fun in terms of laughter and playing. With teens, their concept of what's fun, funny, and play can be a far cry from our own. To be honest, though, when I think of some of the hijinks that I perpetrated either by myself or in cahoots with my friends or siblings, all in the name of fun, I shudder at the recollection and am grateful that I survived my youth. One of the most frustrating moments in our life as parents is when we confront our son or daughter about something they did that we view as potentially dangerous, foolhardy, illegal, immoral, unethical, or just plain stupid, and their answer to the question of why they did it was "I thought it would be fun." In recent years, activities like the "pass-out game"—a form of autoasphyxiation in which kids try to black out temporarily—has led to several deaths. This drives home the point that fun can sometimes go horribly wrong.

Again, as parents, how do you find a middle ground between keeping your child safe and making the child's life joyless? What you may view as necessary and prudent, the child may see as a denial of a fundamental right—the inalienable right to seek pleasure and diversion in all its forms. While it's unrealistic for our children to expect that life is one unending romp of pleasure, we don't want our kids to believe that life is suffering or worse. Again, striking that balance may take some real work, and recognizing how crucial this need is, and how different our adult perspective is from theirs, are crucial first steps.

KEY POINTS OF REALITY THERAPY

In the chapters that follow, we'll examine these five needs, the consequences if they are not met, and how they play such a crucial role in the lives of our teens. Throughout the remainder of the book, we'll come back to some of the crucial points that underlie reality therapy and choice theory. For now, I want you to keep in mind these key points:

- All long-lasting psychological problems are relationship problems. These relationship problems are the result of our losing connection with the people we need.
- When we're deciding how to act, it's important to use the choice theory axiom as a guide: Is what I am doing bringing me closer to the people I need?
- The only person whose behavior we can control is our own.
- All we can give another person is information. How they choose to use that information is up to them.
- What happened in the past has everything to do with what we are today, but we can only satisfy our needs right now and plan to continue satisfying them in the future.
- All we do is behave.
- All behaviors are total behaviors and are made up of four components: acting, thinking, feeling, and physiology.

- All total behaviors are chosen, but we have direct control only over action and thought.
- We can control our feelings and physiology only indirectly through how we choose to act and think.

These are the basic operating principles I use in working with young people. I'm a realist born and bred, and my experience has proved these principles true over the many years I've spent counseling some very troubled kids. While this may not be the only approach to take in working with kids, I think I've laid a good foundation for you to work from. We'll continue our project in the pages that follow.

A FEW MORE CONCEPTS

Before we turn our attention more fully to each of the individual needs, I want to spend some time talking about a few other important concepts: identity, separation-individuation, autonomy, and triangular relationships. At the same conference where Dr. McKinnon spoke, I had a chance to hear John Santa, PhD, discuss these four concepts and many others. I've already talked a bit about identity and individuation, but I feel we need to address them more fully before we talk about the role each individual need plays in your child's development. Dr. Santa's work puts into focus some of the things I'd experienced throughout my career, and he expressed what I'd experienced and understood on a gut level in a way we can all easily understand.

As we all know, and as Dr. Santa pointed out, growing up is really the process of firmly establishing our identity. Often, the acting out that kids do is a product of their struggles with identity. One reason why peer pressure and media representations so strongly influence our kids' behavior and appearance is their insecurity surrounding their identity. As Dr. Santa put it, "presenting an accurate representation of self" is one hallmark of personality development. Some kids try on identities the way they try on pairs of shoes before deciding which one to buy. Some kids maintain a fairly stable identity, but even if they do, they still may feel as if they are stuck between everything, or question whether or not (and where) they fit in. I can relate to that. I was a pretty good athlete and a smart student. At times those two attributes helped me a lot, and at other times they were a hindrance. We'll talk much more later about cliques, but they are a reality, and belonging to one group with one dominant attribute can often prevent a teen from belonging to another group.

Autonomy is an especially tricky subject for parents. We want our kids to be attached to us, and kids need that. We also want them to be independent, but not too independent. That delicate balance often means deciding who's the boss of the elements in your child's life. You and your teen have probably already engaged in these kinds of struggles. You feel it's important to establish a curfew, but he or she feels old enough to decide what "late" and "too late" mean. The list can go on and on. What Dr. Santa said rings true according to my experiences. When children "win" the autonomy battle, they end up feeling entitled. That leads to a greater degree of narcissism. Without enough substance to back up that entitlement, when their ego suffers a blow, they feel like a fake, empty, and they grow angry at being exposed. Many kids put up a great façade but are really afraid of what others will discover about who they really are.

When a child loses the autonomy battle and parents are too controlling, that child experiences frustration and anger as a result of feeling hopeless and powerless. Those two feelings often transform into self-loathing and inner-directed anger. Teens with a sense of never being able to escape from a parent's shadow or from under a tyrannical thumb will most likely beat themselves up and blame themselves for their perceived failures. Often, they will resort to building up a false front, posturing, and presenting an identity to the world that isn't genuine. They will live in fear of being revealed for who they really are, and the cycle of identity crises will continue.

Dr. Santa referred to another important concept: triangle relationships. As we all know, as adults we often have to negotiate among several positions in relationships—especially within the family. Life is filled with complex social structures, and developing an identity separate and apart from the family and the role we play in our family is crucial to personality development. I know so many kids who chafed against their families' (and especially their older siblings') reputations— both good and bad. Being able to develop clear self-boundaries, negotiating for autonomy, learning to accept authority, and finding acceptable role models all contribute to a teen's maturity and solidifying of identity.

As you'll see in the chapters of Part II, looking at each of our teens' needs and how and whether they are met can help us to identify where they are in terms of establishing their identity, and what detours they have taken or obstacles they've swerved around to keep them from progressing to the point where they should be.

When our children are young, it is our responsibility to see that all of their needs are being met. They depend upon on us almost completely for their survival, belonging, power, freedom, and fun. One of the major duties we have as parents is to ensure that our teens continue to have those needs met. A part of growing up is moving outside the circle of family, and it is important that they discover ways to have those five needs met both within and outside of the family environment. Too often, when our teens experience a deficit within the family of one need or another, they will seek unhealthy, negative sources outside the family to fill that need. That is when we need to intervene. Ideally, though, if they understand that we have granted them the freedom to range outside the boundary of family to seek healthy, productive means to have these needs fulfilled, we can avoid that kind of intervention and ease their transition from dependence to independence. We want them to know that they can move freely between their old lives with us and their new lives with peers, classmates, and the world at large, confident that we'll be there to support them and supplement them as the situation dictates.

Part II

The Five Primary Needs of Your Teen

3

Survival

When most people think about survival, they think of our essential needs—water, food, shelter, and the like. While these are all crucial to teens (and everyone else, for that matter), they're only the tip of the iceberg in the larger context of a teen's survival needs. Survival can exist in many different forms, and often problems that on the surface don't seem to have much to do with surviving are precisely that. If teens' survival needs are not met, they'll respond in a wide variety of ways to let you know what's going on.

In this chapter, we're going to take a look at some of the more common forms of this survival mechanism and how you can understand the harrowing and very real survival struggles that your teen may be going through. While some of what I have to say is perfectly in line with Glasser's model, some is culled from my own experiences and work in the trenches. Through my own interactions with teens, I've expanded the definition of survival needs quite a bit, and this is where my work differs in some respects from Dr. Glasser's.

Again, I'm a guy who takes theory and grounds it in reality. In the pages that follow, I'm going to veer from the stricter definitions and approaches of Dr. Glasser's work on needs to include a discussion that turns the tables on how we define survival.

THE ROUGH HISTORY OF GREG

When I first met Greg, I was immediately brought back to my growing-up years and a neighbor's dog named Max. Like Greg, Max was an alpha male—the dominant leader of the pack. There was a bit of physical resemblance between boy and dog, too. Max was a mutt of indeterminate origins, but he clearly had some Labrador retriever and German shepherd in him. He had the same proud head and carriage of a shepherd, combined with the broad thickly muscled chest of the Lab. Depending on his mood and, more than likely, the quantity of food in his stomach, Max could charm you or menace you—he could go from playful to frightening in an instant. Max tolerated neither fools nor other dogs lightly, and you had best tread carefully around him and his territory. More than one kid and many other dogs felt the painful wrath of Max at one time or another. You never knew what would set him off, but when something did, and the dust settled, you could wind up minus a chunk of fabric from the seat of your jeans, your coat sleeve, or, if you were really unlucky (or slow), a bruised and possibly punctured part of your anatomy.

When Max was menacing our area, I had no idea what made him so volatile, but once I heard Greg's story of his childhood and adolescence, I came to suspect that the two might have shared similar upbringings. When Greg was a toddler, his mother abandoned him. Her drug habit and her desire for independence were much more important to her than her first-born son. Greg's father lived a life similar to that of Greg's mother, but he decided he would continue to provide—at least to some degree—for young Greg. Greg's father, Darren, was not a nice man. In addition to his addictions, he struggled with anger issues; worse, he had no concept of what a young boy needs from his father.

When Darren got upset with Greg, he would lock him in his room, often in his closet. Greg would remain in his makeshift cell for days at a time. He received little or no food, and he was allowed only short bathroom breaks and sparse human contact. At the age of five, Greg ran away several times, only to be hauled back home by the authorities or his "father."

Eventually, young Greg learned to hoard food and water in his bedroom closet. He made several more attempts to break out of his prison but was never successful. Over the course of his therapy sessions with me, he revealed that even as a little boy he lived in fear that during one of his father's drug-induced rages, he would kill him or forget about his being in the closet and allow him to starve to death.

Eventually, Greg was removed from that home, and relatives adopted him. Despite a new and healthy environment, Greg still didn't trust anybody, and he feared abandonment. He continued to hoard food, even as an adolescent. He was plagued by nightmares in which he was always getting beaten up or hurt. He became both combative and terrorized. He struggled to respect authority, and he felt he had to defy and stand up to anyone in a position of power in order to defend himself. As he grew up he often used intimidation to control his environment.

All these behaviors were a response to Greg's fears about his personal survival. Though these behaviors were at odds with how much of society operates, they were the survival instincts that he had honed through all his years of living with his abusive father. Working together, Greg and I discussed at great length not only his history, but how he allowed his history to define his current relationships. It took nearly a year for me to gain his trust. It was extremely important to approach conflict delicately with Greg, as he could immediately shut down and internally disappear for weeks at a time. At other times he lashed out ferociously with little regard for the consequences or for the guilt or innocence of his victims. Greg struggled to maintain healthy female relationships—he assumed that every woman was like his mother. At the first sign of conflict in any relationship with a woman— a teacher, counselor, friend, or girlfriend—he would check out of the relationship immediately, knowing in his heart of hearts that it was doomed to failure anyway.

Your Teen's Perspective

While Greg's upbringing is no doubt extreme and a far cry from what you have experienced with your teen, we can still learn some valuable lessons from it. You have to remember that your teens' reality, and anyone else's for that matter, is defined by their perceptions of their experiences. How you view the situation can vary wildly from your teen's estimation of the circumstances. Also, you might be able to get your teens to admit objectively that the facts show that they aren't being locked in the closet, or deprived of food, freedom, and socialization, but you'd be harder pressed to get them to admit that it doesn't *feel* as if their very survival is in jeopardy. You may not be putting them into the kind of literal prison that Greg's father did, but if you deny them something that you see as a privilege and they view as a right, then you've shackled them just as surely as if you'd put cold steel handcuffs on their wrists, gagged them, and put them in an isolation cell.

Remember what we said earlier about teens' brains and development? Given that we now know that those centers of higher functioning are still at various stages of development, you have a ready answer to questions like What were you thinking? How could you believe that? Why would you do that? And many others like it. The answer, of course, is that most teens aren't thinking as much as they are feeling. They're responding to emotional inputs and attempting to make sense of facts and feelings with equipment that is not always prepared and capable of reasoning as it is with you as an adult. Think back to some of the frustrations you may have experienced when you were helping your sixth-graders solve their first algebra equations. What seemed perfectly reasonable and apparent to you was like another language to them. That type of disconnect will crop up again and again as you and your teens struggle with the transition to adulthood.

This is not to say that all of a teen's adjustment issues are a result of brain development, but it's still an important factor that plays a role in behavior that you might take to be irrational. This is why seeing the world from your teen's perspective is so important. The more you can shift into thinking like your teen, the better off you're going to be.

In Greg's case, survival certainly was a real issue for him as a young boy. His existence was tenuous at times, and what we also know from neuroscience is that any experience loaded with emotion is one that we remember with particular clarity. We form automatic and unconscious responses quite easily, and for someone like Greg, any perceived threat to his survival could set him into a downward spiral of aggression and anger.

WORRY AND SURVIVAL

Survival as a dominant need in teens can spring up for other reasons besides threats to their own supply of food, shelter, and other basics. Indeed, worrying can often be a major catalyst causing the survival instinct and behavior patterns of teens to kick in. A former client of mine, Justine, was, in her mother's words, a "worry wart" and an "old lady before her time." While her mother thought Justine's doom-and-gloom temperament was out of proportion to her reality, Justine saw things differently. Justine's father lost his job in a local mine and went on unemployment, and suddenly her world was turned upside down. In a matter of months, she and her five siblings found themselves living in a two-bedroom apartment instead of the five-bedroom home she was accustomed to. As the oldest, instead of being the one at the head of the clothes hand-me-down line, Justine suddenly found herself the recipient of castoffs from her aunt and a cousin. Although the family members weren't starving, meals changed as well. Some of the things they took for granted, like desserts, sodas, and snacks, disappeared from the pantry shelves.

When Justine came to see me, she looked pale and gaunt. Her mother said that her daughter's appetite was gone, and she was worried that Justine was depressed. In time, I learned that Justine's appetite was as healthy as it had ever been, but she was so worried about the younger kids getting enough to eat that she was on a self-imposed and secret diet. Her concern about the family's finances and the state of her parents' marriage weighed heavily on her shoulders. Justine wasn't worried, as Greg was, about whether or not she personally would survive; she was worried about how her family would survive as a whole and how they would manage.

Though Justine's worry was of a much different kind from Greg's, that did not make it any easier to dismiss. The truth was that in a lot of ways, Greg's concerns could be more easily managed—he'd been removed from the environment that threatened him, and hopefully in time when no further obvious threats cropped up, he'd relax into his new life. Justine was still living in her changed environment, and she was somewhat helpless. After all, she couldn't go out and work to support the family, she couldn't tell her father (though she wanted to) that he had to get off his ass and look for a job, and she couldn't reverse the complicated tide of economic circumstances that had closed the mines.

Many of the students I see share similar worries to the ones that plagued Justine. They just express their concerns in different ways. While Greg serves as the example of that worry channeled into aggression, Justine's retreat into a state of near helplessness and resignation shows another example. On one hand, her desire to help her siblings by sacrificing her own interests was admirable, but in the long run she was doing everyone, especially herself, far more harm than good. In many ways, Justine's behavior was a cry for help, and her crisis did result in her mother's coming to realize how much of a toll their financial circumstances were taking on her kids.

Justine's mom had grown up in a "suffer in silence" environment, and despite how much she despised that upbringing, she inadvertently lived out that same scenario and philosophy in her marriage. She expected her kids to dutifully and without question accept the new financial circumstances they had to live with, never thinking about the impact that this type of acquiescence might have on their fears. Justine's mother may have been motivated by a desire to protect her children from the harsh realities of their life, but in this case, what she had hoped would insulate her children from those chilling facts, instead isolated one of them. Saying, "Everything's fine," when that was obviously untrue, was a well-intentioned but harmful approach.

Her mother misinterpreted Justine's actions and failed to see that they were a product of Justine's survival instinct, brought out by the situation. Justine was so afraid of disappointing her mother with her inability to keep a stiff upper lip that whenever her mother approached her to talk about what was troubling her, Justine simply shut down. Justine's response seemed to confirm her mother's diagnosis that something was wrong with her daughter and not with the family or its circumstances. Without those clear lines of communication so necessary to resolving any kind of conflict, things got worse instead of better.

The case of Justine offers an all-too-common tale of how important it is to consider the full scope of the teen's experience. Too often it's too easy to focus on the child who is acting out and not direct our attention to the source of the problem—the larger family and the environment in which they live.

SURVIVING DEATH

One of the most obvious situations that brings a teen's survival needs into focus is the death of a friend or loved one. Many of the young people I've worked with have had a brush with mortality that has fundamentally shaken them to the core.

Tyler was thirteen when his younger sister Taylor died of complications related to leukemia. As you might expect, Tyler was devastated by the loss of his sibling, the pain and anguish of his parents that he witnessed regularly, and to a lesser extent the fear that he might suffer the same fate. In addition, he experienced survivor's guilt, wondering at the most trying times during his ordeal if his mom and dad secretly wished that he was the one who had had the disease. He tortured himself for being angry that his sister was the one who had dominated his parent's time and attention. Though he understood the need for the focus to be on his sister, he couldn't help but feel neglected when he was shunted off to his grandparents, neighbors, family friends, and others when an apparently endless round of doctor's appointments and Taylor's hospital stays took his parents away.

For a long time, being known as the kid whose sister died was a bit in his mouth he chafed against. He beat himself up over the fact that he felt sorry for himself for being labeled that way—especially when he knew that what his sister had gone through was far worse.

Over time, Tyler's anger and emotional confusion found expression in a typical downward spiral. To deflect attention from his situation, Tyler let his grades slip very seriously. He also began to act out in ways so that people would pay attention to him in a different of way. He began to be disruptive in class and disrespectful to his teachers, transforming himself from an outgoing carefree kid into a sullen brat with a hair-trigger temper. Everyone attributed these changes in attitude and behavior to the trauma of losing a sibling, and they cut him all kinds of slack, but their well-intentioned efforts only made the problems worse. Tyler wanted attention from his parents, and he got it to a certain degree by becoming a pain in their ass. Tyler also wanted to be treated just like any other student who was disruptive, but instead of detentions and suspensions, all he got was sympathy and appointments with the school psychologist.

After a few weeks of that kind of special treatment, he figured he'd have to do something more extreme to get school officials to punish him so he could stop punishing himself. Taking one of the driver's education vehicles for a joyride around the practice lot and then playing bumper cars with a few of the autos in the teacher's lot did the trick. He went from "Poor Tyler" to "Crazy Tyler" and felt better. All of his acting out was, of course, a product of the family tragedy he and his parents were enduring, but his behaviors and reasons for them were far more layered than anyone suspected. He finally came to understand, and got others to understand, that he wanted to do anything to put that experience behind him and shed the label of victim. As long as he was viewed as a victim, that meant his survival was more in question than he felt comfortable with.

SOCIAL SURVIVAL

As parents or adult authority figures, we may not consider other people's opinions of us a matter of life or death. Teens, on the other hand, frequently do. In most cases, it is not a literal death but a figurative one that teens face. To them, their social standing and where they fit in the pecking order is a question of survival. While we may benefit from the long-term perspective that our adulthood affords us, there are hundreds of slings and arrows that probably seem like the end of the world to your teen: the ending of a romantic relationship, severing ties with a friend, a crushing moment of public embarrassment over having your zipper down, snot in your nose, or an unfashionable outfit. I know that as I grew older I became keenly aware that I did not dress as nicely as the rest of my classmates; we simply couldn't afford to. I was lucky that I had other positives on my balance sheet—athletic and classroom success primary among them—to offset those debits. That doesn't mean that the looks and snickers didn't hurt.

Unless you were extremely fortunate, I'm certain that you experienced some of those feelings of anxiety and inferiority yourself. These feelings can produce their own set of survival needs and reactions, just as we saw with Greg, Justine, and Tyler. .

Cliques and labeling are part and parcel of the high school experience for teens, and for younger kids as well. Let's be honest: didn't we all want to be a part of the cool group at school? Didn't we sometimes sit in the cafeteria or study hall looking enviously at the table where the king and queen held court? Didn't we all, to one degree or another, use our peers as a measuring stick against which we judged ourselves? No matter what our parents might have said about our appearance, our abilities, or our social skills, what mattered was what those other kids thought of us. And as harshly as we felt our teachers and parents might have assessed us, none of what they said or did could sting like what our peers meted out. We all know that kids can be cruel, and not many of them grow out of that cruelty as they "mature."

Since so much of adolescence and growing up is about forming an identity, social survival takes on an importance that rivals the physiological needs of our young people. To put it another way, they hunger and thirst for peer acceptance and identification. Teens take many of their cues from the media and from their peer groups. As I pointed out before, at times, it may seem as though they try on identities as frequently as clothes, or perhaps more frequently. Kids are going to be judged—by us, by their teachers, but most often and most harshly by their peers. While the criteria your teens' peers use to judge them will most likely seem extremely superficial to you—their style of clothing and hair, how they speak, whether or not they drink, if they get good grades—that's the reality in which they live. Not all of teen culture is superficial, but from an outsider's perspective it may seem that way. As parents we have to be careful to not be too dismissive of our teens' concerns about fitting in.

I've seen this phenomenon work in reverse as well. More and more parents I speak to want their kids to fit in. They're torn about the desire to ensure that their kids are healthy and happy and distinct individuals because they know what can happen to kids who get marked as different. A girl I worked with named Lucy was a good case in point. Lucy's mom once told me that she and her husband joked about Lucy's being an "alien child." Neither of Lucy's parents had much interest in music or the arts, but it seemed to them that Lucy came out of the womb singing and drawing. Somehow, Lucy fell in love with classical music and the cello. How a kid from rural Idaho, whose parents listened only to the commodities report on the radio and whose exposure to culture was clog dancing at the state fair, got a musical prodigy of a daughter is just one of those inexplicable quirks of nature. While most of the kids at Lucy's school were members of the Future Farmers of America, she was auditioning for, and playing with, chamber orchestras and symphonies in Boise.

Life back home wasn't easy for Lucy, and her parents encouraged her to stop listening to the BBC recordings of Jacqueline du Pré and mix in a little Christina Aguilera, Jessica Simpson, or Faith Hill. Lucy cared little about her appearance, and her mother went out and bought makeup and clothes for her after Lucy refused to join her on excursions to the mall. Her mom and dad encouraged Lucy to go to school dances and to go out on Friday nights instead of staying home and rehearsing. They saw their daughter growing increasingly isolated and were nearly desperate to get her to fit in. They suspected that Lucy wasn't telling them everything that was going on at school, but they did hear some of the sniggers and taunts when they were out with her. Lucy seemed not to notice, but they suspected that she felt far more than she let on.

Lucy's parents were savvy and entirely empathetic, and I can completely understand why they were so concerned about their daughter. They believed that without a social network, without exposure to her peers, she would be operating at a deficit. She'd always be separate and apart, and for parents of kids who don't fit in, that situation makes us anxious and sad. Kids are supposed to hang around with other kids and do kid things and not take the bus to Boise to be around a bunch of fuddy-duddy adults, right?

Unfortunately, Lucy didn't see her parents as empathetic or savvy. She translated their efforts to change her into a simple statement:

My parents don't like me. Lucy believed that if her parents couldn't accept her, then no one else would either. She grew suspicious of the attention and praise she received from her fellow musicians, and eventually she abandoned her efforts to play with them. She withdrew and isolated herself even more. By the time I met her, Lucy was in a fairly serious depressive state. With the one thing that gave her pleasure taken from her, her music, she was adrift. School made little sense to her, and she stopped attending classes. Fortunately, she didn't engage in any other real acting out behaviors and didn't stray into a negative peer group. The loss of her parent's acceptance and her music overwhelmed her. Two crucial elements of her survival were taken from her, and as her depression deepened, her parents foundered, completely unsure of what they could do to help their daughter regain her footing.

WHEN THE FAMILIAR IS THREATENED

Despite the wide variety of ways in which survival needs can go unmet, a common thread runs through these examples that we've discussed. In very different ways, each of these stories, each of these types of survival situations, is brought on by an uncertainty about what these teens have come to count on as familiar. I have seen many examples of this, time and time again, with kids who were the product of a so-called broken home or of a home that was on the brink of breaking up. As a result of this dramatic change in their lives and in their routine, they exhibit the kind of survival worry that Justine did. Kids are the main victims in divorce cases and custody battles, and the kinds of acting out we see in these kids almost always have their roots in their concerns about the survival of their family unit.

But whereas Justine's survival worry caused her to withdraw into herself, these reactions can cause a host of different responses. Some withdraw. Some act out in the hope that their misbehavior will draw attention away from the other issues and make the parents feel guilty. Or acting out can simply express a subconscious fear that what has been known is threatened.

Change is frightening to most people's survival. That is supported both by our behavior and by what we know of neuroscience and the formation of neural networks that govern much of our behavior. We learn through repetition, and even when something is bad for us, like living in a home environment in which the parents are constantly at odds, the familiar offers a twisted kind of comfort. The old expression about the devil you know being a preferable option to the devil you don't know applies here. Survival isn't always about threats to our physical existence; threats can also be to our normal, established, regular routine.

Not to make too much of the Max the dog example, but despite Max's unpredictability, he still was, like most dogs, a creature of habit. The same is true for most of us as well. We like to be able to determine with a fair bit of accuracy what our daily round of events is going to consist of. Once that gets thrown off, we can become anxious, irritable, giddy, or subject to one of many other emotional states.

Structure Helps Survival

One thing we tried very hard to do at Spring Creek Academy was to impose as much order and routine as possible on our kids, as this is a successful way to allay concerns over survival needs by emphasizing expectations and consequences. The main reason we do this is that we've seen the positive results when order and predictability are high, and we've seen the negative results when kids exist in a world that seems random to them.

More and more over the past few years, I've heard teens use the word "random" in what seems to me to be, well, random circumstances. They use it to describe events, people, books, movies, songs, and nearly everything else under the sun. Most often, it has negative connotations, but not always. Someone who is considered to be "random" has an element of unpredictability and surprise, as conveyed by the word in its more established context. Depending on the teen and the relative value that he or she places on stability and order, that "randomness" can be good or bad. As is true of most human behavior and attitudes, there's a nearly infinite variability in our appreciation of surprise and spontaneity. In working with cows all these years, I've come to expect a certain continuity in their behavior. Every now and then one of them will do something unexpected, and if it doesn't put me in any physical danger, I'm pleased to observe it.

The Tetherball

With teens, that element of surprise is one of the most delightful and bedeviling aspects of their personalities. In the normal course of the day, we expect people's behavior and moods to change. If you picture the pendulum on a wall clock, that's how the behavior of most adults (and some well-adjusted teens) will swing each day—in a regular, prescribed pattern and distance from the center.

By contrast, many of the teens I work with present a mood and behavior picture that's more like the playground game called tetherball. That ball swings from a fixed point, moving in every different angle, speed, and height, but despite these completely unpredictable movements, the ball remains attached to the same pole in the ground, firmly rooted to where it began. I like that image, because tetherball is usually played by more than one person, and in a lot of ways, every teen that I've worked with has had multiple personalities—not in the clinical sense, but in a way that often seems as if they're engaged in a riotous game of tetherball. The good kid, the rebel, the frightened mama's boy or daddy's girl, the extreme adventurer, and a host of others are all batting that ball around crazily, trying to win dominance.

We have to keep in mind that no matter how wild the range of variation, no matter how chaotic that playground game may appear, there is still something tethering these kids to the center. It could be their values, their faith, their family, their friends, or their education, but something is anchoring them in place. There's some kind of gravitational force at work that keeps them orbiting around something or someone. That something or someone is frequently a representation of the most basic survival need. We all need some anchor, something we can count on when it feels as if everything else is about to fly apart and scatter in every direction.

It's no accident that experts coined the phrase "nuclear family." We all need some nucleus, some center point, around which our world revolves. I'm not saying anything new here, but in today's society, all too frequently the center doesn't hold. The family structure has degraded, and our kids' sense of continuity and stability has been so eroded, that they are like electrons spun off from that nucleus. They're out there trying to join up with something else that will give their lives reason and purpose. Too often that "thing" turns out to be a negative, like drugs, alcohol, sex, violence, or thrill seeking. They become attracted to their peer group because they see in their fellow teens the same need, the same desire for someone or something they can count on.

Now, you have to keep in mind that some of this is a natural part of growing up. Teens need to establish an identity outside the family. We call this process individuation. They want and need to establish themselves as someone other than your child, the brother or sister of Bobby and Sue. That's all normal, natural, and healthy, but it's also a little bit—or for some teens, a lot—frightening. Have you ever been out in the woods at night when you're all alone? Your mind can race, and shadows can take on frightening shapes. Your heart beats faster, your adrenal gland kicks in, and it's a kind of rush. Chances are your survival isn't on the line, but as civilized human beings that's about as close as we get to experiencing our animal fear, our survival instinct.

This is the same kind of feeling that teens experience when they venture off on their own. However, although the thrill of being apparently tetherless can be exhilarating for teens for a little while, in the end they need to feel safe coming back to their nucleus and returning to their fixed point. Any survival risk presented by individuation is offset by the comfort of the tether, but once that tether becomes unreliable, the process of individuation for a teen becomes a whole lot harder.

JEOPARDIZING SURVIVAL

For as long as I can remember, many teenagers have possessed romantic notions of what happens when they purposefully jeopardize their survival. Whether it's the motto "Live hard, die fast, leave a good-looking corpse" or Romeo and Juliet, teens and their flirtations and fascination with mortality have gotten a lot of attention. Most kids today have their physical survival needs taken care of. In spite of that, many of them still experience a kind of reverse survival need—the need to reject the comforts of their privileged lives.

Dave enrolled at Spring Creek about five years ago. He was at heart a really good kid who had gotten himself into a lot of trouble because he fell in love with fear and got hooked on it. He told me that when he was seven or eight, after a snowfall he would go out with his brothers and sneak into a wooded area along a four-lane highway. A chain-link fence separated the woods from the highway, so they felt that they had a secure position from which to launch their attacks on passing cars. "At first," Dave said, "It was a thrill to just hear the sound of the snowball thumping on the car. I'd get this amazing warm feeling in the pit of my stomach. After a while that went away." Dave went on to tell me about a time when one of the drivers got so pissed off by being pelted that he stopped his car.

As soon as Dave and his brothers saw the brake lights bleeding across the snow, they froze. This was something new, something out of the ordinary. When the car's backup lights illuminated, the boys were even more excited. The guy was coming back for more. They furiously made a new batch of snowballs, hit the car with another burst, and laughed in sheer joy at their good fortune. They collapsed into a convulsing, back-slapping heap. When the driver's-side door opened and a hulking figure emerged (Dave said that in his imagination the driver was a combination of Jason—the masked figure from the *Friday the 13th* movies—a *Night of the Living Dead* zombie, and Darth Vader), a jolt of adrenaline had them on high alert. They scrambled into action. They got off a couple of shots, but their enemy was a tough one. In a few quick steps, he crossed the distance between the boys and himself. With a jump and a quick thrust, he scaled the fence.

When they saw the guy on the fence, Dave and his brothers took off running. As Dave said to me, "That rush from being chased was the high that I've been trying to get ever since. I was scared shitless, but that felt so cool. I knew if I slipped, if I slowed, this dude was going to pound me, take me home to my parents, or do something else not good. I never felt so alive. I saw everything with a clarity I'd never experienced before. It was like every sense was fine tuned. It was amazing. I was an animal fleeing a predator. It was totally Discovery Channel, and I loved it."

Dave's history showed that he had tried to reproduce those chase sensations in many different ways. He immersed himself in the world of video games, but eventually the thrill of first-person shooter games like Evil Dead wasn't enough. By his sophomore year in high school, he and his friends were getting into minor (everything's relative) mischief: turning cars sideways in snowy parking lots, then graduating to turning small cars on their sides, first at residences and later at a used car lot. With the last one, he got his wish—they all got chased, but this time by the police. Dave was the only one who didn't get away. Arrest number one.

His frustrated parents couldn't understand how a good kid, an honor role student, and vice president of the student body could have done something so stupid and destructive. Dave was at a loss as well. Nevertheless, the pursuit of the thrill and the high presented by the risk of survival eventually led to alcohol, drugs, and a couple more minor run-ins with the law for trespassing. He developed a fondness for getting into places where he wasn't supposed to be—the high school after hours, classmates' and friends' homes, a couple of stores. Dave never damaged or stole anything; he just liked to rearrange things—swapping the positions of a couch and coffee table with a chair and ottoman, for instance. "Goofy stuff," as he described it.

What Dave came to realize was that the status quo was his enemy. He hated the idea that everyone had him pegged. Underlying all that was his notion that when he was behaving in the way that his parents, teachers, and other adults expected him to behave, he was, as he put it, "a dead man walking." He wanted to be on the edge. He wanted to reexperience the sensation that his actions were putting his survival, his reputation, and his future at risk. In nearly every other part of his life, Dave experienced ease and comfort. He wanted the opposite of that. As you've no doubt told your own teen, Dave should have been more careful about what he wished for.

Many other teens engage in dangerous behaviors in the name of fun (see Chapter Four). Dave was fortunate that his parents had the resources, financial and emotional, to keep him from sliding too far down that slippery slope. In many ways, he was the complete opposite of Greg; in other ways, the two were united in that survival was one of the primary needs that motivated them. They approached the need from different angles, one rebelling out of fear that his very existence would be threatened, and the other out of fear that uniformity and compliance would figuratively spell the end of his existence.

In both cases, what they perceived became their reality. Going back to the image of the tetherball, in both cases there was always the potential that a hard strike could unleash that ball from its mooring. They both bounced around a bit outside their usual orbit and got scuffed up in the process.

Luckily, in both cases, each eventually had someone step forward to try to reattach them to their center point. In Part IV of this book, we look at some of the strategies you can use to identify how this need is at work in your teen's life and how you can help keep your teen centered and in the game. You can't keep a teen from getting knocked around a little bit, but you can make those shakeups seem far less appealing.

SURVIVAL NEEDS—A QUICK GUIDE TO RECOGNITION

Adolescence is filled with changes in behavior and swings in mood. It's not always easy to identify when your kid is struggling with a major issue or just experiencing what my folks used to call growing pains. Ideally, your teen will tell you if he or she is feeling threatened physically or if it seems that survival is at risk, but that's not always the case. If you know that your child has experienced some kind of loss, an accident, or any other obvious trauma, or if you notice changes that don't seem to be connected to any event you're aware of, here's what to look out for:

PHYSICAL SIGNS
- Significant loss of weight, prolonged sickness, excessive or infrequent sleep, reduction in physical activity
- Enuresis (bedwetting)

- Encopresis (defecating in bed)
- Hoarding food
- Distrust of humankind (peeking out the blinds and looking for someone who may wish to hurt them)
- Running away

EMOTIONAL/PSYCHOLOGICAL SIGNS
- Nightmares that include others wishing to do harm to them, running away, and being physically harmed
- Violent reactions to situations that would usually not justify such actions
- Suicidal ideation and gestures, including failed attempts
- SIGNIFICANT signs of depression: weight loss, lack of energy, excessive sleep, frequent crying spells, isolation from friends and family, not engaging in activities that used to be a source of pleasure
- Detachment from loved ones and pets

Teens who struggle with this need not being met will consistently have very low self-esteem, as their self-talk is usually extremely negative. The questions they consistently run through their heads are these:

- "Why me?"
- "What did I do to deserve this?"
- "Why won't they love me?"
- "When will my life get better?"
- "Why do I stay alive?"

We all want to do everything we can to provide a safe environment for our kids' survival. As we all know, we can't protect them from everything. Whether it's school shootings, car accidents, or illnesses, sometimes our worst nightmares as parents intrude. As much as we'd like to build a giant bubble that surrounds our kids to keep them safe, we can't. Maybe just as important as keeping their physical environment safe, and all their physical needs met, is a safe emotional environment for them—one in which they can feel safe in confiding their darkest fears, the struggles they experience in trying to find a place where they can meet our demands and expectations and those that their peers and culture at large place on them.

Sometimes kids just want to be kids and have fun. That's the next need we'll turn our attention to.

4

Fun

At one time or another we've all likely heard somebody say, or said ourselves, "It's all fun and games until somebody gets hurt." Recently, I heard a teen say, "It's not all fun and games unless somebody gets hurt." We also all know that we encourage our teens to enjoy the best years of their lives.

While it might seem obvious to any parent of a teen that kids are motivated by the idea of or potential for fun, the reality is much more complicated than most parents know. Whereas on the surface it might seem as though fun is easy to define and explain, its causes and the various behaviors that this need can elicit are as wide and far-ranging as teens themselves.

Every kid has a different sense and idea of what fun looks like and how to fulfill that need. With such a broad range of emotions and reactions to fun, it's only natural that when this need is not met, it will produce a wide array of responses in the kids themselves. If fun is denied or if teens believe that fun is denied, how will they react? What steps will they take to lash out against those they perceive to be denying them the opportunity to have a good time and enjoy themselves? These and other questions are what we will explore here.

A GIRL JUST WANTS TO HAVE FUN

Not too long ago, I worked with a teen named Christina. Her parents were both in their early twenties when they moved to the United States from Thailand, and they were committed to holding their children to the highest possible educational standards. They constantly reminded their kids of how they'd sacrificed and saved money from working two and sometimes three jobs each in order to save money to make the move to this country. That kind of sermonizing didn't stop once they got here. Neither did their hardworking ways. The parents both worked very hard, and they didn't want their kids to have to struggle at low-earning jobs the way they did. As a result, the value of education was put on a pedestal right next to the value of hard work.

Christina was expected to hold a 4.0+ grade point average while taking honors classes. She often stayed up until two or three in the morning to study, and she followed an equally regimented schedule on the weekends. Literally, she was allowed little time for having fun. All family outings were more like educational field trips than relaxing diversions. She was constantly under her parents' watchful supervision. Being deeply religious, they were hyper-aware of the kinds of temptations that young people in the United States are exposed to, and they were determined that their kids would succeed, thereby justifying their own sacrifices. In many ways, what they were doing was admirable, and they considered themselves model parents.

When Christina began high school, she got her first taste of the kinds of freedoms most kids had already experienced. She no longer attended the local parochial school and was enrolled at the public high school. Her junior high graduating class had contained only twenty-four students, all with backgrounds similar to hers. Her first few days in the tenth grade were eye-opening and mind-expanding. She got involved in several after-school activities and spent more hours away from home and out from under her parents' collective thumb than she ever had. She liked how that felt.

One of her new friends was a young man named Dominick. He was one of the local thugs who partied, skipped school, and had no parental supervision. He provided her with the perfect opportunity to break out of her parent's reign of control. She began to skip a few classes to spend time hanging out with him. One of her parents would drive her to school, and she started carrying an extra set of clothes in her backpack. She always asked her parents to get her to school early, telling them she wanted to study or meet with teachers for extra help. In reality, she spent her time in the bathroom changing clothes and applying her makeup. Eventually, skipping classes or staying after school meant going for drives with Dominick, drinking, and smoking pot. Instead of going to a friend's house to study, as she told her parents, she would meet Dominick and party and laugh until it was time to go home. Eventually, the evidence began to shine through the thin fabric of her deceptions. Her grades dropped, her attitude slid, and home was no longer tolerable for her or her family.

During our first session, Christina's statements were a variation on "I was just so tired of school and studying all the time." The chorus to those lyrics was "I never had any FUN!!!" She discussed the importance to her parents that their children live a life of near perfection. She described the stress she was under as phenomenal. She discussed how good it felt to let go of all the stress and just enjoy her life.

Christina didn't put it this way, but as I sat there listening to her I kept thinking that the pendulum had swung. She was living a life that was way out of balance—both before she acted out and afterward. Getting her and her parents to understand that she needed to have fun and still maintain good grades while avoiding high-risk behaviors wasn't easy. The fact that her parents shipped her off to Spring Creek gives you some idea of how strongly her parents reacted when they discovered the extent to which Christina had strayed from the path they envisioned for her. Through our work together, I had to navigate around Christina's evident anger toward them and get her to focus on how her choices had contributed to her parents' sending her away.

HAVING FUN MATTERS

Christina's story offers a useful glimpse into how the mere denial of this need can have far-reaching ramifications, and Glasser's ranking of fun as the second need in his hierarchy says a lot about how fundamental (pun noted) that need is to adolescent development. One of the great paradoxes of teens, and one of the reasons why I like working with them, is that they are a sometimes comical mix of child and adult. I can be in a group session having a discussion about some serious issue and one of them will pass gas or use the word "booger" or something equally childish, and they revert to their third-grade giggling selves. Frustrating? Yes. Entertaining? Certainly. That may say as much about me as it does about them, but I'm sure you can relate to this lightning-quick rise and fall on the maturity scale.

Going back to the story of Dave in the previous chapter, when his parents found out that he was tipping over cars, they were furious. When they asked him why on earth he did it, he told them the honest truth as he perceived it—it was fun. It was thrilling. It lent itself to telling great stories the day after that would amuse and entertain his friends and classmates. (As a side note, Dave enjoyed greatly his nickname "Scratch." His crony in the tipping, Alan, earned the name "Ding." Those names indicate that they knew they were doing some damage to the cars but didn't fully understand the extent of it.) To all of them, it was just a joke, a prank, a laugh. All the owners had to do was push the car back over—no harm, no foul, just drive off.

Of course, one person's fun is another person's felony, as in Dave's case. I've been sometimes frustrated by my own kids' pursuit of what they consider to be fun. A year or so ago, my two boys thought it would "fun" to take their brand-new mountain bikes to a county highway department facility, where they'd seen enormous piles of gravel and sand. The materials were stored there to be spread on the roads in the winter. My kids had seen the X Games on television and thought that a downhill mountain bike challenge between the two of them would be cool. We always insisted that the kids wear helmets when riding, so thank goodness the only damage they sustained was some scraped forearms and legs and bent-up brake levers and scratched paint. Fortunately, I didn't have to ask them what they were thinking. My oldest came home, looking much the worse for wear and said, "Dad, I came up with a really bad idea."

A more extreme example of fun gone bad is one that I saw recently on *60 Minutes*. Apparently, some genius entrepreneur came up with the idea of creating an Internet site and selling videos for something called "Bum Fight." This is a darker version of the *Jack-ass* television show and films in which a group of guys inflict pain on themselves in all kinds of ways that I don't think you or I could imagine. In "Bum Fight" the so-called "creators" of this enterprise staged and filmed fistfights between two homeless men. The film crew provided them with alcohol and the promise of more if the pair would whale on another.

Using the kind of we-can-top-that mentality that teens are prone to, kids who've seen the "Bum Fight" videos decided it would be cool to film themselves beating up homeless men. Three Florida teens, who said that the videos were their inspiration, took that idea a step further. They didn't just beat the man up; they killed him. When interviewed on *60 Minutes,* two of the teens, clearly remorseful, said that they didn't intend to kill the man. They insisted that the original motivation for the attacks was to have fun. Something clearly got out of control, and both were helpless to explain how or why that happened.

A Matter of Perspective

Everyone's definition of fun is different. That's always been the case. In my youth, some kids took a lot of pleasure in inflicting pain on others. What is frightening is how the level of violence now seems to have ratcheted up. We know that our kids are exposed to more acts of violence because of the relaxed standards (if you can rightly call them that) in video games, television, and movies. As a result, our kids are exposed to things that you and I likely never were at their age. With increased exposure to extreme acts (sanctioned, amateur, professional, violent, risky), teens' temporal lobes begin to process consequences and other acts of higher reasoning much less efficiently. Is it any wonder that we as parents are puzzled by what some kids consider fun? Is it any wonder that some parents go to extremes to protect their kids from what they view as potential threats to their kids' welfare?

More and more of the young people I work with claim that they are "stressed." Their nearly universal lament is that they are under so much pressure from parents and from peers. Their parents want them to get good grades, get into a good college, have friends, fit in. Their peers put a different kind of pressure on them—certainly to conform but also to engage in high-risk behaviors like taking drugs and alcohol and engaging in sexual activity. They crave relief from that pressure. To them, anything that relieves the pressures exerted by those twin and opposing forces is fun.

TOO MUCH STRUCTURE

Several studies have been done to demonstrate the harmful effects of overscheduling on children, and too many activities impose restrictions on teens' natural ability to have fun. Dr. Alvin Rosenfeld, author of *The Overscheduled Child: Avoiding the Hyper-Parenting Trap*, is among the leading experts in the field and believes that this phenomenon has become a problem nationwide. In a sense, this is a case of parents pushing their kids to have too much fun. They go from soccer practice to piano lessons to tryouts for the traveling basketball team. They try to do some of their homework while riding in the SUV from one activity to the next. Believe me, my kids are heavily involved, and we're heavily involved in their lives. We're well intentioned, and I know most parents are.

But in some cases, kids don't view it that way. They sometimes feel that their parents push them into these activities as a way to put another adult in charge of them. James was one of the first kids I worked with at Spring Creek who really opened my eyes to this phenomenon. Both of his parents worked full time, and to keep him occupied and out of trouble they enrolled him in as many activities as they could. They engaged other parents to help shuttle him from one to the other and did what they could to support, fund, and supervise whatever additional activities they could find.

James said that from the time he was seven, his mother had a calendar on the kitchen wall that she used to track all his and his siblings' practices, rehearsals, games, appointments, matches, playdates, sleepovers, parties, and the like. At first it was a simple wall calendar, but as he got older she had to order an enormous monthly calendar from an office supply store that a company might use to track a production schedule. When that wasn't big enough, she bought a magnetic dry marker board and assigned each of them a color-coded magnetic piece. James is a really bright kid, and he said that the board reminded him of the ones he'd seen displaying the various moves for the audience at a Grandmasters' chess tournament. Pretty soon James started to feel like a piece to be manipulated around a board, not a kid. He and his parents were so busy that all of them were seldom together at one place at one time; there was so much structure for their individual activities that they had little or no time for family activities. Every moment was occupied, so Mom and Dad figured that the kids had no time to be unhappy or dissatisfied. They were wrong.

James was so busy that he seldom had any downtime. He was like an adult, feeling overworked with his time stretched too thin. He didn't want to have to squeeze in any family time, because he had no real time to give up. His parents viewed that as a sign that he wasn't interested in spending time with the family any longer, but in truth, James felt exactly the opposite. When his parents stopped suggesting that he do things with them, he interpreted that as indifference, withdrew further, and lost interest in the activities he was assigned to (which his parents felt he was drawn to on his own). Eventually the cycle spun out of control.

Experts also say that overscheduling children with organized activities stunts their creativity and their ability to make fun for themselves. Many kids aren't ever required to use their own imaginations and resources to create fun for themselves. Diane Ehrensaft, PhD, in *Psychology Today*, put it best when she commented, "Creativity is making something out of nothing, and it takes time for that to happen." I know that as parents, when our kids complain that there's "nuthin' to do," we're tempted to give them something to do—either by enrolling them in another activity or by assigning them chores. The latter will typically result in the complaint "That's no fun." Much of the time, I have to hold my tongue when one of my kids complains about being bored. I want to remind them of what it was like when I was a kid and there were stalls to muck out, cows to milk, and fences to mend every day all day.

Fun should be uncomplicated, but when it comes to how it functions in a teen's life, it's anything but that. Finding that right balance, for teens and parents both, is difficult. Too much leisure time and free time can lead kids to explore areas that we'd prefer they stay out of. Too little free time and fun can stress them out, stunt their creativity, make them feel resentful, and deny them what most teens say they really want—more time interacting face to face and one on one with their parents.

WHEN FUN CHANGES

All my kids love sports. They don't all participate in the same ones, but their passion for those they are active in seems about equal. A part of growing up is figuring out what you like and don't like, finding out what you're good at and not so good at, and deciding what you should spend time on. I loved football and played it as a kid and as a high school student. I probably could have gotten a scholarship or had a chance to play at some university, but beyond that, I didn't have a big future in the game. Financial circumstances, and the reality that as a young man who wasn't six feet four inches tall and didn't weigh 240 pounds or run the forty-yard dash in 4.4 seconds, made it clear that I didn't have a future as a National Football League linebacker. I understood all that intellectually, but it was still hard for me emotionally to deal with that reality. I stopped playing the game regretfully, but I knew my decision was the right one.

It's sometimes really difficult for parents to keep up with all of their kids and their scattershot approach to selecting their latest interests. I'm sure our economy would not be as robust as it is if kids decided at an early age what they wanted to do and stuck with it. Generally, though, by the time our kids become teens, they've become more selective about their interests and passions. When our kids suddenly stop being passionate about something they previously cared deeply about, that's a red flag for us to notice and investigate.

Now, I'm not talking about a passing fancy for a particular band or movie star, or dabbling in a particular activity at school like debate or speech team and then opting out of it. That's normal and natural. Kids should be encouraged to experiment and try things— and to stick with them for at least one season once they've made a commitment to the coach and team. Quitting is not a good habit to get into, either.

What I'm talking about is paying close attention when your child abandons an activity or interest for which he or she has demonstrated a real passion and commitment for a significant period of time. I can't give you a magic number of weeks, months, or years that constitutes a "significant period of time." There are too many variables. You have to know your kid and his or her tendencies. For some teens, a passionate commitment to an activity could mean a few weeks or months, while for others it could mean years. You should be able to assess your children's consistency and focus and know what things they do really excite and engage them. If one of those fun interests suddenly goes away, it's worth your time to dig around and investigate what happened to cause the change.

For example, if you learn that your teen has suddenly decided not to audition for the school plays anymore, the first step is to figure out just how sudden a decision this is. A lot of times, our kids don't communicate very effectively, and what may seem like a rash decision is actually one that they've been contemplating for quite a while. If so, you have less cause for concern. Once you determine the suddenness factor, you can proceed accordingly.

While it's natural for some of our kids' activities to lose a bit of their appeal and fun, many times these abrupt changes in interest level are an indication of something deeper at work. This is especially true if your normally sports-obsessed son or daughter quits a team and starts to engage in a pursuit that he or she has previously showed little or no interest in. Again, some of this waffling and switching can be attributed to teens' hyperactive abundance of curiosity. I know too many parents who casually noted a somewhat significant change in behavior and activity but chalked it up to a "phase" and later regretted it.

Rene was one of the top volleyball players at her suburban high school. A tiny mite of a young woman, she was fearless at hurtling her body to the floor to "dig" the ball. When midway through her junior year she decided she'd had enough of the game and walked away from it, everyone was stunned and wanted an explanation.

Rene told them that the game was no longer fun, she realized she was unlikely to get a scholarship, her family wasn't wealthy, she had designs on attending an expensive private liberal arts college, and the time she spent at volleyball could be used more productively at a job. On the surface that all made sense—logically.

What didn't make sense was, what happened to the emotional (fun) connection she had to the sport? This was a girl who had wall-to-wall posters of Olympians and beach volleyball superstars like Karch Kiraly and Misty May adorning her room. As it turned out, Rene had been sexually abused by one of her coaches on her park district team when she was a freshman. The coach was one of the most popular figures in volleyball circles, and he wielded considerable power over the girls' future in the sport. His wife coached the high school team, and all the girls felt that staying in his good graces assured them a coveted spot on the prestigious team that contended for the state championship.

Only after Rene quit the high school team, gained nearly twenty pounds, and started to drink and experience mood swings that had her ping-ponging between despondency and elation did she come forward with her story. Unfortunately, she was ostracized by her former teammates, and with no evidence other than her word against the coaches, her life at home was ruined. That's when I met her.

FUN AND SELF-ESTEEM

Self-esteem once again rears its head in this discussion of fun. What your kid considers fun is often connected to popularity. Unpopular kids often make bad choices that lead to fun leading to popularity. Part of this is natural. We have all joked about the chess club and the mathletes and other nerdy brainiacs. It's hard to insulate your kids from the kind of teasing and stereotyping that goes on. We'll talk at length about these issues in the chapter on self-esteem (Chapter Thirteen) and throughout the rest of the book. While we'd hate to see our kids give up something they once loved because of outside pressures to conform, we need to be especially vigilant about what our kids pick up to replace those activities. Countless kids will engage in substance abuse activities to become "cute, fun, and popular." (This saying has run wild among some of the Spring Creek Lodge Academy girls as of late.)

You saw in Rene's story a variation on this theme. She started to engage in unhealthy activities—binge eating and drinking—as a way to medicate (numb) herself, not to become popular. Once the tide of public opinion turned against her, she was in more pain and needed to numb herself to an even greater degree. More commonly, kids turn to inappropriate and sometimes dangerous fun activities as a means to fit in. Samantha fit this model very nicely. In her small suburban town in Missouri, there wasn't a whole lot to do. When one student showed up at school wearing a pair of rental bowling shoes stolen from the lanes in a nearby community, he set off a fashion and criminal behavior trend. Soon, students were traveling farther and wider to find shoes of a unique color or that had the name of a far-flung bowling center stamped on them. By her own account, Samantha wasn't particularly pretty, smart, or talented. As she put it, "I was one of the sheep."

She did have a talent for stealth, and her plain-jane, girl-next-door looks and demeanor suited her well. She had a trusting face, and even when word spread among the proprietors of the local bowling alleys to watch out for thieving teens, Samantha managed to still get away with theft. When she tired of bowling alleys, she took up shoplifting. As her reputation grew, Samantha began to take orders. "Need a size-eight pair of khaki cargo pants from the Gap? I can get you that."

Previously anonymous, Samantha became as popular as Robin Hood or a daring cat burglar. None of her peers saw any harm in what Samantha was doing. It was just fun, a thrill, a chance to see if Samantha could top her previous exploits with a more daring heist. By the time I met her, she had graduated from shoplifting to joyriding in stolen automobiles—well, at least she did that once. After a few months in a juvenile detention facility, she came to us. Samantha had few regrets. "Dude," she told me, "you don't understand. I'm a legend back home."

From nobody to notorious, Samantha got a shot of self-esteem that she thought she couldn't have gotten any other way. While we want our kids to stand out in positive ways or blend into the wood-work as typical "normal" kids, they are constantly searching for ways to earn recognition—from us, but more importantly, and danger-ously, from their peers. Given the wide variety of things legal and il-legal, moral and immoral, safe and dangerous, our kids believe to be "fun" and their poor understanding of the consequences of what happens when fun turns un-fun, you can understand how Saman-tha strayed down that path.

More importantly, when our teens don't feel as good about them-selves as we'd like them to, they are sorely tempted to take the easy way out and engage in inappropriate behaviors and enmesh them-selves in negative peer groups. The bar is set far lower for acceptance and recognition among those teens, and it's far easier to earn space in the newspaper for being arrested than it is for acing a physics exam. When our teens are focused on receiving validation from their peers, when peer recognition and acclaim constitute one of the only ways they can get a shot of self-esteem, fun offers them the kind of easy so-lution we all seek to our problems.

FUN NEEDS: A QUICK GUIDE TO RECOGNITION

Fun is clearly a vital component of any teen's mental health, and it's important for you as a parent to help your teen strike a balance be-tween meeting his or her need to have fun and providing a structure that will avoid high-risk activities. Here are some quick signs that will help tell you if teens' need for fun is out of balance:

- They engage in activities that may not align with values—from drinking to drugs to shoplifting to dangerous driving and a host of other behaviors. This is a clear warning sign.
- They engage in activities that are dangerous and trigger adrenaline.
- They disengage from activities typically found to be somewhat enjoy-able (sports, family, working, friends, and positive peers) forgoing them to engage in the new maladaptive behaviors.
- They change their interests—dramatically. There is a natural transi-tion from child fun to adolescent fun. Often the transition will in-clude similar activities, for example, Little League transitioning to

Legion baseball. School band becomes a garage band. If you notice a substantial change in interests, they may be seeking new ways to have fun because their need for fun is not being met.

Everybody says the same thing: kids grow up so fast. They're only with us for a short time. How do you know if your kids are over-scheduled? I believe in something I call the twelve-hour rule. If you aren't in the same physical space as your kid for a minimum of twelve hours a week, and your kid is involved in multiple activities, then you've got your answer. Twelve hours a week. That's less than two hours per day on average. Doesn't sound like a lot of time, does it? Even if you don't think your teen is a member of the overscheduled club, I suggest that you track the number of hours for two consecutive weeks to see how you are doing. You may be surprised by what you learn. You can carry a small notebook and jot down the hours, or do a replay at the end of the day just before turning in. You can create a simple grid that looks something like this:

Day of the week	Time in	Time out	Activity	Daily Total
Monday				
Tuesday				
Wednesday				
Thursday				
Friday				
Saturday				
Sunday				

Weekly Total:

What do I mean by the same physical space? Not that you are in the house at the same time. Hours spent sleeping don't count. What I do mean is that you are within a few feet to a few yards of proximity to one another—sitting at the dinner table, in the same room watching television, driving in the car together. Whether or not you are interacting is not the question at this point. Right now, if you suspect at all that there's an engagement gap between you and your kids, then this assessment exercise should help you figure out what's going on. Do not count time spent watching your child engage in a formal activity like a game, practice, or performance.

If after the first week you determine that you are well over the twelve-hour mark, I suggest you tighten the rules up a bit. Only count that time you spend actively engaged in conversation with your kids. Compare that figure with the one you previously tallied. How many of those initial hours you tracked turned out to be empty hours spent near, but not really with, your kids? Proximity is good; active engagement is better.

5

Freedom

Danijela was a bundle of contradictions. She sat at attention, ramrod straight on the chair opposite me, looking like more like one of my former Air Force colleagues than a scared seventeen-year-old girl. I knew it had to take enormous discipline for her to carry herself like that. At five feet ten inches and 110 pounds, she was nearly skeletal, and the ravages of her eating disorder were easy to spot. Her quick, open, and ready smile revealed teeth stained from her purging habit. Her sunken, deep-set eyes were underlined by dark semicircles that only highlighted her obvious intensity and intelligence. Her stillness and her composure hid the frenetic flashes of anger that I'd seen in other sessions. She was like a recently broke horse—skittish, wanting to bolt but still eager to please and avoid being punished.

Danijela's parents had fled Croatia in the early 1990s, just as the last of the occupying Serbian troops were being forced out in a bitter struggle for independence from Yugoslavia. The family was fairly well off, since her father was an engineer. He quickly found work in this country, and the family settled in Chicago in a Croatian neighborhood. Like most Croats, Danijela and her family were Catholic, but her family was particularly devout. Danijela and her older brother and sister were all enrolled in the local parochial school dominated by immigrant families. She spent the first eleven years of her school life living in an environment that sounded like something out of the 1950s. Along with the strict discipline of the church school and the nuns and brothers who taught her, she experienced the same kind of rigidity at home and in her Croatian classes on Saturdays and Sundays.

Each of the kids was an overachiever. They'd studied some English while still in Croatia but were somewhat behind the other kids at first. By the third grade, Danijela was the top student in the school. By the sixth grade, she was the citywide champion in speech tournaments and debate. She followed much the same track when she enrolled in one of the city's elite all-girl Catholic high schools. She had to take the train and two buses to get from her South Side neighborhood to the school on the city's North Side lake shore location. She had to rise at 4:30 each morning, endure the hour-and-a-half commute to get to school before 7:30, and then arrive back home following after-school activities by 8:00 in the evening.

"Mr. Mike," she told me, "I had a day planner that was like Moses' stone tablets. I had the voice of God in my head commanding me to work every hour of the day, seven days a week." Danijela seldom socialized, and then only to attend church-related functions, and her parents were deeply suspicious of anyone who wasn't Croatian. In that regard, Danijela had high expectations to live up to—the summer between her freshman and sophomore years of high school, her older sister Magda went back to Croatia. Danijela accompanied her sibling on (as she put it) this "spouse-hunting expedition." Magda "bagged" a man named Bata, married him there, and returned to the United States to set up a home.

Danijela recoiled at her sister's choice—the new bride was only twenty-one, had just graduated from college, was now a wife, and had a child on the way after only six months of marriage. So much for a career and any kind of independence. Seeing her sister opt for the traditional life that her parents wanted for their children, Danijela shifted into a higher gear. More determined than ever to graduate number one and get a scholarship to an Ivy League school ("Miles, Mr. Mike—I was interested in one thing: putting miles between them and me"), she started to sleep even less, filling her "free" hours with more resume-building activities.

Always what people would call a big-boned girl, Danijela took a look in the mirror one day at the beginning of her sophomore year and hated what she saw. She didn't want "fat girl" on her resume, so she undertook a program to refine that part of her life as well. At the same time her eating disorder kicked in, Danijela had another awakening. Magda confessed that her father had molested her from the time she was ten until she was fourteen. Magda openly confronted her father, and the family was in turmoil. The perfect image Danijela had of a devoted and devoutly religious father disintegrated. In short order, her faith in her father and in her God was shaken. She began to wonder if she'd been abused herself.

Highly respected in the community (her father was a deacon in the church, her mother the choir's director and vice president of the high school's arts booster club), the family had to keep up a good public front despite what was going on behind closed doors. School and her activities became Danijela's refuge. Her bulimia blossomed into full-blown anorexia. In pain, and struggling to figure a way out of it all, Danijela turned to alcohol and drugs. She hadn't been a partyer at all, but she'd heard enough from her school friends to know what went on. On overnight trips to speech meets and debate tournaments, she was initiated into the Booze Club. Her parents, preoccupied with other issues, stopped focusing on Danijela so intently. Eager to keep up good relations with at least one daughter, they agreed to buy her a car so she could commute more easily to school. Saturdays that had been spent in Croatian classes turned into Saturdays spent drinking with her North Side friends. The alcohol she consumed brought her down, and diet pills and Ritalin brought her back up.

By the middle of her junior year, Danijela was having sex regularly with an assortment of partners. She continued to get good grades, however, so much of her high-risk activity escaped her parents' notice. Distracted by what was going on elsewhere in their lives, and fearful of losing another daughter's love and respect, Danijela's parents loosened the shackles that had bound her. Danijela had never had a curfew before, since she was never really out of the house unsupervised. Now her weekends became her own. Danijela's mother confided in her that she was afraid of what her father might do to her, so she allowed Danijela to spend weekend nights at the homes of school friends.

One night during the Christmas break her senior year, while Danijela was traveling to a party at Northwestern University in Evanston ("How pathetic was that, Mr. Mike? Going to NU to party with a bunch of other overachieving eggheads?"), the car she was riding in got into an accident on Lake Shore Drive. Everyone in the car was under age, and because they were all slightly injured and taken to the hospital, routine toxicology tests showed that they were all over the legal alcohol limit. Only the driver was cited, of course.

That should have been enough to get Danijela and her parents to recognize that something was not right. But sometimes parents won't see what they DON'T WANT to see; the accident didn't stop Danijela or her get her parents to intervene. After years of being under their thumb, she was literally intoxicated by the taste of freedom. To her credit, Danijela never let her grades slip and kept attending school regularly, but she also partied harder and longer than before. The physical toll on a system already weakened by her weight loss, her habit of keeping long hours on the go, and drug and alcohol abuse finally landed her in the hospital after a case of bronchitis persisted and worsened into pneumonia.

Severely weakened physically and emotionally, and spiritually devastated, Danijela confessed all to her mother. As soon as she was well enough to travel, her parents transferred her to Spring Creek. They thought the source of her problems was the negative influence of her North Side peers back in Chicago. Danijela felt they were too exhausted from dealing with the rest of their lives to be bothered with helping her. In our first meeting, Danijela told me that she felt like a car being dropped off for service—her parents wanted us to call them back when she was fixed enough, so they could drive her again.

After a year and a half of being essentially on her own, Danijela struggled at first with the discipline and demands of our program. She'd gone from one extreme to another before coming to us—from being penned up to roaming free—and she'd never learned how to navigate between those two extremes. The other issues aside—the eating disorder, her father's abuse of her sister—she had spun out of control because she became primarily motivated by her need for freedom.

A DELICATE BALANCE

Danijela's experiences are not out of the ordinary. A lot of kids end up in programs like Spring Creek because they weren't properly prepared for dealing with the responsibility that comes with freedom. If you have teens, I'm sure you've struggled with getting them to understand the apparent contradiction in that statement. Teens want freedom. Who doesn't? One of our most important roles as parents and authority figures who work with teens is to assist them as they become (warning: big word here) autonomous. We want our kids to be able to function independently of us, but here's another of those contradictions. Simultaneously, we still want them to remain dependent on us.

What I've learned from talking with hundreds of teens about freedom is that they experience this contradiction from another perspective. They want to be independent, but they also want and need to know that as parents and teachers we support them and will be there when they need us. The problem is that they don't want us to know that they still rely heavily on us as they experiment with freedom, and the last thing many of them want to do is to ask for our help when they need assistance. Somehow, we're supposed to sense where they are drawing the line between support and interference and between independence and indifference. I wish I had a nickel for every time I heard a kid say, "I could do whatever I wanted. My parents didn't care." I'm sure that in the course of my career there were a few cases of parents who were truly indifferent, but they were few and far between.

Trying to walk the tightrope between freedom and dictatorship is probably the most difficult act a parent has to perform. Judging when your child is developmentally capable of handling the responsibility is very difficult. That's especially true when you have more than one child. If your first child is allowed to go out with friends of the opposite sex at age twelve, when your second child reaches that age he or she will expect to be granted that same privilege (your word) or right (their word) at that same age. Problem is, the second child may not be as mature emotionally or intellectually to deal with the challenges and responsibilities that bit of freedom entails.

MATURITY SCORECARD

It makes sense that teens need freedom and that how well or how poorly they handle the freedom they earn is an essential part of their maturity scorecard. I don't play golf myself, but I understand how it should be played. In some ways, I wish there was a "par" score that every teen had to shoot for. That would make it much easier to evaluate where they stand.

Of course, kids aren't standardized, but there are some markers along the way that do function kind of like par. For example, when kids turns sixteen, the government has determined that they possess the skills, intelligence, and maturity to handle the responsibility of driving a car. You and I both know that not every sixteen-year-old possesses that complex of skills and attitudes. (I'm not convinced that every twenty-six-, thirty-six-, or forty-six-year-old does, either.)

With that prize dangling in front of their eyes like a side of beef in front of a wolf, for lots of kids a driver's license represents those proverbial keys to the kingdom. I've been in this position, and I know how hard it would have been for me to say to one of my kids that he or she wasn't ready to be granted that privilege (my word) or right (their word). To teens, a driver's license is like a freedom card. It means that they don't have to rely on their mom and dad to pick them up and drop them off all the time. It means that they can venture out on their own, free of adult supervision. However, the privilege to drive a car can be a slippery slope and lots of kids end up going down the wrong road shortly after they are able to do it legally.

Am I against kids driving at the age of sixteen? Certainly not, but the point I'm trying to make is that as parents we sometimes feel a great sense of relief when one of our children starts to drive. After all, it's a good thing to have someone else in the house we can count on to run to the grocery store when we need something and don't feel like hauling our butts out of the chair or are otherwise too busy to do it ourselves. Our teens remind us of how big a deal driving is, but does it really register with us just how much else is piggybacked on that little laminated rectangle? For us, a teen driving may represent additional expenses—insurance, gas, another car. For them, driving may represent a whole bunch of other stuff—freedom, sure, but also a passport to the country of "Coolistan" and the temptations and the pressure that come with the idea that when in Coolistan one must do as the Coolistanis do.

Obviously, we have to communicate clearly the freedom=responsibility equation and how that equation is balanced by the right versus privilege theorem. I took every opportunity I could when my kids were in the car with me to talk about driving and the responsibilities that go along with it. I didn't want to wait until the day they came home from the Department of Motor Vehicles with that license in their pocket and pride pumping through their blood as I stood there holding the keys. At that point, it's like trying to lecture your dog on good behavior when you've got a Milk-Bone in your hand. They hear the sounds, but their attention is so riveted on the object in your hand that they don't really understand the words you're saying.

When our kids were younger, Janna and I hammered home the point about responsibility and freedom. We let them know at every turn that sometimes we gave them additional freedoms and sometimes they earned them (more on this important distinction in a moment). Regardless of whether they were earned or granted, those freedoms were conditional. Our love for them was unconditional, but the respect we had for them and for the freedoms they'd earned or been granted were not. That's a tough thing for a kid to hear later in their teens when they've perceived that everything is theirs for the asking. Kids get spoiled when responsibility is left out of their upbringing. I told you early on that I had a heap of chores to do, and if I didn't get them done, not only would there be hell to pay with my dad, but everyone else would suffer because some essential task wasn't completed. Janna and I have made sure that our kids have had age-appropriate chores assigned to them from the time they were toddlers—whether it was putting their toys away or carrying their plates to the kitchen sink. If they failed to clean up after themselves and toys were left lying around, those toys went into the penalty box. The kids could get them out only after they'd demonstrated that they could put away all the toys consistently when asked.

One of the great battles waged between parents and teens is over the condition of their rooms. Janna and I struggle with this one, and, surprisingly, it's not with the boys that the most fevered struggles occur. Alicia is a young woman who needs her privacy, and we all respect that. We allow the kids to decorate their rooms as they see fit, and the only thing we ask in return for that freedom is that they keep their rooms tidy. We try not to invade their space and to let them have the sense that their rooms are their sanctuary, but we've always made it clear that while that room is "theirs" it is a part of a larger thing called "our house." In a sense, they are renters and not owners, and while they have some freedoms, they exist within a larger framework of rules and regulations. The same is true with most things we buy for them.

For instance, when we bought the kids their bicycles, we let them know very clearly that yes, that is "your" bike, but your continued possession of it depended upon following some rules. The bikes had to be put away in the garage every night. No exceptions. The bikes could be ridden only on certain roads at certain times, and as the kids got older that area expanded. You get the point. As they demonstrated more and more responsibility by caring for those bikes well, and by adhering to the rules, they got more freedom. When they failed to abide by those rules, they lost freedom. This also reinforced cause and effect, a key concept that many kids lack the developmental capabilities to understand. They need to be exposed to that reality more frequently.

KIDS HAVE CHANGED

I know that kids are probably tired of hearing about the "old days," and though in some ways, kids are a lot different today than they were back then, in some ways they are the same. One way in which I can say they are different, with few exceptions, is their sense of entitlement. We are fortunate that in our family we've had only some minor skirmishes with the kids over this issue. We had to bust our butts to get them to understand the difference between something that's earned and something that's given. It's an ongoing struggle with a generation whose definition of freedom is somewhat different from our own.

The other day, we were all in the truck driving into town. We were all talking and laughing and having a good time. A story Jessy was telling was briefly interrupted by the sprightly ring tone of Alicia's cell phone. She was in the backseat, and I heard her start to chat with one of her friends. I reached back with one hand palm up, and in a few seconds I heard Alicia say, "Hold on." Then I felt the phone nestle in my palm. I said hello and asked who I was speaking to. I heard Robin's familiar voice, and we talked for a few minutes before I handed the phone back to Alicia.

Janna and I do this somewhat regularly. We have no qualms about "invading" our kid's privacy in situations like that. I tell this story because it illustrates a couple of points. First, it reinforces in our kids' minds the idea that what's mine is mine and what's theirs is theirs is only temporary, because their mother and I have allowed them to have it as long as they understand and demonstrate the responsibility required of that privilege that's been granted to them. Alicia's phone is on our family's plan, and she can't abuse or overuse the minutes that plan allows us. We don't allow the phones to be on during our meals together. The kids know and understand these guidelines, and as long as they don't violate those guidelines, everything's cool.

When I was a kid, I had to ask permission to use our home phone. I had to be certain that no one else needed to use it or was expecting a call. I'm willing to concede on some of those points with Alicia by allowing her to have her own phone. I get it that social networking among kids is vastly different from what I grew up with. That doesn't mean that just because I've adapted to the new technologies, the old values have to change as well. Alicia needs to use her phone responsibly, and Janna and I have made sure that we've granted her the privilege of having a cell phone as long as she does use it responsibly.

I also tell this story as a kind of preview of things to come and to demonstrate how freedom works in our family. I'm not about to censor or eavesdrop on my kids' phone conversations. In one sense, my speaking with Robin wasn't a way to check up on Alicia to see with whom she's talking. In another way, that was exactly what I was doing. Janna and I want and need to know who our kids' friends are. We want their friends to know us and how our family operates and what our values and rules are as well. Teens don't want us to dictate the people they can and cannot socialize with. They consider that one of their essential freedoms. In our view, if our kids want that freedom, they have to demonstrate the ability to choose wisely. That's the responsibility that comes with that freedom. How do they demonstrate that responsibility? By proving to us, by letting us get to know their friends, that they can choose wisely and have done so.

So many parents I've talked to lament the negative peer groups their kids have enmeshed themselves with. I understand the desire to share the blame and to feel that their kids were influenced by the wrong crowd and led astray. By reinforcing the notion that our kids are not entitled to as much as they believe they are, by making clear that they have a responsibility to us and themselves to understand and demonstrate compliance with the rules we've laid out for them, we can go a long way toward getting them to understand the crucial distinctions between rights and privileges. I know it's a bumper sticker truism, but there's a lot to be said for our kids understanding that freedom isn't free.

We'll talk at length about other strategies you can use early on to lay the groundwork for enabling your teen to understand that as parents we don't establish boundaries to restrict their freedoms but to ensure them. I'll also provide you with some strategies you can use if that groundwork hasn't firmed up enough to support your authority. If you haven't yet gotten the message across clearly, don't despair. There is still a lot you can do to reign your kids back in if they've jumped the fence and gone wandering. For now, go into observation mode, note how often issues of freedom come up, and see if you can figure out how your teen defines it.

FREEDOM NEEDS: A QUICK GUIDE TO RECOGNITION

Understanding when and where your teen needs freedom is probably the most recurring problem in parenting a teen, and understanding when your teen is pushing normal, healthy boundaries and when your teen actually has issues that stem from his or her need for freedom can be incredibly difficult. This fine line doesn't make your job any easier, but I hope this will give you a sense of where your teen falls on his or her own maturity scorecard. In Chapter Sixteen we will address how to alleviate and solve these issues that deal with freedom, but for now, here are some common actions of teens with freedom difficulties to help you recognize whether or not your child is struggling with this need.

If your teen is having a hard time with freedom, then he or she

- Consistently pushes limits preestablished and previously agreed upon
- Consistently complains he or she does not feel as if he has his or her own space
- Claims to lack autonomy and isn't able to make even the most simple of decisions
- Strikes out for "freedom" by not coming home at agreed times, running away, or strongly defying your wishes

While many of the behaviors on this list seem that they could be true of just about every teen, keep in mind the frequency and fervor with which these actions and conversations take place. Though freedom issues are incredibly common, which can make them easy to identify, the widespread nature of freedom problems is also a large part of the risk that they carry. Many people are quick to dismiss extreme reactions to freedom needs as being merely an age-appropriate behavior, but in most cases this could not be further from the truth.

6

Power

For many teens, the desire for freedom and the desire for power are difficult to separate. When we grant our kids freedom, we are telling them that we trust them, that we respect them, that we believe they are capable of handling the responsibilities we've tasked them with, and that we recognize their accomplishments. As a result of our positive inputs, they feel a surge of power—and that's a good thing.

One of my fondest memories of growing up took place on an Indian Summer day when I was about twelve. I was out working with my dad on a row of fencing. Most of that summer vacation, I spent hour after hour with a posthole digger and shovel, prepping the site and then setting the posts. By the time school started after Labor Day, the calluses that had developed over the calluses on my hands had started to slough off. This particular Saturday, we'd been stringing wire between those posts. We didn't have a come-a-long (a mechanical tool that helps pull the strands taut), so I had a stout broom handle running through the center of the wire spool like an axle. I'd pull as hard as I could while my dad did the tacking.

When the sun had nearly set, Dad whistled and waved me in. I took the wire cutters and snipped through the strands of barbed wire and hefted the remainder of the spool over my shoulder like a hobo carrying his load. My father stood leaning on a fence post, one leg crossed over the other. Squinting into the last rays of the sun and the smoke from his Camel cigarette, he pointed past me as I drew up alongside him. "Look at all we got done today." I turned around and admired the straight-as-an-arrow row of posts that bobbed up and down the rolling field. "A good day's work, son. A damned fine job."

I walked to the house with my chest puffed out like a full-of-itself rooster. That feeling of accomplishment and my dad's praise lasted through Sunday and on into Monday when I went back to school. When one of my classmates asked me what I'd done that weekend, I was proud to tell him what I'd helped to accomplish. He was one of the so-called city kids and was duly impressed, though he didn't want to admit it. I asked him what he'd done, and he just shrugged his shoulders and said he had done a bunch of stuff.

I figured it didn't amount to a whole lot, and that's one thing I see that troubles the young people I work with. Many of them don't have anything tangible that they can point to as an accomplishment. As a result, they haven't experienced the kind of positive power trip that comes from being able to validate yourself through those kinds of efforts and results. Getting to the next level in a video game doesn't produce the same kind of long-lasting effect; turn the game off, and what you've accomplished disappears except in that console's memory. Not the same thing as being able to point down a row of fencing and know that it stands there, and will be standing there for many years, because of what you've done.

PRAISE AND THE PROBLEM OF POWER

Some of my fondest memories as a parent are of the "me do" days when my kids were toddlers. Exerting control over your environment is one of the main developmental functions we all experience as we grow and mature mentally, physically, and emotionally. Of course, looking back at my kids using utensils to feed themselves for the first few times, I can smile at the mess they made of themselves, the high chair, the floor, and the dog. I also know that as they got older, the potential existed for them to create worse messes as they performed more advanced tasks than eating. That's always going to be a part of the bargain, I suppose.

For most teens, exerting their power through accomplishing tasks is a positive step in their development. One of our primary responsibilities as parents is to help our kids develop mentally, physically, and emotionally. When our kids are really young, we all fixated on the percentiles for weight and height that we used as a kind of scoreboard. We had a lot of ourselves invested in our child's physical wellbeing. Later we wanted to make certain that our kids were on track academically—we beamed with pride or had to mask our disappointment when we found out whether they were at, above, or below grade level for reading and math.

Some of you may be thinking that you'd love to be able to praise your kid about the good things he or she has accomplished—if only you saw something positive. I'm not a big believer in mindless praise of anyone for the simplest of things. Kids see through that.

By all accounts, Randy's father was a tough, old school S.O.B. A former Marine, Mr. Anderson had left the military after a ten-year stint of service and had started his own home construction business. He applied the kind of discipline that the Corps instilled in him to his new work life and grew his business from a shoestring operation to one in which he had a waiting list of clients eager for him to construct million-dollar-plus custom homes.

Randy told me that he had grown up idolizing his dad, who was a caring and surprisingly affectionate father. Then Randy started to work with his father during the summer after his eighth-grade year. Gone was the doting father, and in stepped the guy who'd learned his lessons well from his drill sergeant on the infamous Parris Island. I have to admit that I could relate in a lot of ways to Mr. Anderson. He was a man's man, good with his hands and, from the way Randy described him, someone who could make power tools sit up and beg and do his bidding. He had a way with machines and inanimate objects that allowed him to be successful. He also was great with his clients, but overly demanding and in some ways abusive toward his employees and other subcontractors. He got the job done and got what he wanted from people, but he was far more feared than respected.

Randy admitted to me that he wanted nothing more than to be like his father, but he needed more training. He started out as a laborer, mostly toting lumber, offloading supplies, and doing all the grunt work necessary to keep the more highly skilled carpenters busy. "At first, Mr. Mike, I didn't know a stud from a rafter or an eight-penny nail from a sixteen-pound sinker. My dad just assumed that I did. When I asked him a question, he'd mock me a bit. When I didn't ask a question and tried to figure it out myself, he'd get all over my shit for doing something stupid."

Randy was a quick learner, and over the course of several summers he went from errand boy ("I only mixed up the orders from McDonald's once after my dad's head exploded over it") to actually doing rough carpentry. When he screwed up, as he did occasionally, his father, in what he considered a joking punishment, told him to go get the "widow maker" (a legendarily temperamental circular saw) and cut some of the scrap wood and cutoffs into smaller pieces—an essentially useless task. Mr. Anderson wanted his son to be able to think for himself, to solve problems, and to demonstrate that he understood the larger picture behind each of the tasks he was assigned.

"It got to the point, Mr. Mike, that I dreaded getting up in the morning. I loved my dad, but he was like Dr. Jekyll and Mr. Hyde. I don't know what his deal was, but he always had to put me down in front of the other guys on the crew. He'd find the nitpickiest thing I'd done wrong and hound me about it. If I did something right, I never heard about. Never a 'good job' or nothing. I figured I sucked at carpentry, so why bother."

With his father's never-ending stream of criticism ringing in his ears, Randy grew paranoid, and his self-esteem and level of motivation plummeted. Once he figured out that no matter what he did it was going to be wrong, he stopped trying. That lack of effort infuriated his father. Their relationship deteriorated, and Randy's lack of self-esteem and sense of powerlessness spilled over into his school life.

"My dad saw me as just another slacker. He thought I couldn't cut it, and he kept telling me that if I wussed out at this, I'd wuss out of everything I ever tried to do."

The next thing Randy knew, he was enrolled in a military academy for his junior year in high school. He hated it there, and, determined to show his father who was really in control, he dug in his heels. He refused to do any of his schoolwork and completely rejected the marching and other military disciplines that were part of the program's training.

"I figured out that I couldn't beat my dad in a fair fight. So if I just laid there like a turtle and tucked myself into a shell, he could beat on me, but he couldn't hurt me. My failing at everything was more painful to him than it was me. Apathy was a great weapon."

By the time Randy and I met, he and his father hadn't spoken in nearly six months. "All I ever wanted to know from my dad was that he respected me and what I could do. I knew I screwed up sometimes, but I was a kid out there working with men. Why couldn't he ever just let up on me?"

Mr. Anderson believed that his son should learn from his mistakes and that the only way anyone ever learned anything was from criticism. He told me he'd grown up in that kind of environment, and his military training had reinforced all those notions. He wanted his son to be tough, to be a take-charge kind of guy, but the lack of praise Randy experienced did just the opposite. It made him feel powerless and incapable. While the father wanted his son to develop an internal sense of accomplishment, the son wanted some tangible sign of his father's approval and respect. When Randy quit trying, he pushed the exact wrong button on his father, and he knew it. Learning to appear helpless got Randy what he wanted—a way to injure his father. They were locked in an unequal power struggle—Mr. Anderson not recognizing that his need to put his son down was a way to maintain his top-dog status, and his son taking the energy directed against him and using it to throw his father further off balance.

Time and again, I've seen kids exaggerate the perception they believe their parents have of them. "If you think I'm incapable, then I'll show you just how big of a screw-up I really am" is just one variation on that theme. When our kids don't feel capable and we don't reward them with praise (in the communication chapter [Chapter Fourteen] I'll make specific recommendations for how to do this well), we take one kind of positive power away from them, and they find less appropriate ways to express that very real need.

One way or another, our kids will find a way to get their need for power met. When we praise them, we are empowering them in the most positive way possible. When we don't, they will either feel helpless or seek other ways to find the power fix they need.

POWER NEEDS AND ABUSE

Unfortunately, like any of the other needs I've covered to this point, when that need for power is out of balance it can produce some real developmental and behavioral problems. The teens that I mentioned previously in the chapter on fun, who watched and reenacted the "Bum Fights" videos, claimed that they were doing that because it was entertaining and amusing. Teens aren't always the most reliable judge of their motives and actions. I'm certain that to a degree they resorted to first beating up and then killing a homeless man because of their need for power. In all likelihood, they were the kind of kids who either got picked on or ignored by their school's elite. I can think of no better example of the need for power gone wrong than any of the school shootings that have gotten national headlines. Putting an end to bullying became a national rallying cry and is an issue we'll discuss in more detail in Chapter Ten. The powerful and the powerless exist on a sliding scale in every classroom, on every block, and in every household. How our teens learn to navigate that slippery slope is crucial to their success in life.

Meghan was an only child, and her parents indulged her every whim and need. When Meghan didn't feel like going to school, her mother called the office to excuse her absence. When Meghan was frustrated by a homework assignment, her parents would sit with her and help her "do" the task. Meghan's mom and dad wanted her to learn about spending, so they set up a checking account for her. That was a good idea in theory, but they had to fill out the application, balance the account, monitor her spending online, and put more money in the account when she was in overdraft territory. Essentially, Meghan's parents did everything for her. In one sense, Meghan was extremely powerful. As a fourteen-year-old just starting high school, she had two employees in their mid-forties who did most of her work and smoothed her life's path for her.

In most other ways, however, Meghan was helpless. Whenever she encountered any kind of difficulty, she cried for help and her parents rescued her. She was always the victim and never took responsibility for her actions. As a result of this powerless side, Meghan was ripe for the picking and could be easily taken advantage of. She had grown so accustomed to having others care for her needs that she was extremely compliant. If anyone in a position of authority told her to do something, she did it without much thought.

When she struggled in an advanced algebra class her freshman year, she was assigned a student tutor to help her—a young man in his senior year. They worked together during study hall, and soon their work sessions extended to after-school sessions at Meghan's house. Both her parents worked, but they trusted her tutor and allowed the two to spend unsupervised time in their home. The tutor was a brilliant kid, a National Merit scholar bound for a prestigious West Coast university. He was also universally scorned and abused by the other students as the typical brainiac nerd type. As bright as he was and with as promising a future as he had, he still wasn't immune to the kind of abuse leveled at him.

They were the imperfect couple. He preyed on her weakness and convinced her that he was in love with her, and they soon engaged in a sexual relationship. He was also verbally abusive toward her. By constantly putting her down, he kept his position of dominance over her and made her feel as if only someone like him could care about her. She grew completely dependent upon him, and he found great gratification in her neediness. This kind of unequal power dynamic plays out in lots of relationships, but not only was Meghan underage, she was also extremely immature emotionally and socially. She had grown so accustomed to playing the victim that his treatment of her felt right, not like abuse at all.

It took a long time before Meghan could trust me enough to let me know what had happened to her. With her parents' constant attention to her every need, she felt powerful. She also understood on one level that one way to get what she wanted was to appear powerless. Her tutor, on the other hand, felt completely at the mercy of his peer group. When he found someone who was even weaker than he was, he took advantage of that opportunity to fulfill a need that had gone previously unmet. The strong find a way to prey on the weak, and the weak often search for someone even weaker than themselves. Meghan's story is an object lesson in just how complex this need for power can be and how it may, and often does, play out in teen dating relationships (see Chapter Ten).

Whether it's at the hands of bullies or an adult, the power need is typically very important for those kids who are survivors of physical, emotional, or sexual abuse. These survivors have had their core power needs challenged, since they have been dominated in the most primal sense of the word. Not every teen who has power issues is a victim of abuse, but there is a correlation. As you think about your own teen's situation, be aware of this risk, but don't jump to conclusions without researching the subject. The Web site www.helpguide.org has a useful list of warning signs regarding abuse and your teenager.

POWER STRUGGLE

Teens don't have to resort to physical violence to act out problems with power needs. I'm sure that if you have a teenager, you've found yourself locked in a power struggle with your teen at some point. One reason why we have such a clearly defined set of expectations governing behavior at Spring Creek is that we know what can happen when a student wants to engage in a power struggle. The vast majority of the students at the school and whom I see on a regular basis in my office are experts at entangling adults in general, and authority figures in particular, in these kinds of futile battles.

Henry was a master manipulator and a genius at entangling his parents and teachers in power struggles. The youngest of three, Henry felt that he was always being denied the privileges his older brother and sister enjoyed. I met Henry when I was working in private practice before taking my position at Spring Creek. If I had known then what I know now, I would have definitely handled the situation differently.

Henry, his parents, his sister Heidi, and his brother Paul all came in to see me. It soon became clear that Henry enjoyed his position at the center of whatever family upsets existed. One discussion in particular illustrated what these power struggles can look like. The family had only one television, and frequent squabbles about what program to watch erupted. Henry's parents decided that each child should have one half hour of TV choice. Since Henry was the youngest, he got the first choice in the evening, followed by Heidi, and then Paul. Henry's bedtime was an hour before each of his siblings. He was eleven when I first met him, and he had to be in bed by 9:00 on school nights and 10:00 on weekends.

I have some grudging admiration for Henry. He played the game well. Some nights, Henry voluntarily surrendered his time to his older brother or sister. His parents thought that Henry was showing some maturity, but they didn't realize that Henry was far more mature in some ways than they imagined. At the end of the first week of the TV time-share, Henry announced that Saturday night that he had given up three of his half hours during the week and he was going to cash them in that Saturday night with two hours' worth of his choices. Of course, his siblings objected, especially since Henry knew that if he started his watching at his usual time, 7:00, he'd dominate the screen until 9:00. That would leave his siblings with their usual half-hour allotment. How could they complain, he reasoned, when they were getting exactly what his parents said they could have? If they could have what they said was theirs, then why couldn't he have what was owed to him?

Henry's parents tried to be reasonable, and they had to admit that they'd left some loopholes in their rules that Henry had exploited to his advantage. They tried to reason with him but kept butting their heads up against the stone-cold logic of Henry's argument: "But you said we get a half hour each night. That's three and a half hours a week. You didn't say we had to use it or lose it."

When his parents explained their intention, Henry wasn't buying into it. "You can't change the rules now. Not in the middle of things. You're always telling me I have to learn to play fair, so why don't you?"

Henry's parents relented, and the next week, each of the kids tried angling for an advantage by giving up some of their time. The problem was, Henry had first choice each evening, so if he elected to not select a show and passed that privilege on to Heidi or Paul, he was going to be able to accrue whatever hours of television watching for the weekend that he wanted. Another round of negotiations began, and Henry's frustrated mom and dad said that they would alternate each day who got first choice, regardless of bedtimes and age differences.

The whole thing got convoluted and confusing, with Henry and his siblings using the hours of television time owed to them on the weekends as a bargaining chip in extending bedtimes. At every turn, Henry or one of his siblings would play the "but you said . . ." or the "right and wrong" card until the parents sought harmony by buying a second television set. They weren't exactly rivaling the biblical wise man Solomon, and they needed the math and time tracking skills of an accountant to keep straight who was watching what shows when and on what screen on what day.

In this case, the struggle was nearly comical, but it revealed a deeper set of issues, and the kids exploited the "you play favorites" and "X always gets his/her way so why can't I?" friction that seems to exist in all families with multiple siblings. Who got to watch what show was really more of a battle over who was going to set the rules, who was going to gain Mom or Dad's favor, and who ultimately had the most power in the family. My money was on Henry, and though I saw that family for only a short while, the crafty little guy, who also had a mean streak a mile long, left an indelible impression on me. As the youngest he had to work the hardest to get the power he needed. When his parents compensated for his age and gave him a break, his older siblings pounced on every opportunity to claim, "NO FAIR!" Henry picked up on all those cues pretty darn fast. I've always wondered what happened to Henry, but I'm sure he succeeded at whatever he chose to do.

POWER NEEDS: A QUICK GUIDE TO RECOGNITION

How to tell if your teen's power needs are not being met:

- Teen often engages in arguments and plays the right/wrong game.
- Teen dominates younger or weaker siblings.
- Teen complains about not feeling heard or understood.
- Teen consistently attempts to manipulate the environment (makes physical changes in room or home).

The old adage that power corrupts and absolute power corrupts absolutely doesn't have to apply in your family. Power can liberate and encourage your teens. Power—yours and theirs—needs to be managed carefully and with great sensitivity. We all want it, we all need it, but when we struggle over it, we all ultimately lose it. (Balance is as important with power as it is with any other aspect of our lives.)

As adults we understand the role power plays in our lives, and even with all our experience and accumulated wisdom, it is very easy to either get caught in a power struggle with others or be a victim of someone else's power play. Maturing into an adult involves learning how to handle our own power appropriately and to deal with other people and their power-related issues. Probably the best thing we can do as parents is to model appropriate behaviors. By not abusing our own power and authority over our children, by not exercising or abusing our power over others, and by having the proper respect for other authority figures we come into contact with, we can go a long way toward helping our children understand what's appropriate and what's not.

7

Belonging

Andrew was an intelligent student at a Midwestern high school. Despite his high grades, or perhaps because them, he was far from being the most popular kid in school, and as the story so often goes, this shy unassuming kid was so overlooked that he nearly blended in with the beige lockers. At a school with a proud history of athletic accomplishment, it was kids like Andrew who served as extras brought in as background filler for a crowd scene.

Michael was Andrew's advanced placement physics teacher, and because of his background in carpentry and electricity, the school's principal assigned him to be the technical director in the theater, making the sets and lighting the school's theater, dance, and music productions. Michael had a soft spot in his heart for kids like Andrew. He bantered with students like Andrew in class and greeted them in the hall, but his motives for going out of his way to acknowledge these kids weren't completely unselfish. He needed kids to enroll in his class to keep it from being dropped, and he needed kids to work on his theater crew. While the students who tried out for the acting roles in the productions tended to be extroverts, anyone who wanted to work behind the scenes was either someone who failed to get an on-stage part or someone who didn't mind not being seen or heard. Tech crew, as it was not so fondly known, was just a step or two ahead of chess club and on a par with Spanish club or the ill-fated AV club. It tended to attract students a lot like Andrew—self-proclaimed "loners, losers, and loonies."

Excluded, by choice or by vote, from most other school activities, tech crew kids developed a reputation as a band of misfits. Michael didn't mind that at all. By giving the kids who joined his crew any identity at all to associate with, they were better off than the anonymous, drifting, faceless beings they had started out as. Andrew's trajectory was pretty similar to that of others who joined. At first he barely spoke to anyone but Michael, and he preferred to be given a task he could work on alone and unsupervised. Soon, though, he proved to be really handy and loved working with the power tools, eventually confessing that he had taken woodshop all three of his first years at the school.

Being an honor roll student in a shop class further isolated him, since shop tended to be the last resort and refuge of what we used to call burnouts. Andrew had adopted some of the habits of that lowest rung on the school's social ladder: he wore his hair long, dressed mostly in concert T-shirts (black only), and instead of the hip-hop look with oversized baggy jeans and chinos that nearly every other male wore, he favored slimmer-cut Levi's or Carhartt work pants. Once Michael got to know him better, Andrew told him that he tried to dress as much like the custodial staff as he could. He said, "I felt like that was what my role was—keep the place up and running so the elite kids could trash it."

In time, Andrew discovered that the others on the crew shared some of his interests—Japanese animation and comic books, classic speed metal rock music, and beyond terrible B movies like *Toxic Avenger*. He began to open up; he had a quick sarcastic wit and a cynicism that seemed as much a part of the group's identity as their role as outsiders. Over time, he became one of the tech crew's leaders and assumed the role of chief carpenter and electrician. One of the young women in the group recognized him for the diamond in the rough that he was and asked him to the homecoming dance his senior year. He declined, but after some talking-to from Michael and from his AP English teacher, he agreed to go. The two dated for the remainder of the year and the summer before they went off to college.

At graduation, Andrew's parents sought out Michael to thank him personally for how he'd helped their son. Andrew had concerned his parents. He spent a lot of time by himself. He didn't have a computer of his own, so it was easy for his parents to monitor how much time, and where he spent it, on the Internet, and as far as they could tell he spent little of it instant messaging anyone or hanging out on any of the social interaction Web sites like MySpace or Facebook. They had encouraged him to participate more in school functions, to get out and meet new friends, but Andrew had mostly ignored those suggestions. Andrew's mother and father knew that it was important for their son to form an identity outside of the role he played within the family structure. They understood that a natural part of growing up is differentiating oneself from one's parents. Andrew wasn't really taking those steps until Michael intervened.

AN UNEXCEPTIONAL EXCEPTION

As we've discussed earlier, all teens need to go through the stages of individuation—separating themselves from the family and establishing an identity independent of family. Andrew's father was somewhat of a recluse himself, and he and his wife didn't socialize much, so Andrew really had no role models for typical social interaction and interpersonal relationship development. Whatever belongingness needs he felt were met by his extended family. His case is somewhat atypical because he had to be encouraged to form new bonds. Most teens are eager to do this, and in many cases, parents are more concerned about applying the brakes on their teens' explorations with peers than they are in getting their kids out of neutral.

In many ways, freedom and belonging are intertwined here. As we saw in Danijela's case, it is difficult for a teen to establish an identity independent of family without having some freedom to explore. When Danijela realized that she was like a clone, producing the desirable traits that her parents had programmed into her, she rebelled. Fortunately for Andrew, freedom was never an issue, and his parents' sensitivity to the pressures he faced in overcoming his reluctance to separate himself from family and find another place where he fit in helped him make the transition more smoothly than many kids.

THE BENEFITS OF BELONGING

For many teens, the idea of belonging is one of the most important and complex. I read somewhere once that exclusion is a form of inclusion, and after hearing Andrew's story from Michael, I had a better understanding of what that contradiction meant. Because the social climate he existed in and his natural temperament excluded him from participating in most other school activities and social cliques, Andrew was automatically discarded by the mainstream, along with others like him. Some of those discards gravitated toward tech crew, and others were recruited into it, but they formed their own group and developed that group's identity as well as their own, based on the fact that they were—in the minds of the cool kids at least—castoffs.

One positive benefit of the desire to belong is that like-minded individuals can find comfort in being cast out from the larger group—or from being a part of that larger group. Some people think of themselves as the independent type—what was once called the lone wolf, and they go out of their way to push other people away and prevent them from entering their circle. A true lone wolf (one who really prefers and enjoys isolation) is a very, very rare breed. Teens (or adults for that matter) who adopt that identity usually do so as a means of protecting themselves—they are needy sheep in a wolf's clothing.

What I've always found interesting is that teens who isolate themselves, who want the world to view them as unique and independent, who proclaim to march to the beat of their own drummer and choose to walk a different path, usually are marching to music someone else has written and are walking down a path that someone else has already made. They also happen to be wearing whatever uniform of the outcasts of their day or a previous generation have worn. They act as if they don't care what the world thinks of them, but in behavior and appearance they are almost shouting, "Hey look at me! What do you think of this?" In truth, they care about what others think of them as much as most people do. They are also usually found in pairs or groups. So much for the myth of the lone wolf.

The Company You Keep

Whether it is Goths with their piercings, black clothes, and distinctive makeup; fashionistas with their UGG boots, Lucky jeans, and little dogs in designer handbags; or jocks with their jerseys and ball caps, most teens use clothing to announce their affiliation with the group they choose to be identified with. Though they claim to hate to be judged on their appearance ("Just because I dress slutty doesn't mean I'm a slut"), they intentionally choose a manner of dress, language, and attitude that aligns them very closely with a particular group. Again, we face a contradiction that many teens aren't quite capable of grasping intellectually. As parents we know that they are books who are judged by their cover; the company they keep, and nearly everything else about them, are subject to someone's judging them and making assumptions on that basis.

Has this really changed at all for today's teens? Weren't we all subjected to the same kinds of lumping conclusions? An Air Force buddy of mine, who grew up near Chicago, told me about the raging debate that kids in his junior high had about what radio station you listened to the most—WLUP or WLS. Whichever one you declared your allegiance to revealed a whole host of other things about you—whether you were a "stoner," whether you drank Bud or Miller, whether you were a virgin or experienced. To that extent, things haven't changed a whole lot. What is different is how information is exchanged. As I've mentioned before, teens are so much more savvy about the media and technology than before. They have far more tools at their disposal to announce to the world who they are. Whether the face they present to the real world or the world of cyberspace is an accurate reflection of the truth hardly matters.

Online Belonging

If you spend any time at all on the MySpace or Facebook Web sites, you can also see some of the ways people try to reach out to one another and make connections—in other words, to belong. Just as kids in the past compiled lists of their friends on paper and rank ordered them, MySpace allows them to display photos or lists of their "friends." These decisions are based on a few lines of text in which they describe themselves and the e-mail exchanges they have. Another Web site that I find somewhat troubling, but many teens I've spoken to claim is just innocent fun, is www.hotornot.com. On this Web site, individuals can join up and post pictures of themselves. (As I write this, nearly twenty-six million photos have been posted.) Anyone viewing the Web site can select the gender and age and sexual orientation of people whose photos they'd like to view. Nude photos aren't allowed, but viewers are asked to rate the person's appearance on a one-to-ten scale. Once they make their choice, that person's overall rating is updated, and the viewer moves on to another photo to rate. (To date, twelve billion votes have been cast.)

We make judgments based on appearance all the time, and while the people posting their pictures can provide a short blurb about themselves, the superficiality of it all stunned me the first time I viewed the Web site. I do think it's interesting, since it says a lot about the strength of our need to make connections, to be accepted, and to find a sense of belonging. Making new friends is easier for some people than for others, and I'm trying to remain nonjudgmental and simply accept this as a tool for this era that is probably different only in format from a newspaper lonely hearts ad or one of the many other variations on that theme that exist. I'm still a bit old-fashioned, and I haven't quite come to embrace the notion that the Internet offers community and connection in the same way that face-to-face meetings outside of cyberspace do. I'm still puzzling over this digital belonging and trying to figure out what it says about us. The key for you as a parent is to recognize that this need is strong in your teen, to talk about it, to view some of these Web sites yourself, and to make the determination whether you feel that they're appropriate or not. The fact is that no book can keep current with the latest trends in cyberspace that currently occupy your teens' time and attention. Monitoring their Internet usage is always a good idea.

JILL BELONGS

Jill's story is pretty typical. She was born and raised in Bellefonte, Pennsylvania, a small town fairly close to Penn State University. Her family had lived in the area for years, first farming, and then running a hardware store in town. Her mother was more ambitious than any of Jill's other aunts and uncles, and she had put herself through school at Penn State. She was content to help her husband run the family business for a few years after graduation, but the tension between Jill's parents grew as each "one more year" turned into another. During Jill's freshman year in high school, the divorce was finalized. Tired of the small town life, and with a nice inheritance from her grandmother, Jill's mother took advantage of a former classmate's offer to work at an Internet startup company in New York City. They weren't prepared, or able to able to afford, housing in Manhattan, so Jill, her younger brother, Jason, and her mother settled on a leafy suburb across the river in New Jersey.

Maplewood was a commuter town, a cluster of tidy homes around a quaint town center and a few strip malls. By all appearances, it wasn't that different from Bellefonte. Tree-lined streets and city parks were a far cry from Manhattan's congestion and commotion. In truth, Jill found Maplewood to be a world apart from Bellefonte. Though she had spent only one year in high school at Bellefonte, Jill had established herself as one of the more popular kids in her class. She wasn't a top student, but her A's and B's put her near the top. She was popular with her peers and well regarded by the faculty. She'd grown up at the store, was used to being around adults, and was polite, respectful, and at ease around adults. In almost every away she was an ideal kid, and her mother, now thinking of Jill as much as a valued friend as a daughter, trusted her implicitly and knew that if anyone could make the transition to a new life in New Jersey, it was Jill.

Jill wasn't thrilled about the idea of leaving her close circle of friends, girls she had been in school with since the first grade, but she was excited to leave Bellefonte. Jill loved clothes and fashion. She had read *Elle*, *Seventeen*, and *Cosmopolitan* at an age when many of her peers were just weaning themselves from *Highlights* magazine. She also loved movies and music, and she devoured the celebrity gossip magazines and daydreamed of being the "It" girl at some point in the future. All of that was just a dream in Bellefonte, but in Maplewood, that reality was just a few stops away on New Jersey Transit—the island of Manhattan.

The first few weeks at school were tough for Jill. As the new kid she had to endure a series of examinations by her peers. Fortunately for Jill, she wasn't too attractive, too thin, too smart, or too talented to pose a real threat to the pecking order. She was also pleasant enough and knew enough about what her peers were also interested in to be accepted on the fringes of the most popular girls at the school. In a sense, as Jill later told me, "It was like I was on the team but I wasn't a starter or anything. A couple of groups of girls wanted me on their team because there's strength in numbers. The group that I chose to go with was effectively the JV team. More of a chance for me to get playing time." Sports metaphors came naturally to Jill, who had been a pretty good soccer player back in Bellefonte, but one passing mention by a member of her new clique that "All girl jocks are dykes" convinced Jill that her soccer career was over.

Cut off from most everything that was familiar to her, and with only a six-year-old brother, whom Jill described more in terms of his being a pet ("He could be cute and fun sometimes, but he was mostly a pain in the ass to have to take care of—and he smelled funny"), than a family member, Jill was eager to latch onto whatever connections she could find.

Under the influence of her new-found friends, Jill went from being a somewhat serious athlete to a mall brat. Her mother was working long hours and reaping the financial benefits of that hard work, so she had no problem with hiring part-time help to watch Jason on the weekends. This left Jill with plenty of free time. Feeling guilty for having uprooted her daughter and for not spending as much time as she used to with her, Jill's mom compensated with a credit card and a thousand-dollar spending limit. She was reasonable and told Jill that the money had to last for three months.

Very quickly, Jill realized that a thousand dollars wasn't going to go as far as she hoped. The fashionable attire bar was set pretty high at her school, and she noticed that the while both brands of watch ended in "ex," her Timex wasn't going to cut it when most of her friends were sporting a Rolex on their wrists. Rather than deal with embarrassment of being seen with an inferior product—which had been a graduation gift from her grandparents—Jill tucked it away in a drawer. "Who needs to know what time it is?" she told everyone. Jill later realized the significance of that decision. She was adopting a new carefree persona, shedding bit by bit the remnants of her past.

Over time, the trips to the malls in New Jersey got old. What better place to shop and bargain hunt than Manhattan? By the end of her sophomore year, Jill was sipping eight-dollar lattes while roaming arm in arm with her girlfriends down in SoHo, dressed and made up more like twenty-four-year-old models (with the prerequisite cigarettes dangling from their lips) than the sixteen- and seventeen-year-old girls they were. It didn't take a lot of effort, just a flirty glance at some of the guys out on the streets, to get escorted into a bar for a drink. Later, her sleepovers with the girls in the neighborhood were mere disguises for nights spent clubbing in Manhattan and for her first experiments with the drug Ecstasy and a bag of marijuana she kept in her purse and used to calm her from all the stress she was under.

"My name was Jill, and my two best friends were Amy and Sara, but in our minds we were Lindsay, Paris, and Britney," Jill later told me. Jill's drinking and drug taking weren't, by her standards, "a problem," but when her funds ran low she resorted to other measures—stealing money from her mother, blackmailing her father with guilt to send her cash ("Mom won't let me have anything"), and having sex with guys she knew would give her drugs and in some cases cash. She looked at those exchanges as "gifts," vehemently denying that she was ever turning tricks.

Fortunately for her, but unfortunately for Sara, fate intervened and kept her from sinking any lower than she had. One night the trio went to Manhattan. By one in the morning, Jill and Amy had had enough. They wanted to head home, but Sara, both high and drunk, insisted on staying out. They tried to convince Sara that she should go home, but she insisted she would be fine.

"The biggest regret of my life, Mr. Mike, was being so scared of getting in trouble myself that I let one of my friends do something that stupid."

The next morning, Jill learned that later that night, Sara had hailed an unregulated gypsy cab to take her back to Jersey. She was raped and beaten and dropped off just across the Hudson River near the Lincoln Tunnel. Too drunk to remember much of the incident or her assailant, Sara was little help in the investigation.

Jill was devastated and despondent. She'd violated a kind of code that existed in her clique by abandoning her friend, and she was outcast. She slipped further into depression. When her mother sent her back to Bellefonte to live with her father, she exploded into a rage and ran away several times before coming to Spring Creek.

BELONGING MATTERS

As is true in all of these case studies, a variety of the person's needs aren't being met to some degree. In Jill's case, her parent's divorce, the move to a new location, and the change in the nature of her relationship with her mother all point to that need for belonging not being met. What she did to meet that need in a new environment (once again, a loss of familiarity rears its head) included abandoning a previously important identity as an athlete and "good kid," adopting a new persona, latching on to a new kind of peer group, and experimenting with drugs and alcohol. All these actions demonstrate how Jill's need to fit in and belong to some group led her down a very dark and disturbing road.

I've also seen this work in reverse. When a teen's need to belong goes unmet—because he or she is either rejected by peers or lacks the kind of self-esteem necessary to move beyond the circle of the family—that teen can become overly clingy. I know of one young woman in her late teens who still insists on sitting in her mother's lap. Being affectionate and close is one thing, but this young woman has few friends and socializes seldom, and at an age when most of her peers are anxious to go to college or move out of the house, she shows no signs of desiring any kind of independence. In this case, freedom and belonging are intertwined.

I've said before that teens need and want to feel a connection to family. That connection is different from what it was like when they were younger, but it still exists, though it may be well disguised. Whether we admit it or not, flaunt it or hide it, express it quietly or loudly, we all want and need to belong to some group of other humans. Belonging can make teens feel free of parental control and influence, powerfully proactive, provide many opportunities for novel experiences and fun, and on several levels ensure their survival.

BELONGING NEEDS: A QUICK GUIDE
TO RECOGNITION

Teens all feel and are motivated by meeting these needs to different degrees. While some of the signs and indications of that need may overlap from one need to another, we can get a glimpse inside a world that we sometimes feel cut off from by paying close attention to our teens' behavior and by having frank and open conversations with them regarding their thoughts and feelings. Looking at our teens' needs is not merely a diagnostic tool to determine what's wrong with them when they are acting out—though that is certainly an important component of parenting—but offers insight into what really makes our teens tick: what motivates and drives them, what delights them and discourages them, what frightens them and encourages them.

This is a quick guide to recognizing when behavior needs aren't being met. Be on the lookout for sudden changes in behavior like these:

- Adopting a new style of dress
- Listening to a new type of music
- Abandoning a previously favorite activity and taking up a new one
- Using language or slang that is unfamiliar to you
- Changing radically the amount of time spent either at home or away from home
- Hanging out with a new group or individuals
- Spending more or less time on the phone or Internet or other forms of communication and interaction

While these are indicators, they are by no means the only determining factors to spotting problems with belonging needs. Thinking of your teens' needs is just one of several lenses you can use to examine their behavior and personality. As we make the transition to the next part of the book, we will look at what happens when those needs aren't met and how we can solve many of the problems associated with those unmet needs.

Part III

When Teens' Needs Aren't Being Met

8

The Emotional Consequences
of Unmet Needs

About four years ago when my sons, Cody and Jessy, were age eleven and nine, one of the joys of their lives was playing video games on their Nintendo 64. One of their favorite games was Mortal Kombat. In it, they could select from a series of different characters to square off against one another in Ninja-like fights. The violence in the game wasn't excessive by today's standards, and while I didn't have Mortal Kombat when I was younger, my brother and I scuffled pretty frequently when I was growing up, so I knew that some roughhousing between my kids was inevitable and in most ways healthy. One thing Janna and I noticed was that after the boys first got the game, and more especially after they had been playing it frequently, the level of violence in their real-world play went up. They didn't take bloodletting swings at each other with broadswords or sticks the way the characters in the video game did, but their play went from relatively harmless pushing and shoving and slapping to all-out wrestling and arm twisting.

After a particularly rough day when Janna had to handle more than her share of one or the other boys complaining to her that the other had roughed him up somehow, she shared this information with me. Together, we told the boys that if that kind of violent behavior continued, we would have to take the game away from them. Well, we were still learning parenting lessons at this point, and after the two had an equally difficult day that same week, Janna and I wised up. We realized we hadn't made the consequences clear enough, so we sat Cody and Jessy down and told them the new plan: If their violent behavior continued, the first time we witnessed it or heard about it from one of them, we'd take the game away for a week. If it happened a second time, we'd take it away from them for two weeks. If there was a third strike, the game would be gone for good. Eventually the boys got to strike two, but they never did get a third strike against them, and the level of violence went back down to its old run-of-the-mill level.

I tell this story because it illustrates how my sons' need to have fun could be used to modify their behavior. To them, there was no greater fun than playing that game on their Nintendo 64. If you have kids, I'm sure you know how addictive those games can be. After a while, your kids crave the pleasure they get out of playing them. The whole point of needs and how they function in governing our behavior is that when those needs are met, we experience pleasure. When those needs are not met, we experience some form of pain. Knowing that, Janna and I had to set up a plan that would deny them the pleasure they got from playing the game in order to modify their behavior.

Simple stuff, right? Humans seek pleasure and try to avoid pain. Nothing new here. Our first effort (instant denial) at getting the boys to stop banging heads physically probably wouldn't have produced the same results. Why is that? The point of the consequence wasn't just to get them to stop playing the game; it was to get them to understand the boundaries between rough play and violent play. If we had simply taken the game away from them immediately, they'd have had only one experience to learn from. Also, the punishment would have been swift and definitive—no more game, ever. Chances are, we would have been tempted to backtrack on that action and let them play with the game again. But going back on a promised consequence is a major no-no (see Chapter Twelve).

It was better for the kids to experience a little bit of pain and then a little bit more pain before the game was gone completely. Not only did we get to reinforce the message more than once, but a consequence remained in place. If they'd gotten the ultimate punishment immediately, we'd have had to come up with another consequence to get rid of the behavior we didn't want and to reinforce the learning we did want. We'll return to this example later on. For now, the main thing to keep in mind is that when needs aren't met, we experience pain. Most of us want to avoid pain and seek pleasure.

In the chapters on the primary needs, I told you stories of teens driven by different needs. As those stories progressed you also saw what happened to those kids when their primary needs weren't met: most of them acted out inappropriately. For now, I want to concentrate on the three emotional consequences—pain, anger, and frustration—all of which, along with the various acting out behaviors, are byproducts of the failure to satisfy a teen's needs.

FROM PRIMARY NEED TO PAIN

In the strictest sense, pain isn't an emotion but a sensation. In behavioral terms, it is the response to a stimulus. If someone sticks you with a needle, you feel pain. The needle pricking your skin is the stimulus; the sensation of pain is the response to that stimulus. Next, that pain causes you to cry out, cover your arm, or make some other appropriate response. In other words, a response becomes a stimulus that produces another response, and the stimulus–response cycle goes on and on.

If only the connection between stimulus and response were that clear and direct when it came to human beings and our complicated behavioral scenarios. If somebody walks up to you and stabs you with a pin, you pretty much know immediately what the cause of your pain is. You may not know why that person hurt you, but you have a clear understanding of cause and effect once the action has occurred. So many of the teens I've worked with don't know what is causing their pain; they only know that they are in it. Even when they do know who or what is causing their pain (someone like Greg, the boy I talked about in Chapter Three whose father abused him, and that led him to struggle with the need for survival), knowing the cause of their pain isn't a magic solution to ending it. That whole stimulus–response behavioral model takes on a lot of layers. It's almost like a river depositing sediment and piling debris on top of debris. First one thing happens that causes pain, then another, and then another. Most of us don't often process the stimulus–response, cause-and-effect chain thoroughly enough. We ignore the pain, move on, and do that little trick we mental health care pros like to call sublimation. We bury it. Sometimes that river bed gets so piled up with the dirt we've thrown over our shoulders while digging to bury our unprocessed, unresolved pain that the waters overflow the banks, flooding the area and doing damage on a wider and wider scale. If we were to deal with the emotional consequences of our experiences regularly and immediately, we'd likely not have the kinds of problems that plague most of us.

Conversely, there are times when our physical pain can't be traced to a single source. Unless we have an accident that results in a specific injury, most of our physical aches and pains are the result of overuse, not one-time trauma. This same scenario is true of our emotional and psychological pain. Danijela, the young Croatian woman whose parents kept her under strict control and who struggled with issues of freedom in Chapter Five, was someone who, to lesser extent than Greg, knew the source of her pain. In her case, as well as in Greg's, she had multiple sources of pain—the burden of her parent's expectations, her father's incestuous relationship with her sister, her separation from her old country, and being the "different" kid in a new school. That gradual buildup over time of nicks and scratches rather than deep gashes and gouges can make it hard for us to identify why we feel bad. How many times has someone asked you "How are you doing?" and you've responded with a cover-up: "Fine" (translation: I'm not really feeling great, but it would take too long to explain) or with the other alternative: "Not so good." When pressed for an explanation, we use the shorthand, "Life."

Your Perspective Is Different from Theirs

Just because teens haven't had the same amount of time as adults on the planet, we sometimes make the mistake of thinking that every single experience they have is easy to differentiate. We think they should be able to pinpoint exactly what is causing them to be upset and feel pain because it had to have happened fairly recently. Alternatively, we think that it should be easy to recall because it is such a fresh new experience, not like the experience of adults, who have a enough aches and pains the world has heaped on us that we've become numb to it all. That "get used to it, kid," sentiment has a close cousin: "you think you got it bad?" It's best not to let either of those two family members in the room when you are talking with your kids about the kind of pain that they are in.

One of the great joys—and, I have to admit, frustrations—about working with young people is the extremity of emotion they feel. Everything that happens is loaded with such emotional mass that it's any wonder they can move around at the rapid rate of speed they do. Just listen to your teen's conversation—it is filled with superlatives. Everything is "you never understand," "it was the WORST," "it was the BEST/ugliest/hottest/coolest"—you get the picture. As a result, when they feel pain, they feel PAIN. It's easy for us as parents or authority figures to dismiss this as exaggeration, but one of the most important things you can do is keep their feelings in perspective. A wound, a slight, a look, a word may not seem to you to be source of considerable pain, but it is to your teenager. And for the most part, they aren't acting. They are feeling that amount of pain. They lack the emotional and cognitive skills to deal with that pain in the way you and I would. In some ways that's good—they express their anger and frustration immediately and don't stuff it down inside themselves the way many adults tend to do—but their expressions of pain and anger and frustration are sometimes inappropriate and don't involve any kind of learning from the experience.

Think about the last time you wallowed in pain over some real or perceived slight at work or over a personal relationship or one of the world's injustices. You get off the train after work, and the new car you got just last month has had its driver's side door scratched and dented. You feel that pain in your gut and in your head. And what follows immediately after that? Anger. How could somebody have done this? Why can't stupid people control their doors? Why does this always happen to me? Why does this have to happen to a BRAND NEW CAR? Chances are, if you're like me, that pain and anger get together and either play out a revenge fantasy, get exorcised with a few choice words, or get extinguished with a couple of palms slammed on the steering wheel. Or we cram it into a mental storage space labeled "Life Sucks" and let it sit there and fester. We pull ourselves together (sooner or later) and put it into perspective.

As I've mentioned earlier, teens' higher cognitive centers in the brain are still developing, so they lack the intellectual tools needed to put painful events into perspective. Because of this, what might seem to us like an obvious next emotional step often eludes them. They are simply unable to make that connection by themselves, and without a guide, their pain will continue to escalate until it becomes something new altogether. Because teens don't have the kind of experiences and mechanisms to understand the nature of their pain, their lack of understanding causes more pain.

FROM PAIN TO ANGER

When I am in physical pain and can't figure out its source—whether it's a stomachache, a headache, or back pain—the level of intensity seems greater. That's true in many cases of emotional or psychological pain—because we don't understand its source, the pain intensifies. The reason is partly that we are focusing on it more. It's like when we were kids losing our baby teeth. We somehow couldn't get our tongues to stop probing and poking at the tooth, and the pain was as much self-inflicted as it was a result of the natural process of the new tooth cutting its way through gum tissue.

Because teens experience pain as a result of a need not being met, they are sometimes not fully aware of the source of the pain. This in turn leads to anger. When anger isn't connected to any real source, it attaches itself to anyone or anything that comes near it. It's almost as if anger has an indiscriminate magnetic field—it will attract anything to it and convert it into an irritant. You've probably experienced that transformation yourself. You're in a bad mood and don't really know why, and your spouse starts to talk to you about some issue that needs discussing. You're watching television, and the interruption really becomes a burr under your butt. At any other time, having a topic raised like this wouldn't be a problem, but for some reason, whatever energy was powering that bad mood gets transferred to this situation, and you flare up.

It sometimes seems as if teens are in a constant state of flare-up. Their anger seems to come at you from all directions and in all levels of intensity that have nothing to do with the circumstances at hand. That's difficult to deal with, because as humans we expect some kind of proportionality and rationality of response based on cause and effect. Going back to our pin prick example, if someone stabbed you with a pin, and you pulled out a gun and shot the person, most people would agree that your response was out of proportion to the stimulus.

Beware Eruption

Teens can act like volcanoes, erupting violently, seemingly without provocation. However, like that natural phenomenon, they often give off signals before they let loose. Often their seismic rumblings can be picked up only by delicate instruments, and given the many responsibilities we have as adults and as parents—especially if we have more than one teen at home—it can be nearly impossible to fine-tune our sensors to be sensitive to every nuance and change in their rapidly fluctuating mood states. Unfortunately, our teens often don't tell us about their painful experiences, and the only way we learn about them is after a display of anger. Here's a brief checklist of signs and symptoms of a teen who is likely to have experienced some kind of emotionally painful experience and who could possibly erupt in anger:

- Isolation: Has your teen stopped spending time in common areas in the house and retreated to his or her bedroom or other private space away from others?

- Reduced social contact: Has your teen stopped or reduced the amount of social interaction with friends? Have you spotted a noticeable decline in the amount of phone calls or time spent on activities like instant messaging?

- Changes in sleep patterns: I know it seems as though some teens spend most of their lives sleeping, but any changes in their sleep habits—going to bed much earlier, staying up much later, remaining in bed far longer—could be the result of emotional pain.

- Changes in eating behaviors: Some teens (I have two teenage boys, so I've seen this) seem to view life as a nonstop all-you-can-eat buffet. I also have a teenage daughter, who eats, in comparison with the boys, very little. If you observe any change in eating habits, this may be a sign that something is troubling your child.

- Decline in academic performance: Any contact from the school regarding your child's progress should be treated seriously. The vast majority of teachers prefer not to have to contact parents with bad news.

- Reports of behavioral issues at school: Much like academic performance, when the school reports that your son or daughter is acting out—whether it's being a disruption in class, fighting, or skipping classes—you know that you have to intervene at that point.

- Noticeable shifts in mood: If your teen is usually chatty and now clams up, that's a signal, and so is the inverse of that. If your happy-go-lucky upbeat son or daughter goes into a funk, you need to pay attention to that. Those are easy shifts to spot, but you also need to pay attention to subtler shifts as well.

- Significant change in appearance: Clothing can often be an indicator of a significant shift in self-perception. Such a change in the son who once wore clothing you considered "normal" and is all of a sudden wearing skintight pants, black nail polish, and lipstick is a significant indicator. Multiple piercings, tattoos, and even makeup and hairstyle changes may indicate emotional upheaval.

- Noticeable increase in disrespect: This could seem as simple as your child becoming overly argumentative. We have all seen disrespect from our teens, so it may be difficult to pick out a shift in disrespect.

In all of the situations above, the key is to notice the change and take no other action but to monitor it. The goal of this monitoring is to spot the development of anger before it actually comes out. Ultimately, being aware of your teen's anger can make the difference between a small skirmish for the two of you and an all-out blowup. While there aren't always clear signs that your teen is in pain, once that pain has reached the anger stage there are bound to be a few side effects. (See Chapters Fourteen and Fifteen for how to talk to your teens when is it clear that they are in the anger stage.)

Watching for Signals

As you observe your teen and try to discern whether he or she is just being a teen or is expressing his or her pain as anger, keep in mind that one night of your teen going to bed early or skipping a meal is not a clear indication that something serious is going on. First, put yourself on notice to be more vigilant in your observation. If you notice that a trend is beginning to form—that for three or four nights your kid came home from an after-school activity and went immediately to his or her room and skipped dinner with the family—then it's time to put that teen on notice. It's important to be nonjudgmental here. Simply say, "I've noticed that _____." Fill in that blank with a clear statement of observations or facts. Don't frontload it with assumptions or accusations or conclusions. Just ask the next question: "Is there something going on that you want to talk about?" If the answer is "no" or "nothing's going on" or "I'm just tired" or whatever, take that response at face value, but make sure you let the teen know that you are aware of the trend in behavior and that you are going to continue to monitor it.

Letting your teens know that you are monitoring them is a dual-edged sword. Context and past history are the key. If your kids grew up in an environment in which you had these kinds of open and direct conversations with them, they will likely not think twice about your letting them know you are watching them. If you are new to this kind of strategic parenting, then there's a danger that you will force your teen, or at least that behavior, underground.

Since freedom and power are such a major part of your teens' life and needs, knowing they have you looking over their shoulder may not sit so well with them. The reason I recommend you alert them to the fact that you are observing them is that in my experience so many teens have the perception that their parents just don't care, aren't involved, or don't have a clue. I would much rather err on the side of being vigilant and up front about my vigilance than try to sneak around to observe them. Calling their attention to your attention is a way of saying, "I care and I'm concerned." That phrase should preface the remarks that let them know you will continue to pay attention to what they are doing. Too often words like that go unsaid because we assume that our teens know we feel that way about them. Too often teens don't read between the lines or understand the subtext of our messages to them. Direct and clear is better than presumed and not stated.

Finally, if after you've first noticed a change and let your teen know that you've noticed this new pattern, you then observe that it is continuing, it is time to have a more direct intervention. Again, the key is to be as direct and fact-filled in your presentation as possible. I don't mean that you have to take detailed notes and state each of the number of hours that they've slept for the past seven nights and provide a PowerPoint presentation to graphically illustrate the decline in their hours of wakefulness in that period versus the same period one month earlier. The important thing is to remind them that you've spoken to them about this before and your concern is greater because the behavior has persisted.

FROM ANGER TO FRUSTRATION

Many mental health experts define depression as anger turned inward. I agree with that, but not all anger is necessarily a sign or symptom of depression. The trigger that I believe turns anger inward and puts a person into a depressed state is the last of the three emotional responses to a need not being met—frustration. Depressed people feel that their situation is hopeless, and that's because they have experienced—or perceive that they have experienced—persistent frustration. Most often, in discussing depression, you hear the feeling that results from persistent frustration expressed as hopelessness and helplessness. We'll deal more specifically with depression in Chapter Eleven, so for now I want to concentrate more on this idea of frustration.

"Thwarted"

The word I like to use when talking about anger being transformed into the next stage is "thwarted." That's what happens when you try every option you can think of and you see no results. Not a lot of teens use that word, but when I hear them talk to me about their feelings of frustration, what they describe is exactly that. To me, thwarted isn't what happens when you try to remedy a situation and fail to get the desired results; instead, thwarted is what happens when your efforts never even get off the ground. You met Lauren in the first chapter—she's the young woman whose parents were both academics at a small private college. Her parents were so wrapped up in their careers that they could intervene on Lauren's behalf only after she vandalized the school and had developed an alcohol problem.

In Lauren's mind, all her attempts to let her parents know how she was feeling were met with indifference. Not only that, any attempts she made to let them know how she was doing in school, or what was going on in her social circles, were all ignored. These were all Lauren's perceptions, of course, but she felt as though any time she wanted to talk to her parents, they were so pressed for time or had such a problem-solving mindset of their own that they would immediately cut her off and tell her what to do to resolve the issue. Since she never got to express herself fully, she felt thwarted. In pain because she was an outsider, angry that her parents seemed to have little time for her, and frustrated that her positive efforts to communicate her feelings were unsuccessful and cut short, Lauren acted out.

I see similar cycles all the time. When your attempts to make yourself feel better only make you hurt more, you get angry, and your anger results in more pain, your pain and anger frustrate you, and you take actions that result in more pain, anger, and frustration. I don't know if you've ever seen the inside of a baseball, but it's all wound up with a long strand of yarn around a rubber core. That yarn is like the pain, anger, and frustration cycle that results when teens' needs aren't being met. It gets wound around and around, and it's difficult sometimes to unwind it to determine exactly where it all started and at what points each of the three overlap. I guess my job is to help unwind that strand of yarn to get to the center.

Often your kids are trying to do the same thing themselves. It's hard work and it's often painful, so they make the move that most of us do—they walk away from the pain and toward something they think will give them pleasure. Unfortunately, in the long run, the choice they make to break the cycle of pain, anger, and frustration leads them—and you as their parents—to even more pain, anger, and frustration. In the next three chapters, we'll take a look at the various forms of behavior, and frequently misbehavior, that acting out takes.

9

Acting Out Behavior I: Eating Disorders, Drinking, and Drugs

Over time, even if you keep an eye out for signs that your teen is suffering from the three emotional consequences of an unmet need, you may still miss some signals. If your teen suffers alone through these emotional consequences—pain, anger, and frustration—for long enough, he or she will act out because the pain, anger, and frustration have boiled over. This reaction will be a dangerous behavior, and it is up to you to spot the signs as soon as they start to manifest themselves.

In the pages ahead we will take a close look at the different types of dangerous behaviors that are the consequence of unmet needs. Some may apply to your child, and some may not, but keep in mind as we proceed that emotional consequences of unmet needs can manifest themselves as behaviors in many different ways. Just as every child is different, every child's reaction to unmet needs will be different. Not every teen suffering from unmet needs will join a gang, just as not every teen will develop an eating disorder or take up binge drinking.

Nevertheless, the underlying cause of all of these behaviors and actions is the same: at least one of the five primary needs is not being met. This is the problem that we have to solve, but before we can do that, let's examine what that problem looks like.

EATING DISORDERS

As a result of the generalized pain, confusion, and anger associated with adolescence and the blows to their self-esteem that are easy to acknowledge but difficult to quantify, our adolescents and teens are binging and purging or gorging themselves in unprecedented numbers. As we saw in the chapter on freedom, Danijela, the daughter of Croatian parents, fell victim to anorexia and bulimia. Even before she discovered her father's secret, she struggled with her self-image. Her parents were different from most, they insisted she attend Croatian school to preserve her heritage (and in Danijela's mind her status as an outsider), and they were acutely aware of the oversexualized image they felt most American girls flaunted, so they did their best to make sure that Danijela didn't present such an image. Danijela thought of herself as fat and dumpy, and she started dieting at an early age. She also wanted to live up to the high standards her parents set for her. All that contributed to her eating disorder.

Anorexia and bulimia are the two most common eating disorders diagnosed in teens. Anorexia, or more technically anorexia nervosa, is a psychiatric diagnosis. Individuals with the condition are easily identified by their low body weight. Not every thin person is anorexic, of course, and since this is an emotional and psychological condition, we have to look at what underlies its physical manifestation. Individuals with anorexia have body image distortions—they think of themselves as fat even though they appear to others to be of normal weight or even underweight—and they have an obsessive fear of gaining weight. Of all the psychiatric disorders, anorexia is one of the most life threatening: approximately 10% of those diagnosed with it die of complications from the condition.

What makes anorexia of particular interest and concern is its link with our discussion of teens and their primary needs. Anorexia is about control. Control is all about having power over something or someone. Control is also a reaction to the absence or presence of a teen's freedom. For anorexics, dieting starts out being all about weight loss and body image, but it transforms over time to also be about exerting control over the body. While no one has definitively determined what causes anorexia, many experts agree that the demands of society generally, and family specifically, can combine to exert a lot of pressure on adolescents (primarily young women—in fact, 95% of anorexics are female). We live in a thin-is-beautiful world, and women with poor self-esteem are particularly prone to anorexia. While young women may not have power over what is taking place with their bodies—the onset of menstruation cycles and breast development, among other secondary sexual characteristics—they can seize power over their relative size and shape.

Also, researchers are discovering that there is a type of dysfunction within families that may produce anorexia in susceptible individuals. We've talked about individuation and establishing an independent identity as it relates to a teen's freedom needs. What researchers have found is that in families with an anorexic, family members are so interdependent that individuals can't attain an individual identity. In other words, they can't separate their own identity from the family's. In some anorexics, this dysfunction includes a fear of growing up—by starving themselves they either delay or stop their physical maturation, and they can return to being children and hold on to the parent–child relationship that was so familiar and comfortable. These individuals don't want to give up that family identity.

Again, in light of what we've discussed about teens' needs, you can see the importance of freedom, power, and belonging to healthy development. When our teens don't experience freedom, when they feel powerless, they are less likely to branch out on their own and establish relationships with others. Their sense of belonging is completely tied up with their parents and siblings. We saw this earlier with Danijela. She was predisposed to anorexia because of her fixation on appearance, but when her family exploded as a result of her father's incest, the ideal mental picture of her family that she'd held for so long was destroyed. Her mother and father had held her under such tight control for so long that she couldn't handle her freedom well. She felt powerless to control the situation, so she exerted power over the one thing she could control—her intake of food. Couple that with her perfectionism (another typical symptom of anorexia), and it's easy to see how she fell prey to this obsessive and dangerous set of behaviors.

Bulimics, unlike their anorexic counterparts, binge on food, or engage in frequent and repeated episodes of significant overeating. Bulimics experience a sense of loss of control—they know they shouldn't eat an entire bag of potato chips, but they feel helpless to stop. Once they've binged, they purge to prevent weight gain. To do this they use various methods, the most common of which are vomiting and laxative abuse. Many but not all bulimics are also anorexics.

Those who suffer from bulimia may engage in eating as often as several times daily for many months. After a binge, self-loathing often sets in, and to make up for their weakness, bulimics will either purge or engage in excessive exercise. Whether they use vomiting, laxatives, diuretics, or enemas to prevent weight gain and to make up for their lapse in control, bulimics are doing serious damage to their bodies, just as anorexics are. Body weight for bulimics is usually normal, but just like anorexics, bulimics have a distorted perception of their own bodies and think of themselves as overweight.

Researchers attribute many of the same causes as anorexia to bulimia—the excessive emphasis on weight, perfectionism, and family dysfunction can play a part in its development. In much the same way as for anorexia, teens' needs for freedom, power, and belonging play a real role in the development of this disorder. Both disorders have serious consequences for your teen's health, and those who engage in them are at great risk.

Overeating

As much as we think of eating disorders such as anorexia and bulimia when it comes to body image, many teens are moving in the opposite direction. We hear a lot about obesity in America. The startling number now is that 40% of all Americans will be considered obese by the year 2010. What is most alarming, however, is the number of young people who can be classified as either overweight or obese. Among teens sixteen to nineteen years old, the number of obese individuals doubled between 1980 and 2002. The number of overweight individuals in that same age group increased threefold. While twenty-two years is a long time, and you may think those changes are slight given that span of time, let's take a look at even more recent developments:

- From 2000 to 2004, the number of obese girls and young women in the sixteen to nineteen age range increased from 13.8% to 16%.
- In that same period and age range, the number of obese boys and young men increased from 14% to 18.2%.

Clearly, food issues—overeating, purging, and extreme dieting—are taking their toll on our teens regardless of gender. We all know that food issues are really emotional issues, but the question that remains is this: which of the five primary needs produces problems with food?

A DIFFICULT NEED TO PIN DOWN

When you consider Glasser's list of needs and look at the broad demographic of teens who are affected by problems with food, I'm sure you recognize that for many kids with eating disorders, the need not being met isn't likely to be survival. These issues cross race, gender, and economic lines. Our kids are in pain, and they are acting out in a variety of food-related ways. Greg, the young man whose mother abandoned him and whose father abused him, isn't a typical example. Greg hoarded food out of fear that he wouldn't be given any; he didn't struggle with body image issues. Danijela, as discussed above, is a more typical case. As we saw, there was no single need that her anorexia met; it was a complex combination of power, belonging, and freedom that contributed to her developing the disorder.

Tony, a seventeen-year-old I worked with, is also typical of a teen with body image issues that resulted in an eating disorder. As a young boy Tony was overweight. He endured the abuse from his peers all through elementary school and middle school. When he entered junior high, he decided to make a change. Dieting was tough, but he stuck with it as best he could. He started to lift weights and saw some results. He wanted better results, so he started taking energy- and performance-enhancing compounds from a local health food store. He heard about steroids and decided to give them a try. He'd go off his diet and his weight would balloon; then he'd starve himself again.

By the time I'd met him, he'd become addicted to speed in the hope of jump-starting his metabolism. It took some time, but eventually we got to the source of Tony's unhappiness and pain. In part it was because of the teasing he received, but it also had to do with his perception that his stepfather belittled him and made unfair comparisons between Tony and his biological son. Tony hated his stepbrother, a young man who excelled athletically and had movie-star good looks. Food became a comfort and a bitter pill for Tony.

Much of Tony's obsession with food and body weight was attributable to his belonging needs. Both at school and at home, Tony was considered a kind of misfit. With his biological father seldom in the picture, and as a child of divorce, Tony felt excluded from his family and felt the stigma of being from a broken home. (This was more his perception than reality, since many of those kids who tormented him were also children of divorce, acting out because of their own deficit of needs.) He hoped that by transforming his body he could win his stepfather's approval. Also, he'd enjoy the additional benefit of not having to endure the teasing from his classmates, and he just might fit in better with them. What Tony didn't understand was that he was also motivated by power. Lifting weights and being in control of his eating habits constituted a way to take command of his life. A lot of young men engage in sports and fitness activities as a way to feel powerful and in control. For someone like Tony, weight training was ideal. The plates of iron couldn't talk back, and in time he could dominate them.

While power, freedom, and belonging are likely the most common needs being addressed with eating disorders, survival and fun can play a part as well. With Greg, we saw what his survival fears did to him in terms of hoarding food. Some teens will tell you—and as the father of two teenage sons I can verify the truth of this—that eating provides some kids with real pleasure. For a lot of boys, being able to pack away large amounts of food is a way to earn recognition. That recognition can lead to belonging, belonging can lead to power, and so on. It's interesting to note how in our country, the ideal body types for men and women differ. In the past, powerful, influential, successful men were usually very large and robust—well, overweight—while women were expected, to one degree or another, to be petite and slender. That hasn't really changed that much.

Signs of Eating Disorders

The National Eating Disorders Association (NEDA, www.National EatingDisorders.com) has produced this list to help parents and others identify the presence of an eating disorder.

Warning signs of anorexia nervosa:

- Dramatic weight loss
- Preoccupation with weight, food, calories, fat grams, and dieting
- Refusal to eat certain foods, progressing to restrictions against whole categories of food (e.g., no carbohydrates)
- Frequent comments about feeling "fat" or overweight despite weight loss
- Anxiety about gaining weight or being "fat"
- Denial of hunger
- Development of food rituals (e.g., eating foods in a certain order, excessive chewing, rearranging food on a plate)
- Consistent excuses to avoid mealtimes or situations involving food
- Excessive, rigid exercise regimen despite weather, fatigue, illness, or injury; a need to "burn off" calories taken in
- Withdrawal from usual friends and activities
- In general, behaviors and attitudes indicating that weight loss, dieting, and control of food are becoming primary concerns

NEDA lists these as potential indicators:

- Evidence of binge eating, including disappearance of large amounts of food in short periods of time or the existence of wrappers and containers indicating the consumption of large amounts of food
- Evidence of purging behaviors, including frequent trips to the bathroom after meals, signs and/or smells of vomiting, presence of wrappers or packages of laxatives or diuretics
- An excessive, rigid exercise regimen, despite weather, fatigue, illness, or injury; need to "burn off" calories taken in
- Unusual swelling of the cheeks or jaw area
- Calluses and scars on the back of the hands and knuckles from self-induced vomiting
- Discoloration or staining of the teeth

- Creation of complex lifestyle schedules or rituals to make time for binge-and-purge sessions
- Withdrawal from usual friends and activities, or mood swings
- In general, behaviors and attitudes indicating that weight loss, dieting, and control of food are becoming primary concerns

As helpful as these warning signs are, we can be proactive to head off any possible development of an eating disorder. As we know, the media sends powerful messages to our kids about what constitutes beauty and attractiveness in our culture. The Web site www.aboutourkids.org offers tips for parents regarding body image and self-esteem. I've adapted some of them to make more them gender neutral:

- Monitor your own comments about yourself and your children.
- Don't bemoan your looks.
- Avoid general comments about looks and beauty.
- Point out positive attributes in people.
- Comment on bad media messages, and ask your child what he or she thinks of those messages.

Our role as parents is to monitor what our kids consume—what they put in their mouths as well as what they allow into their brains. When our kids are young, I think it's easier for us to understand that we are their role models and that they look to us for guidance. As they age, and as they exert their own independence, we tend to think that we aren't as strong an influence on their attitudes, beliefs, and values as we once were. That's not the case. While they may outwardly pretend to ignore us, in fact, our kids pay very close attention to what we say and do. If we are constantly self-critical and obsess about food consumption, they will take note of that and likely will copy our behaviors in some way. The same is true of our self-image.

While I think it's important that we be honest with our kids and allow them to see us struggle with issues, we have to balance that honesty with the effects our negativity will have on them. What's crucial is that if we allow them to see us struggling with an issue—any issue, be it our weight, our appearance, or whatever—we also have to let them see us seeking solutions to those problems. If you've spent time complaining about your spare tire or your love handles or your saggy buns, then model for them a strategy you use to improve on those problem areas. Kids will follow our lead, and many of the students I've worked with who had food issues reported that their parents were major contributors to their problem—either because they were obsessive about weight and food consumption or because they modeled really bad eating habits.

Media and Body Image Issues

The media also exert an influence. Again, much of the focus of this element has been on teenage girls and body image issues, but lately we've been seeing more research about boys and body image, particularly as it relates to the use of steroids. For girls the issue revolves around being slimmer, for boys about being more muscular. A 2000 Harvard University study revealed that 86% of teenage girls are on a diet or believe they should be on one. According to NEDA, 51% of girls as young as nine and ten years old report that they feel better about themselves when they are on a diet.

While it may be too late to deal with body image issues with teens in this way, sometimes presenting them with facts can help. They may simply respond "That's great, but the reality is I still have to deal with unrealistic expectations," but knowing how unrealistic those expectations are might prove helpful. These numbers are also a sobering reminder of what the media, their peers, and in some cases parents are doing to teenagers and their body image:

- The perfect supermodel is 5 feet 8 inches tall and weighs 115 pounds.
- The average American woman is 5 feet 3 inches tall and weighs 144 pounds.
- 67% of women believe they are expected to be more physically attractive than their mother's generation.
- 75% of eight- and nine-year-olds said they liked their looks.
- 56% of twelve- and thirteen-year-olds said they liked their looks.
- 80% of girls report experiencing harassment about their looks.
- 7 million girls and women have eating disorders.
- 1 million boys and men have eating disorders.
- 20% of college-age women are bulimic.

Again, you probably don't want to cite these numbers chapter and verse to your kids, but they're helpful to know and can help put your thoughts into perspective as well.

ALCOHOL

Among the other ways our kids act out as a result of emotional upheaval is the consumption of alcohol and drugs. It's hard for me to imagine, given all that we know about teens and drinking, that any parent could feel a sense of relief that their child is drinking and not doing drugs. I'm also stunned when parents are stunned to learn that their kids are experimenting with alcohol and drugs. And the number of kids who experiment with alcohol and drugs is not that far removed from the number of kids who abuse alcohol and drugs. I may be a bit of a hardliner when it comes to this issue, but I believe that any kid who is below the drinking age and who experiments with alcohol, who drinks sporadically or regularly or who binges, is abusing alcohol. It's illegal for them to consume alcohol, so any teen consuming it in any way, shape, form, or amount is abusing it, in my estimation.

Drinking Is Everywhere

Legal and semantic issues aside, alcohol and drugs are a scourge preying on our kids. According to the 2004 (the most recent date for which this information was available) National Survey on Drug Use and Health (NSDUH) administered by the Substance Abuse and Mental Health Services Administration (SAMHSA), and the U.S. Department of Health and Human Services, alcohol abuse among young people follows a trend you'd likely imagine. Please note that I'm going to use the word "abuse" throughout, though the people at SAMHSA don't. They discovered that the prevalence of alcohol abuse increased as kids got older. Among adolescents age twelve, only 2.3% self-reported consuming alcohol (beer, wine, mixed drinks, straight liquor) in the thirty days before the survey. By age eighteen, that figure rose to slightly more than 50%. More disturbing are the percentages of young people who report that they engaged in binge drinking—five or more drinks on the same occasion—at least once in the previous thirty days. For twelve-year-olds, 1.1% of them responded "yes" to binge drinking—in other words, half of the twelve-year-olds who drink, binge. Slightly more than 41% of eighteen-year-olds admitted to binge drinking. The last category of consumption was heaving drinking—five or more drinks on the same occasion on at least five different days in the previous thirty days. Less than 1% of twelve-year-olds reported fitting in that category, but 15% of eighteen-year-olds did.

I don't want to belabor you with numbers, just show you the trend. I think it's noteworthy that for this survey at least, no significant statistical difference was noted by gender. Among young people age twelve to seventeen, 17.2% of males reported currently using alcohol, versus 18% of females. Interestingly, those who were attending college (eighteen-year-olds) or were employed were more likely to abuse alcohol than those who weren't attending or weren't employed. Also, alcohol abuse levels were higher in small towns and suburban areas than in major metropolitan areas. Many of the myths and stereotypes we may carry around as parents might be coloring our perceptions of who the "good" kids and "bad" kids are, where they live, and what their lives are like.

Why Teens Drink

The U.S. Surgeon General's Office compiled a report on teens and drinking. Here are the conclusions drawn regarding why teens drink:

- 40% drink when they are upset.
- 31% drink when they are alone.
- 25% drink to get high.
- 25% drink when they are bored.

If teens' needs aren't being met, then they become confused, frustrated, angry, and in pain. To get rid of that pain, they take what our society tells them is an acceptable route to dulling that pain—they drink. Alcohol is the almost perfect solution, teens discover, to their problems. Of course, we know it's not a solution, but it does do a pretty good job of dealing with symptoms quickly. When you look at the list of "reasons" above, you can see how this needs deficit works in regard to alcohol. Belonging and fun needs are most clearly represented, along with the pain numbing—which points to survival.

If there's one word I'd use to describe teens, it's "anxious." They tend to be impatient, and they tend to worry about their social standing, their grades, their appearance, their sexuality, and a host of other issues. If alcohol is good at one thing, it's good at reducing anxiety. If you aren't anxious, what can you do? Have FUN. If your inhibitions are reduced, what can you do? Have FUN.

How else do you feel when you're under the influence? You feel POWERful, you feel FREEdom. If you are FUN, POWERful, and FREE, then what happens? People like being around you, and you BELONG. If four of your five basic needs are being met by a substance, then you may come to believe that your SURVIVAL depends on consuming it. If you are in pain, your SURVIVAL feels threatened. You now have gone from having four of a kind to a royal flush. Can't get any better than that.

Is it any wonder, then, that so many teens succumb to the temptation to drink? Like eating disorders, drinking can be a reactive pattern that ties into every one of the primary needs—especially fun. Is it also any wonder that many of the teens I worked with, when asked why they drank for the first time and continued to drink, answered, "It was fun. There was nothing else to do. I had fun when I drank." Although it starts with that simple need, it grows more complex—and many teens don't understand all the needs that drinking meets. As parents we have to understand these needs and how they function in the lives of our kids.

DRINKING TO BELONG

For boys, and increasingly for girls, drinking is a rite of passage. How a young woman holds her liquor isn't a sign of her femininity, but how much a young man can drink certainly is a measuring stick used to determine masculinity. Now, I'm kind of an old fuddy-duddy in a lot of ways, and I don't want to believe this because I was some sort of all-American boy who believed my body was a temple and I didn't want to defile it with alcohol. After all, I was a jock, a football player. Well, today that attitude is anachronistic at best and laughable at worst. Among teens, male athletes drink more than nonathletes. We have a whole complex of associations among sports, alcohol, and men in this country, and many of our teenage and adolescent boys seek role models in athletes and their fathers. What do they see their fathers doing? Watching sports and drinking, perhaps? Teenage boys are firmly impressed by this mixed drink of alcohol, masculinity, and athletics, but I believe the connections extend beyond that.

Bill was a high school baseball player. While many of his friends first started to drink and experiment with drugs in middle school and junior high, Bill viewed himself the way I viewed myself at that age—as the all-American boy. He wouldn't be tempted. His father was a teacher at his school and also coached the basketball team. When Bill got to his senior year of high school, he decided he'd had enough of abstinence. He was tired of being left out of all the good times he was hearing about. Soon he became a fixture at all the parties. Bill would try to keep up with the boys, and he'd often drink to the point where he couldn't remember how much he had drunk. He began to ask a teammate to count for him. Bill was as competitive as could be, so he wanted to drink at least one more beer each night he went out drinking than he had on the previous occasion.

So, what's going on here that we can learn from Bill? First, drinking became a bonding experience. I've already said that it is a male rite of passage, and the camaraderie associated with drinking buddies and wingmen and all of that solidifies a young man's shaky standing among his peers. You may be a geek who doesn't know a zone press from hitting the cutoff man, but if you can drink, and drink a lot, you're okay in most jock's books—and let's face it, jocks tend to earn the highest status among teens.

Girls Want to Fit In, Too

Girls also frequently use drinking when their need for belonging goes unmet, but for girls, the results of this belonging often look quite different. As Rosalind Wiseman points out in her book *Queen Bees and Wannabes*, drinking allows girls to engage in activity, often sexual in nature, that they want to engage in (and sometimes don't), but they are too shy, awkward, and afraid to do so when not under the influence. Wiseman also points out that a girl can earn a positive reputation among her peers by consuming alcohol. Drinking someone under the table is not the sole province of males; the rewards (from a teen's point of view) are simply different. The world of teen drinking isn't fair to young women in this regard. A male who hooks up with a young woman while drinking, even if his peers view her as unattractive, undesirable, and beneath his standing, gets rewarded ultimately for his conquest. A young woman who engages in the same kind of behavior under the same set of circumstances and social standing gets punished with a bad reputation. Alcohol has the same numbing and erasing effects on teen women as it does on teen men, but somehow that eraser leaves a clearer afterimage behind when it's wielded by a woman. Not fair, but true.

DRINKING FOR FREEDOM

For many teens who are suffering from the unmet need of freedom, consuming alcohol helps fill that void. Drinking can offer a freedom from expectations and the anxiety that surrounds those expectations. It can offer a temporary freedom, a freedom they think they need to express the true versions of themselves. With their inhibitions broken down, they can tell people how they really feel.

This is especially true of young men who lack emotional fluency. Somehow, alcohol turns them—or at least so many young men believe it turns them—into articulate, expressive, sensitive souls. Any mothers reading this book will likely be able to recall at least one young man in her romantic history who expressed his undying devotion to her in an alcohol-fueled torrent. She can also probably recall a late-night, long-distance phone call from a would-be or once-was suitor who could thank his good buddy Jack Daniels for putting him up to it. For many teens, it is better to drink than to think. It is better to fuel than to feel. Alcohol, at least temporarily, numbs the pain of the social and emotional awkwardness that most teen boys feel—again, their lack of self-esteem comes into play.

In their best-selling book *Raising Cain: Protecting the Emotional Life of Boys,* Dan Kindlon, PhD, and Michael Thompson, PhD, did an amazing job of lifting the veil of secrecy from an area of boys' lives that we seldom look at or talk about. As Kindlon and Thompson point out, alcohol is literally a pain reliever. It acts on the brain, and the body produces a compound very much like morphine. Our brains and bodies also do something similar when we exercise. You've probably heard of endorphins. Endorphins and the chemical response to drinking both produce opiates. Our opiate system is also involved with our emotions through our sense of touch. We feel comforted emotionally and physically when we are caressed, our skin is stroked, or we experience close bodily contact. All emotions are chemical in nature, so alcohol can serve as a substitute for the kinds of physical expressions of affection, compassion, and comfort that most kids, particularly males, no longer receive the way they once did as children and to a lesser degree as adolescents. If you are not comfortable with those kinds of physical displays of affection, and yet you crave them and need to fulfill your need for belonging, you can always find it in a bottle or a glass.

Boy, Was I Wasted!

Not only does alcohol provide freedom from anxiety when someone is drunk, it also continues to offer that freedom the morning after. As the great eraser, alcohol offers a solution to the memory of awkward or embarrassing moments. One of the most painful things teens experience, and one of their greatest anxiety-producing fears, is being awkward and doing something stupid in front of peers or adults. Alcohol frees them from that fear. Christina, the young woman I wrote about earlier whose parents put extraordinary expectations for good behavior and success on her shoulders, once told me, "Mr. Mike, I had to do everything perfect to please my parents. One little mistake and they'd jump all over me. When I was with my boyfriend and we were drinking or smoking pot, I could say or do anything. If we were out with a bunch of his or my friends and we were drunk, we could do totally stupid things. Didn't matter. You could always say you were drunk. The perfect excuse for anything was, 'I was so wasted.'"

Teens can use that excuse to cover up a variety of sins, and whether they realize it or not, every time they use that justification, they feel as though it satisfies their need for freedom. They can have fun without any fear of embarrassment. When being wasted is their excuse, they can do whatever they want—or at least, that's what they think.

THE DOWNSIDE OF ALCOHOL CONSUMPTION

With a few exceptions, it sounds as if I'm presenting you with a paid advertisement from the liquor and beer industry touting the beneficial effects of their latest cure-all. I'm no snake oil salesman, so I'll let you know the downside. As much as alcohol is that empowering, bond-creating, freedom-enabling substance, it is in fact a depressant. Ultimately, the fun high ends. For a lot of teens, especially those who binge drink, the depressive effects show up about the time they fall asleep, pass out, or, in the most severe cases, black out. (Studies show that three of ten high-school-age boys will pass out from too much alcohol at least once in their careers.)

As a result, they either are not aware of those depressive effects or figure they are a small price to pay for the benefits derived from alcohol. Unfortunately, sometimes those depressive effects are more serious. A recent incident in a suburb north and west of Chicago brought this painfully home to several young men and their families. According to a report in the *Chicago Tribune*, an eighteen-year-old boy was at the home of some friends, and toxicology reports later indicated that his blood alcohol content was over the legal limit, so the presumption was that he was drinking. Whether it was the depressive effects of the alcohol that made him say that none of their lives were worth living or not is difficult to say. Very likely it did contribute to his feelings and definitely contributed to what he did next.

Two of his friends tried to console him. Unfortunately, they didn't prevent him from getting behind the wheel of his car; instead they climbed in along with him. The disconsolate teenager then drove along a main highway, exceeding the speed limit considerably before veering off the road and crashing into the side of a building. One of the young man's friends was killed, while he and his other friend sustained serious injuries. Police investigators noted the absence of skid marks, interviewed those at the gathering who had heard the young man's remarks, and concluded that he intentionally drove off the road in the hope of killing himself. Instead, he killed a friend and now faces first-degree murder charges.

No fun, power, belonging, or freedom in that story, and certainly not enough survival to go around. Studies also show that four of ten high-school-age boys will drive while intoxicated. Teenage boys are ten times more likely than their female counterparts to get arrested for an alcohol-related criminal offense.

You may be saying to yourself that all of your teen's needs are met. He or she doesn't have to worry about survival, seems to have plenty of fun, enjoys freedom and power, and has a sense of belonging from plenty of friends. That may be true, but it doesn't mean that your teen won't drink. For many teens, consuming alcohol provides them with a privileged glimpse of the adult world. Year after year, they have probably heard you and teachers and others warning them about what these forbidden beverages can do. At the same time, they've likely witnessed adults drinking and seeming to enjoy themselves, and enjoying many of the benefits of alcohol I've previously discussed. Again, the temptation likely proves to be too much for them. They are at a stage in their lives when they want to become adults—not necessarily assume adult responsibilities, but enjoy the pleasures of being an adult.

To put it simply, even good kids do it. Even if you ensure that all of your kids' needs are met, they may still do it—the chances of them doing it are lesser but still there, but that doesn't mean that your cause as a parent is lost. While many kids abuse alcohol, the difference between those who experience severe problems with the substance and those who don't is that those with problems are trying to fill one of their primary needs. Whether it is fun, belonging, power, freedom—or, to a lesser extent, survival—problems with drinking can be the behavioral consequences of unmet needs in a variety of ways.

As parents, it's our job to keep our eyes open to the signs of these behaviors and to the emotional signals that something is wrong. Once you have identified that your teen is suffering from an unmet need and relying on alcohol to solve it, you can design your approach to help your teen (see Chapter Fifteen).

DRUGS

Much of what was said above about alcohol and its ability to satisfy the unmet needs of your teen is true of drugs as well. I've used alcohol as an example throughout, but you can substitute the word "drugs" in most places, especially as it pertains to how the consumption of any type of drug serves the purpose of numbing pain, reducing inhibitions, providing an escape, and allowing your teen to feel a much-needed sense of belonging.

The good news, courtesy of the same NSDUH study I referenced for the numbers about alcohol consumption, is that illicit drug use is not on the rise among our young people. Here are the general conclusions and numbers provided by that study:

- In 2005, an estimated 19.7 million Americans age twelve or older were current (previous month) illicit drug users, meaning they had used an illicit drug during the month before the survey interview. This estimate represents 8.1% of the population age twelve years old or older.
- The overall rate of current illicit drug use among persons age twelve or older in 2005 (8.1%) was similar to the rate in 2004 (7.9%), 2003 (8.2%), and 2002 (8.3%).
- Marijuana was the most commonly used illicit drug (14.6 million previous month users). In 2005, it was used by 74.2% of current illicit drug users. Among current illicit drug users, 54.5% used only marijuana, 19.6% used marijuana and another illicit drug, and the remaining 25.8% used only an illicit drug other than marijuana in the previous month.

Compare the 8.1% of teens abusing illicit drugs with the almost 50% abusing alcohol, and you can see why I put so much emphasis on drinking. Most parents agree that drug use is a serious issue. I'm not convinced all parents agree that consuming alcohol is a problem.

The trends we see among teen drug abusers are similar to those among teen drinkers. As teens grow older they are more likely to use drugs. In other words, more eighteen-year-olds use drugs than thirteen-year-olds do. Less than 4% of twelve- and thirteen-year-olds and slightly more than 22% of eighteen-year-olds reported using drugs. As you can see, your teen is far more likely to experiment with and use alcohol on a regular basis than they are illicit drugs.

Despite the alarm about the increasing use of methamphetamines (crystal meth), marijuana remains the drug of choice among abusers. That's not especially good news, since the potency of the marijuana available today is far greater than it was in previous decades. Males smoke marijuana only with a slightly greater frequency than females—a difference of just 1.2% overall across all ages.

For most teens, then, their consumption of illegal substances consists of alcohol and marijuana. Why teens choose to take other more powerful illicit drugs has less to do with which of their needs is being unmet than with the degree to which they feel the pain of that unmet need and a host of other factors that are beyond the scope of this book to discuss. For our purposes, the kinds of self-medicating our teens are doing is less important than the fact that they feel they have to self-medicate at all. Once we decide to treat all substance abuse as a high-risk behavior, very few if any differences exist. Getting to the reason why teens are abusing is more crucial than determining what they are abusing.

I'm not trying to diminish the seriousness of drug consumption. Instead, I'm trying to establish the importance of treating alcohol abuse with the same degree of tenacity and vigilance that we have illicit drugs. Though it was likely being implied in the "Just Say No" campaigns that talked about alcohol and illicit drugs, a bit of a wink and a nudge existed in our culture that told our kids that drinking was acceptable, because most of us have set that example for our kids. Perhaps it's time to refine that message. Also, it's time we let our kids know that while they may think of alcohol and drugs as the great need providers, they in fact create far more problems and needs than they solve.

10

Acting Out Behavior II: Violence and Sex

If our kids believe alcohol is the great liberator and pain reliever, then we have to do everything we can to let them see that alcohol is the big liar. They believe that they are more attractive, better dancers, funnier, smarter, and more charming when under the influence than when they are not. Just as anorexics or bulimics believe that they are overweight or look better when they are skeletal, teens under the influence are delusional about its positive effects. Convincing someone that what they believe to be true is false is really hard. Replacing one reality with another is equally difficult. What we have to do is demonstrate to them that two realities can exist simultaneously. Yes, alcohol can temporarily relieve your pain. It can make you feel freer, more fun, and more powerful, and bond you to your friends in a way that makes you believe your very survival depends on them and, by extension, on it.

The truth is that alcohol, especially, sits at the apex of a triangle of very negative and potentially life-threatening behaviors. The other two legs of that triangle are violence and sexual promiscuity. Within that triangle are a whole host of other dangerous reactions to unmet needs that are either a direct result of, or have alcohol as a contributing factor to, injury and death from car accidents, drowning, cigarette smoking, illicit drug use, sexually transmitted diseases (STDs), and suicide.

For teenage boys and girls, alcohol abuse is a dangerous behavior that paves the way for other dangerous behaviors. While the reactions that stem from alcohol abuse can take many different forms, the two most common are violence and sexual promiscuity. Now, as I'm sure you know, these can occur in both boys and girls, and they can occur in very different ways. That said, statistics have proved the truth of certain trends about the role boys play in instigating both violence and sexual promiscuity.

ANGER AND ALCOHOL

I have no statistics to support this contention, but I'd bet the ranch that those teens I referred to earlier who were involved in attacks on the homeless fashioned after the "Bum Fight" videos had been abusing alcohol in combination with those assaults. Sadly, a recent article on CNN.com documented the increasing number of violent attacks for "fun" on the homeless. A few studies have shown a direct causal link between alcohol and violence among teens. It's estimated that a teenage boy who has been drinking is twice as likely to get into a fight than a sober one.

It is also estimated that one half of all murders committed by men are under the influence of alcohol. The link between alcohol intoxication and physical and sexual abuse of women has been clearly established. Researchers as yet don't know the exact role alcohol plays in triggering violent episodes, particularly among habitually violent individuals, but whether acting out violently is a regular part of an individual's routine or represents a sudden and unexpected flare-up, if a fire no matter how small exists within a male, drinking alcohol is like pouring gasoline on it.

Regardless of the statistics on the connection, what I know is that I see a lot of angry young men. Whether or not they abuse alcohol, they are pissed off and deeply wounded, and far too many of them lack the emotional, intellectual, and moral intelligence to deal with their anger effectively. The National Center for Juvenile Justice reports that boys commit 95% of teen homicides. Though I don't have the numbers for other violent crimes, such as assault and forcible rape, experts say that they are as high as or higher than the percentages for homicide.

What's the cause of this? Why are boys so angry? For many of them, the answer lies in their unmet needs. Because of the pain, anger, and frustration they feel as a result of an unmet need, boys are driven to drink, and some of these same forces that lead boys to drink also lead them toward violence. A boy's inability to express and find positive release for the emotional turmoil that swirls within him will eventually find expression. In too many cases, that expression is a high-risk, negative behavior that is frequently violent in nature. All too frequently, when a male's belongingness needs are not met, he lashes out. While serial killers are certainly an extreme example of this, most of them are very quiet, very shy, very withdrawn individuals. In the case of the teen shooters at Columbine High School in Colorado, their thwarted sense of belonging and their desire to exact revenge for being made outcasts was very clearly expressed in the writing they left behind. As I wrote this, a very angry, very troubled young man who clearly viewed himself as an outcast shot and killed dozens at Virginia Tech University.

One thing we know about boys is that they lag behind girls in the important area of developing impulse control. We also know that being able to verbally express your feelings improves impulse control. Boys don't have those verbal skills to the same degree that girls do. In school and at home, boys are subject to more frequent and harsher forms of discipline. Corporal punishments are meted out on boys at a 6:1 rate compared with girls, according to a recent study by the U.S. Office of Education.

Despite how much more enlightened we are, the belief persists that boys need to be toughened up. The kinds of punishments we exact on them often reflect that notion of what manhood is supposed to be. We may expect and demand that the young men we are in charge of be more thoughtful, less impulse driven, and emotionally expressive, but we seldom teach them how to express those qualities. When they fail to exhibit those traits, we punish them. From a male's perspective, the rules of this game aren't fair: I'm being punished more harshly, more often, for not doing something I haven't been taught to do or am far less capable of doing. How is that fair?

In a school setting and elsewhere, if you react against what you perceive to be an unfair punishment, you're beaten down even more harshly. Wouldn't that make you feel powerless? Would you feel that your freedom was being impinged upon? Would you find school or work or home a lot less fun place to be? Wouldn't you feel as if your place in the pecking order was being threatened? Wouldn't you feel as if the only ones who understood you, the only ones who would accept you, were the other guys who were being treated the same way? Wouldn't that make you angry? And what if your anger over this caused you to act out and be punished again and again? And what if you lacked the ability to express how this unjust, unfair system made you feel? What choices would be left to you?

The end result is that many boys find themselves with an overwhelming sense of being thwarted. They feel that there is nothing at all they can do to make their situation better—nearly every one of their needs is being unmet or is somehow distorted. The last few questions and statements above are pretty much the perfect example of how someone can wind up feeling thwarted. Eventually, some boys lash out violently or sexually—and sometimes in a combination of those two.

VIOLENCE AND BELONGING

Another factor that contributes to this anger/violence/thwarted complex is the culture of cruelty in which boys exist. Peer pressure has an impact on boys and girls alike, and boys want to fit in, they want to belong, and the group they want to belong to is often dominated by boys who are older and bigger than they are. Older boys taunt and tease younger and weaker boys. Those younger and weaker boys, reeling from the psychological effects of this taunting, take their deflated sense of self-worth and inflate it by finding boys younger and weaker than themselves to pick on. They take their feelings of powerlessness and offload them onto other weaker boys. Boys learn to not show weakness, to remain loyal to the pack, to adhere to a code of silence, and to live with fear and insecurity. Just when a boy thinks he's earned his right to be among the "cool" kids, he can be struck with a sudden blow that has him reeling. He feels betrayed, and he won't let that happen again. He stops trusting. His need to belong goes unmet, and he retreats inward.

So, what happens when you lack empathy, learn not to trust, and have at best tenuous relationships with others? Hurting another person becomes easier—especially when you've been drinking. Hurting someone else becomes a way of proving yourself to others. Hurting someone else strikes fear in the heart of others and offers you what little security you have. I know this all sounds like something out of *The Lord of the Flies*, but one of the reasons that book is a classic is that it represents much of what boy and teen culture is like. Piggy, Ralph, Jack, and the rest of the boys stranded on that island enact in a very dramatic fashion what goes in our adolescents' and teens' lives. Add in the kind of hyperviolent culture our kids are exposed to with video games, television, and films, and you've got a recipe for disaster.

It's Just as Tough at the Top

Even boys at the top of the pyramid suffer from the same kinds of fears and insecurities that come with unmet needs of power and belonging as the so-called bottom feeders. Robert, a seventeen-year-old client of mine, seemingly had everything going for him. He was a star point guard on his high school's basketball team, he was dating the head cheerleader, he was ranked in the top twenty-five of his class academically, and in everyone's estimation he was the leader of the most popular clique. He was a regular at parties, he was the ringleader behind several legendary escapades—among them breaking into the community indoor swimming pool, vandalizing a rival school's sign to read "Pussies" instead of "Panthers"—and he developed a prodigious tolerance for alcohol. By the time I met him, that alcohol abuse had led his parents to pull him out of school after a second DUI arrest.

Robert walked into my office exuding the charm that had won over family, friends, and faculty. Soon I was able to see behind that image. "Mr. Mike, remember when you were a kid and played king of the hill? That was a blast, but you had to have eyes in the eyes of the eyes in the back of your head. People were coming at you from all directions, trying to knock you down, throwing dirt clods at you. That was what it was like for me. Some guys hated me because they were jealous, and they'd constantly challenge me—funneling beers, funneling shots of grain alcohol. I could have gotten into a fight every weekend if I wanted to. Sometimes I'd just walk away, but sometimes I had to step up and represent. It got to be ridiculous. It wasn't like I could enjoy myself. I always had to be on the defensive or the offensive, cutting somebody off before they could get to me. Sometimes I'd have to fuck up somebody just so people would know I was still in the game. I hated all that, so, I drank. I figured live it up while I could and enjoy it."

Robert's need to belong was constantly being threatened and put under stress. The power he held over his peers was something that others wanted to take from him. Unable to articulate the anxiety he was feeling over these constant threats to his primary needs, he turned to alcohol and violence to ease his distress. Robert is far from alone in this reaction. In this country we like to think of people who are at the top of the social pyramid as having it easy and having complete control over every aspect of their lives, but being at the top is often just as difficult as being anywhere else. Fighting was not Robert's first choice, but often he saw it as the only way he could protect his need to belong.

It's Not So Easy at the Bottom, Either

While Robert was at least aware of what he was doing and why he was doing it, Dave, the young man who started out throwing snowballs and later vandalized cars, who would have been one of Robert's likely targets for violence, could not see the connection between his behavior and his needs. The interesting thing about Dave, who was rebelling against being pigeon-holed, was that he really didn't understand why he took on innocent people's automobiles as a target. When I first asked him why he did it, he said it was for fun, just "shits and giggles," as he put it. I asked him more about what his life was like in high school, and along with what you already know about his desire to not be pegged the "good kid" his whole life, he also revealed that he'd been humiliated a few times by some of the older alpha males.

At first he didn't want to talk about it, but he later confessed that at one party he was so drunk that he could barely move. He was slumped in a chair, and a series of other guys came along and placed their penises on the back of his head. Dave pretended to be passed out, but after several instances of these boys doing this to him and laughing and calling him their "beeeyotch" (bitch) and saying they could do anything to him, he stood up and staggered from the table. Everyone knew that he'd let those guys humiliate and demean him in that way.

When I asked Dave if there might be a connection between what he did with the cars and what happened to him, he looked completely confused at first. As we explored the issue a bit more, he told me that he guessed that he wanted to get even with the guys who'd humiliated him, but he couldn't. Instead, he found someone at random, some innocent victims, and punished them for what he'd experienced. What better to pick on than an inanimate object that can't fight back? Why not choose a victim at random? Why not sneak around in the dark of night instead of confronting his tormentors head on? I asked Dave if he'd ever thought of tipping over the cars of the guys who'd treated him so badly. His response: "Fantasized about it. Hundreds of times I thought about it. Drove past their houses, but I couldn't pull the trigger on that. Somebody would have figured it out. I'd have been a dead man walking."

For Dave, violence became an option for precisely the opposite reason as for Robert. Because his need to belong had been so clearly thwarted, he responded by taking up the dangerous behavior of committing acts of violence and vandalism toward other people's property. The need to belong pushed him to drink, and when that didn't make him belong, he turned to tipping cars. He felt powerless against the people who had really done him harm, so he exerted his control on something that couldn't fight back.

GANGS—NOT JUST A CITY PROBLEM

Though drinking can be a tremendous catalyst for teen violence, it is far from the only reason that teens engage in violent acts. When most people think about the link between these types of violent behaviors and their role in a school's social hierarchy, they probably get a mental picture of inner city gangs and their hazing rituals. Increasingly, however, gangs have spread to the suburbs. They exert their own kind of control over teens, enforcing their codes of conduct with a ruthless efficiency that produces the kind of conformity and obedience that, if the behaviors they got their members to perform weren't so illegal, would make parents envious.

I simply want to make note of the ever-expanding sphere of influence of gangs. It is not an inner city problem exclusively. According to the National Youth Violence Prevention Resource Center (NYVPRC), reporting on a Department of Justice survey, there were more than 24,500 different youth gangs around the country and nearly 750,000 youth and adult gang members. While those figures represent a relatively small number of teens—most youth gang members are between the ages of twelve and seventeen—they are responsible for a disproportionate amount of crime and violence. A survey in Denver showed that while only 14% of teens were gang members, those members were responsible for 89% of the serious violent crimes. Gang members are sixty times more likely to be killed in an act of violence than the rest of the population.

The good news for you as a parent is that roughly half of the gang members active today are older than eighteen. If your child doesn't have a gang affiliation by the time he or she is in high school or is about to leave high school, chances are that he or she won't join one. In fact, of those who do join, one half to two thirds leave the gang by the end of their first year. If you have a teenage daughter, you can't rest at ease thinking that she's exempt from the lure and temptation of gang affiliation. Roughly 39% of gangs have female members, and they make up only 6% of the total number of gang members. That's good news for you parents of girls, but given what we know about the kinds of activities these gangs engage in, even if the numbers are small the potential for harm to your child is great, regardless of gender.

Gangs and Needs

When we look at the reasons teens join gangs, Glasser's structure of needs once again rises to the forefront. Belonging is certainly one of the most obvious needs that a gang fulfills. Many of the young people in gangs cite this as a reason for affiliating themselves with a gang. The word "affiliated" is an interesting one that has at its root "filial," or brotherhood. Gang members often use words typically associated with a family to describe their relationship with one another, and they use them as a form of address. In a culture in which a fractured or completely broken family structure is almost the norm and not the exception, is it any wonder that some teens are drawn to the sense of belongingness that gangs provide?

We all know the old adage about there being strength in numbers. If you feel powerless and fear for your survival, what better thing to do than to join up with a group of people who will help protect you and not be one of your enemies? Having someone who has your back gives you a feeling of power and less vulnerability.

The list below is a compilation of the reasons teens have cited for joining gangs. I've added to that list of reasons by providing correspondences to each of the five primary needs. Certainly, others are possible, but this represents how unmet needs can function in the kinds of faulty decision making that some teens make.

Reason	Need
Attention	Belonging
Peer pressure	Belonging
Low self-esteem	Belonging, power
Fear or need for protection	Survival, freedom
Sense of power	Power, freedom
Long tradition by older family members	Belonging
Access to drugs, guns, money	Fun
Media glamorization	Fun

SIGNS OF VIOLENCE

As I write this, the nation is reeling from the horrific events at Virginia Tech University, where thirty-two people fell victim to a single extremely disturbed gunman. Every time a school erupts as a result of a violent act, we're all stunned. School shootings perpetrated by students are awful, terrible events, and they demonstrate violent behavior taken to the utmost extreme. We have learned some things as a result of them. In many cases, including this most recent one, the perpetrator demonstrated behavior that, in hindsight, made it clear that he was filled with rage and posed a potential threat. This underscores the need for vigilance and the importance of taking seriously any suspicions we may have about an individual. Here is a list that parents can use to help identify whether a child may be prone to violence:

- Withdrawal from school either partially (skipping days) or totally
- Feelings of isolation and being alone, not having any friends
- Intense feelings of rejection by peers and/or family
- Being a victim of violence or abuse
- Feelings of being picked on, bullied, teased, singled out for ridicule or humiliation
- Little interest in school and poor school performance
- Expressions of violence in drawing or writing
- Fascination with violent video or computer games
- Being "set off" by small things
- Cruelty toward animals
- Bullying and aggression
- Discipline problems over a long time or in recurring cycles
- Intolerance of differences
- Drug and alcohol use
- Depression (can present differently in teenagers than in adults)
- Gang affiliation
- Access to weapons in home
- Threats of violence
- Exposure to violence in the home
- Physical or sexual abuse

As is true with the previous warning signs, you will see some overlap, and just because you can identify a few of these traits, that doesn't mean your teen is necessarily involved with a gang or is on the verge of committing a violent act. Common sense should dictate your approach. If, however, you feel very strongly that the indicators are there, taking swift action—notifying a counselor at school, a mental health professional, or even your local law enforcement agency—is a wise move. I've had experience with parents who lived with violent teens and had to install locks on their bedroom doors with the deadbolts facing inward to keep their teens out. These parents lived in daily fear that their teens would harm them. I don't know how or why they put up with that kind treatment or how they existed in that kind of environment.

Clearly, if you feel threatened or if your child has threatened or harmed your other children or neighbors or strangers, it's your duty to intervene immediately. Better to act than to regret not acting. We will talk more about the steps you can take if your situation degenerates to the point at which you feel unsafe in your teen's presence. It's also important to take action when you or your teen is threatened by others or notices violent tendencies in others.   /

SEXUAL PROMISCUITY

Most teens are preoccupied with sex. I'm not going to spend a lot of time on the subject of teen's emerging sexuality at this point, except to point out that many sexual behaviors begin as a product of unmet needs. As parents we all have different values and beliefs about the appropriate age at which we hope our kids will wait to engage in sexual intercourse. It's difficult to say with any certainty what that age should be for any given teen, and most of us understand that our kids are physically capable of performing sexually long before they are ready for the emotional complications entailed in a romantic relationship.

I'm not about to tell you how to have the "birds and the bees" discussion with your kids, but I will say this, based on my experience in working with young people: Our kids are having their first sexual experiences at a much younger age than ever before, many of them view oral sex as a form of casual sexual contact, and they are engaging in higher-risk sexual activity—anal sex, sex with multiple partners, unprotected sex, and sexual competitions.

Teens have always explored their sexuality, and sexual experimentation is an important part of growing up. Having a healthy attitude and taking pleasure in sexual intimacy is a hallmark of a healthy individual. What troubles me, and most likely troubles you, is that the trend among young people seems to be to separate the physical act from the emotional connectedness that true intimacy brings. Certainly, intercourse can be pleasurable without the emotional bonds we normally associate with sex in the context of a committed relationship. In other words, sexual contact with another person meets teens' need for fun. Gender differences do exist that influence attitudes toward sexuality, and it is true that for males, the procreative act does have a biological imperative attached to it. Males, on a very deeply subconscious level, feel the urge to engage in sexual activity to meet their survival needs.

As is true of drug and alcohol consumption, the component of peer pressure may make your teen feel as if his or her social survival depends upon being sexually active. The "everybody's doing it" mentality can drive most parents crazy, but the reality is that teens, whether because of poor self-esteem, the delayed onset of brain development and higher reasoning capabilities, or other factors, believe that this rationale is a sound one.

While sexual activity can meet two of those most basic needs—survival and fun—it can also meet the three higher-level needs—freedom, belonging, and power. Just as getting a driver's license is a rite of passage that indicates a teen's emerging adult identity and independence, so does having intercourse for the first time. As I've said time and again, freedom = responsibility. Janna and I have made sure, in talking to our kids about sex, that they understand completely that engaging in sexual activity entails taking on a lot of responsibility and that the intended end product of sexual intercourse—producing children—involves a whole lot more responsibility than they can ever imagine. We've had to strike a delicate balance between making sure they understand the responsibilities they have to undertake (including, but not limited to, practicing safer sex) and dissuading them from the idea that sex is carefree fun. We've also had to tread carefully because we don't want to lead them to believe that sex is something dirty and not pleasurable. Talking about the responsibilities that accompany being sexually active also ties in with disabusing them of their distorted notion of freedom and sexual activity.

We've also made it clear to them that while it may seem as if being sexually active admits them to a club that will help meet their belongingness need, it's not an exclusive club with cachet attached to its membership. This is also tricky, because what we've talked to them about is becoming sexually active for the right reasons. If they are having sex because they want to fit in with a group of their peers, then what they're really doing is creating a false sense of belonging. The reason we as humans engage in sex is to feel a connection to our partner, not to our peer group. As adults we likely can't imagine choosing to have sex with someone because we think it will solidify our standing among our friends or colleagues. That is ludicrous, but for some teens that's reality and their perception.

Finally, sexuality and power are intertwined in both positive and negative ways. Taking part in any kind of activity that is considered adult, like drinking or having sex, has an empowering effect on teens. Similarly to how many boys are able to achieve some status among their peers for drinking, they will engage in sex, or brag about it, as a means to fit in and raise their status. With status comes power, and many boys who can't compete academically, athletically, or in other areas can make up for those deficits, real or imagined, by engaging in sexual activity.

Unfortunately, when one person is empowered by involvement in a sexual relationship, too often the other partner's power can be diminished. The relationship between power needs and sex is a complex and troubling one.

Don't Want to Know

Many parents approach discussions of sexual matters with about as much anticipation as they do an IRS audit while simultaneously having root canal work done without anesthesia. The Big Deny that we all have to deal with is that our kids grow into, and in some cases out of, their identity as beginning sexual beings.

- The present generation of teens has a very different attitude about sexual intimacy than you and I do.
- For many of today's teens, sex isn't intimate at all—it's something they are very open about and don't believe has to have any kind of emotional component.
- Our teens today have been exposed to more sexually explicit and not-so-explicit images and concepts than in any previous generation.

- Sex isn't so much about procreation or establishing the bonds of a romantic relationship as it is recreation.
- Our kids may have more information about STDs and birth control than in any other generation, but they still engage in high-risk behavior at levels equal to, or greater than, those in any other previous generation.
- Despite the level of education and information many of them have about sexual matters, a lot of them subscribe to the belief that if there is no penis-to-vagina contact or penetration, then no sex act has taken place.
- Among those teens who pledge abstinence, the rate of sexually transmitted diseases is higher than for those who don't formally pledge, even though they are less likely to get tested. Those teens who do pledge delay their first sexual encounter by eighteen months, but they quickly catch up in terms of the number of partners they have.*
- Along with this early development come problems with sexual abuse.

What these numbers don't reflect is the number of sexual partners our kids have. I've worked with some young women who have had sex with as many as thirty to forty different males. Sure, these young women have serious self-esteem issues, but they are also representative of the more casual attitude toward sex that kids have today—sex is not something that you engage in only in the context of a romantic relationship. "Hooking up" with someone (or whatever term is currently in use for this practice) means having sex with someone outside the boundaries of a dating relationship.

At the most extreme end of this spectrum is something that kids I've worked with call "sport fucking." This turns having sex into a contest, and points are kept based on the kind of sex engaged in over a period of time. To get this idea of the impersonal nature of sex

---

*Source: *New York Times* article on National Longitudinal Study of Adolescent Health (May 10, 2004). The study was financed by the National Institutes of Health, the Centers for Disease Control and Prevention, and the National Science Foundation. Our kids are physically maturing earlier. Adolescent girls are beginning to menstruate and develop breasts as early as ten or eleven. Adolescent boys' secondary sexual characteristics—pubic and facial hair—are developing earlier as well.

across even more strongly, I've had young women who engaged in these contests tell me that they could earn the most points for having intercourse without kissing the partner. I've also read accounts of kids as young as middle school and junior high being involved in this activity. We're a long way from sneaking a kiss under the bleachers of the football field or blind groping in the backseat of a car with your steady girl or guy.

Some numbers for you to consider from the Centers for Disease Control and Prevention:*

- In 2005, 47% of high school students had (*never*) ever had sexual intercourse, and 14% of high school students had had four or more sex partners during their life.
- In 2005, 34% of currently sexually active high school students did not use a condom during their last sexual intercourse.
- In 2002, 11% of males and females aged 15 to 19 had engaged in anal sex with someone of the opposite sex; 3% of males aged 15 to 19 had had anal sex with another male.
- In 2002, 55% of males and 54% of females aged 15 to 19 had engaged in oral sex with someone of the opposite sex.
- In 2004, an estimated 4,883 young people aged 13 to 24 in the thirty-three states reporting to the Centers for Disease Control and Prevention were diagnosed with HIV/AIDS, representing about 13% of the persons diagnosed that year.
- Each year, there are approximately 19 million new STD infections, and almost half of them are among youth aged 15 to 24.4.
- In 2000, 13% of all pregnancies, or 831,000, occurred among adolescents aged 15 to 19.5.

I keep asking you to be specific in dealing with your teen, so let's take a close look at what we mean by teens engaging in sex. This table also comes from the U.S. Centers for Disease Control and Prevention (CDCP) and its 2005 Youth at Risk Behavioral Study. The study will be administered again in 2007, but the results were not available when this was written.

*Source: www.cdc.gov/HealthyYouth/sexualbehaviors/index.htm#1.

**PERCENTAGE OF STUDENTS WHO HAVE EVER HAD
SEXUAL INTERCOURSE**

	Grade	T	9	10	11	12
Sex	T	46.8	34.3	42.8	51.4	63.1
	F	45.7	29.3	44.0	52.1	62.4
	M	47.9	39.3	41.5	50.6	63.8

Sex: T = Total, F = Female, M = Male.
Grade: T = Total, 9 = 9th grade, 10 = 10th grade, 11 = 11th grade, 12 = 12th grade.

Making Sense of the Numbers

What can we learn from these statistics about our desire to take an attitude of denial?

- Nearly half of all the students enrolled at any high school have engaged in sexual intercourse.
- The older our teens are, the more likely they are to have sex.
- A higher percentage of younger teen boys have had their first sexual experience than have girls in the same grade.
- By the time our teens reach their senior year in high school, the difference in gender and sexual activity has almost disappeared.
- If your daughter is going from her freshman year to her sophomore year, she's at a particularly vulnerable point, when nearly 15% more girls report having had their first sexual experience.
- For teenage boys, the largest increase in percentage occurs between their junior and senior years, when we see a 13% increase.

Do these numbers confirm what we believe about girls maturing faster than boys? As far as I'm concerned, those assumptions don't really matter. What matters is that we face the realization that our kids are engaging in sex—orally, anally, and vaginally. They're better educated than ever before, but they seem to be less concerned with preventive measures, such as using condoms, despite what they know about STDs and pregnancy.

If our kids are being assaulted by media images and peer pressure and the pervasive attitude that sex is something to be experienced early and often, regardless of emotional connections, then we have to do a gut check. As parents, do we see our values reflected in these statistics? Are we unwilling to discuss sexual matters because of our discomfort, or because whether or not we want to admit, we don't view our teens' sexual activity as bad? Are our kids more open and honest, and do these surveys reveal in stark numbers what we experienced and perceived in our youth? For better or worse, our kids take their lead from us. Given what we know about sexual activity among young people, it's likely better to talk about sexual matters earlier and more often than we anticipated we'd have to—shortly before they become teens.

I talked earlier about the need to check into the reality hotel. We have to be realistic about our values and attitudes as they relate to sexuality. We know what's going on, but do we want to do something about it? Do we just pay lip service to the "save yourself for marriage / till you're older / till you're ready / till you're out of my house" schools of thought? An unfortunate reality—the disturbing connection between violence and sex may force our hands.

VIOLENCE AND SEX

We know that one reason why boys like to throw parties and have girls attend them is that alcohol reduces everyone's level of inhibition. I don't condone this, and as the father of a teenage daughter and teenage sons I find that act reprehensible in the extreme. I've taught my sons to have respect for women, and I firmly believe my daughter has enough respect for herself that she will act appropriately when and if she finds herself in that kind of situation. I have faith that she can exert control over nearly every situation she will encounter. A part of me feels a great deal of empathy toward any boy who would like to date her—she's a formidable and independent force of nature.

Unfortunately, the kind of force we're going to have to talk about is one in which my daughter, and millions of other young women, are the controlled rather than the controllers. The combination of dating and violence is one of the unspoken realities of teen life. I've heard horror stories from many of the students I've worked with. For example, Lisa, who came to us as a tenth grader, told the story of how she fell victim to a "scammer" at her school. Only after she'd been victimized did she find out that the young man (and I use the term "man" very loosely here) had used this scheme several times before. Lisa was an attractive but shy young lady. She was a member of the school's dance squad, a group with a reputation for having the most attractive and adventurous girls at the high school. She met Brett when he was asked to be part of the squad's winter dance recital. Brett was a popular kid, a wrestler who had won two consecutive state championships at the one-hundred-forty-eight-pound weight division.

He was slight but powerful, only an inch or so taller than Lisa. Dating him was the dream of most of the girls in the school. When he expressed an interest in Lisa, she was flattered but unsure. Brett was a senior, eighteen, and Lisa had just turned sixteen. Brett was flirtatious, but Lisa resisted. After graduation, Brett and Lisa met at a party hosted by one of the other girls on the dance squad. Feeling that she was a little older and wiser, and that if Brett's attentions hadn't yet wandered to someone else his interest must be genuine, she agreed to go on a date with him.

By August they were a couple. Brett was getting ready to go to college, and as a farewell celebration Lisa agreed to go out on Lake Michigan with Brett on his family's boat. They had done so before, but only with other family members. This time, it was just the two of them, the boat, and miles of water between them and the shore. That's when Brett, who'd been gently pressuring Lisa to have sex with him, decided the time was right to insist. Fearful, far from anyone who could hear her cries for help if she chose to make them, and feeling trapped in that confined space, Lisa broke down and cried. Rather than relent or offer her any comfort, Brett mocked her. When she offered little resistance to his removing her clothes, he got what he wanted.

Lisa never said a word to anyone about what had happened, but she vowed to never see Brett again. Everyone assumed that her withdrawal was over her first real heartbreak. The rumor mill spun it that Brett had told her the long-distance thing wasn't going to work when he went to college. Lisa spiraled deeper into a depression and eventually was hospitalized for it. The rumor mill cranked up again, and Lisa's depression was transformed into a pregnancy and an abortion. When Lisa returned to school, she was appalled to hear that story going around. She decided to break her silence. She told a few girls on the dance squad about what Brett had done. None of them believed her, and Lisa's reputation as a "psycho-bitch" was secure. Two other underclassmen on the dance squad told her privately that Brett had done the same thing to them. They made Lisa promise not to tell anyone—their lives would be ruined.

As far as Lisa was concerned, her life was already ruined. Her father had slipped and injured his back over the summer. Lisa knew where the Percocet was kept, slipped ten of the pills into her mouth, and lay down on the couch in the living room. Her mother discovered her when she returned from a quick trip to the grocery store. An emergency room visit, discussions with her school counselors, and Lisa was on her way to Spring Creek.

Whatever empathy I have for boys and their emotional illiteracy and the difficulties they face with peer pressure, and with unrealistic and unfair expectations of what manhood constitutes, ends when a young man abuses anyone. Especially if it is dating violence—physical, emotional, or sexual abuse. According to a study conducted by the CDCP, one in eleven high school students reports being physically hurt by someone he or she was dating. One in four adolescents reports being a victim of verbal, physical, emotional, or sexual abuse each year. With teens, males and females both use violence—the difference is that boys tend to act out in anger and girls in self-defense. One in eleven teens also reports being forced to have sexual intercourse when he or she did not want to, again according to a CDCP survey.

VIOLENCE, SEX, AND THE PRIMARY NEEDS

When violence and sex are intermingled, the catalyst at work causing that reaction is nearly always power. Sexual assault and rape are all about dominance. Aggression of all forms, in particular sexual aggression, is rooted in the need for power. Our typical conception of someone who commits sexual assault of any kind is a hulking, brooding savage. The truth is that those who commit crimes of a sexual nature are just as likely to be the shy, quiet, slightly built, unassuming type. We saw that in the story of Lisa and Brett. Brett was the typical boy-next-door type, polite and refined, yet it's clear that he was also deeply troubled beneath that calm exterior.

We all want to feel powerful and in control of our lives. As I've said before, power accrues status in this culture. Most of us would like to be rich and powerful. In our minds the two go hand in hand. Power sits at the top of the hierarchy of primary needs. That means that is the most difficult to attain for teens and is also the most important to them. When we talk about individuation—the development of an adult identity—freedom and power are the two most important needs teens have to have met in order to achieve it.

When teens aren't given power and freedom in appropriate ways (by earning it, mostly), they will seek it in other inappropriate ways. Sexual violence among teens is an extreme form of bullying. It is about taking power from another person, exerting one's will over them. It's about seizing someone else's freedom. To many teens, in particular males, one of the easiest ways to have the power need met is to take sexual advantage of another person. Why? First, there are the physical differences between teenage males and females. The size difference makes it easier for many males to physically dominate females. Second, males can prey on the unmet needs of females. If a young woman wants to have her need for freedom, belonging, and power met, she can do so by engaging in sexual activity.

How many young women have fallen prey to the "If you really cared about me you'd do this" ploy? And how many young women have caved in to the pressure to have sex out of fear of abandonment and the consequent loss of status, belonging, and power that would result from being broken up with?

In these cases we are talking about borderline consensual sex. In some ways it would be better to think of it not as consensual but as coercive sex. Coercive sex is a form of emotional abuse. Though I don't know of any studies that have looked at trends in coercive versus truly consensual sex among teens, I'd be willing to bet that the vast majority of sexual encounters between teens is the former, not the latter.

Where the power differential is greatest and where the power need is met to the greatest degree is when physical violence is involved. Our teens need to feel powerful and in control, and they need to feel in control of themselves. As parents we are obliged to make clear to our kids that taking power from someone else is always wrong. As I mentioned earlier, we can make sure that our kids feel powerful by recognizing and praising them for their positive accomplishments.

Some of the most disturbing kinds of acting out teens engage in is when sex and violence are linked. In the next section I'll look at this in the context of dating relationships. That's not the only kind of sexual violence we see teens committing. One disturbing case comes to mind. A New Jersey high school football team went away for a pre-season training camp. In what they considered a type of hazing or initiation ritual, a group of upperclassmen "welcomed" a few of their younger classmates to the team by pinning them down and violating them anally with objects.

Where did they get the idea to do such a horrible thing? Well, not too soon before this incident, officers in the New York City police department made national headlines by abusing a man in its custody with a broomstick by inserting it into his rectum. Both these cases involve a kind of ritualized sexual abuse. Both took place in stereotypically male-dominated, macho, violent worlds. This cult of violence and aggression and homoerotic torture is deeply disturbing, and it reflects a series of unmet needs and aberrant responses to them. It also says some deeply disturbing things about the influence of the media and our adult world being reflected in the lives of our young people.

THE LONG-TERM EFFECTS OF DATING VIOLENCE

Here is what a CDCP fact sheet has to say about what happens to victims of dating violence:

> Teens who are abused are more likely to do poorly in school. They often engage in unhealthy behaviors, like drug and alcohol use. The anger and stress that victims feel may lead to eating disorders and depression. Some abused teens even think about or attempt suicide. Abused teens often carry the patterns of violence into future relationships. Physically abused teens are three times more likely than their nonabused peers to experience violence during college. In adulthood, they are more likely to be involved in intimate partner violence.

The legacy of sexual abuse is long and torturous. I've worked with so many kids over the years who have been the victim of abuse and have become victimizers themselves. Here are a few things we know about those who do the abusing, again from the CDCP:

Studies show that people who abuse their dating partners are more depressed, have lower self-esteem, and are more aggressive than peers. Other "red flags" for dating abuse include the following:

- Use of threats or violence to solve problems
- Alcohol or drug use
- Inability to manage anger or frustration
- Poor social skills
- Association with violent friends
- Problems at school
- Lack of parental supervision, support, or discipline
- Witnessing abuse at home

The NYVPRC provides the following list of things your teen can do to keep from becoming a victim of dating violence. As parents we have to alert our kids to some of the more unpleasant aspects of life. It is likely best to let them know about dating violence before they become involved with anyone. If you wait until they are in a dating relationship, you run the risk of your child's thinking that you are accusing his or her "partner" or being too judgmental. Here is that list of factors you can share with your teenager.

Early Warning Signs of a Dating Situation or Relationship with Potential for Violence

- Your boyfriend or girlfriend pressures you, soon after you begin dating, to make the relationship very serious, or presses you to have sex.
- Your boyfriend or girlfriend becomes extremely jealous and possessive and thinks these destructive displays of emotion are signs of love.
- Your boyfriend or girlfriend tries to control you and to forcefully make all decisions for the two of you, refusing to take your views or desires seriously. He or she may also try to keep you from spending time with close friends or family.
- Your boyfriend or girlfriend verbally and emotionally abuses you by doing such things as yelling at you, swearing at you, manipulating

you, spreading false and degrading rumors about you, and trying to make you feel guilty.

- Your boyfriend or girlfriend drinks too much or uses drugs and then later blames the alcohol and drugs for his or her behavior.
- Your boyfriend or girlfriend threatens physical violence.
- Your boyfriend or girlfriend has abused a previous boyfriend or girlfriend or accepts and defends the use of violence by others.
- If you're in a dating relationship that in any way feels uncomfortable, awkward, tense, or even frightening, trust your feelings and get out of it. It could become, or may already be, abusive.

The NYVPRC also suggests that teens become aware of some signs of abuse so they can recognize them in their friends. This is another opportunity for you as a parent to reinforce this message regarding the possible negative consequences of dating in a more general way.

Friends in abusive relationships may also do some of these things:

- Radically change their style of clothing or makeup
- Seem to lose confidence in themselves and begin to have difficulty making decisions
- Stop spending time with you and other friends
- Begin to receive failing grades or quit school activities
- Turn to using alcohol or drugs

Obviously, this is a difficult, extremely complex, and ultimately painful situation for those involved. No parents want to suspect that their child is either the victim of date abuse or committing date abuse. If you see a pattern of anger in your child's response to problems, if the child threatens or commits acts of violence against you or siblings or peers, it's your obligation to get help for that child. I can't imagine what it would be like to be a parent who has to phone another family asking them to check on their son or daughter to be sure that your child isn't harming their child. It would take great courage to do that, but great courage is needed to make sure that all our children are safe. Keep in mind that the legacy of violence can extend for generations. Someone has to put a stop to the violence.

11

Acting Out Turns Inward:
Depression and Suicide

The steps that many teens take to remedy the pain, anger, frustration trio resulting from unmet needs—binge eating, excessive dieting or exercise, consuming alcohol and drugs, engaging in acts of violence, participating in sexual activity—are all stopgap measures to keep themselves from hurting. In many cases, those negative behaviors do achieve the teen's desired effect, at least temporarily. But what happens when teens either don't take those inappropriate measures or find that they are ineffective against the onslaught of pain, anger, and frustration they believe can't be resolved? What happens when a teen truly feels thwarted at every turn?

Hilary could easily answer that question. At just an inch under six feet tall, and with the broad-shouldered physique of an Olympic-caliber swimmer, Hilary was the very picture of invulnerability. In fact, at one point in her young life she had been a promising swimmer who seemed destined for Olympic glory. Growing up in swim-happy south Florida, Hilary began her competitive swimming career at the age of six. "I was addicted to the smell of chlorine, Mr. Mike," she reminisced in one of our first sessions.

Encouraged and supported by a mother who had been a collegiate diver, and by a father whose passion for polo was rivaled only by his passion for other women besides his wife, Hilary grew up in an intense environment as an only child. Her parents separated when she was ten and divorced three long years later. Throughout the dissolution of the marriage, Hilary kept her focus on the positive—several national under-sixteen junior national championships in the individual medley and the butterfly. "I loved the butterfly and IM because they were just so painful. As long as I was beating on my body, I didn't have to think about all the other crap going on."

What was going on besides the contentious divorce was the realization that her father had sired two other children out of wedlock with different women. While he wanted Hilary to be part of the one big happy family he envisioned, she recoiled at the thought. Though the court-ordered visitations with her father never seemed to go well, it wasn't for lack of effort on her father's part. "He couldn't show up at our designated meeting locations without some big-bucks gift. It was like 'Hi honey, just for playing our game and as a consolation prize you've won a personal DVD player from Sony.' "

In some ways Hilary loved her dad, but she hated being forced to interact with her half siblings—a young woman a year younger than she and a boy of seven. Her father had married the mother of the young woman. Her stepmother and father also had sole custody of the boy, James.

"He had this whole Brady Bunch fantasy running in his head. Maybe it was because he was an architect. I wasn't about to let him have that."

Ultimately, Hilary had no choice. In short order, her mother was diagnosed with ovarian cancer and soon died. Hilary went to live with her father. A month after that she felt a pain in her shoulder and upper chest. She thought it was a muscle strain and figured that rest would help. When it didn't, her coach took her to a doctor. Hodgkin's disease and chemotherapy treatments kept her out of the water for six months. Inactivity and her chemotherapy caused her weight to balloon by thirty-five pounds. Between bouts of nausea, she ate to dull the pain. Always an overachiever and a perfectionist, she hated the person she now saw in the mirror. Friends commented on how strangely dispassionate she seemed over her mother's death, but behind closed doors, Hilary mourned hard and obsessed about death. She filled notebooks with ramblings about mortality and the larger questions of life. She found the saddest songs she could find and played them endlessly on her stereo.

She cut herself off from her swim team friends and stopped going to the pool to watch practices or meets. It was too painful to not be participating, and sitting in the stands was where her mom, not Hilary, was supposed to be. Without the imposed discipline of 6:00 a.m. and 3:00 p.m. practices, Hilary became an indifferent student. There was always time now on the weekends or weeknights to get schoolwork done. She didn't sleep well, and ultimately she gave up trying. Long after the house fell silent, she sat up in bed, mindlessly clicking through the channels, her interest held by real estate infomercials for a few minutes, the rest a blur.

Everyone was sympathetic. She was sick, she'd lost her mother, and she was living with strangers. Her own survival had been threatened; what activity she'd engaged in for fun, belonging, and power had been taken from her, and she felt trapped, imprisoned by her condition and her living arrangements. She didn't eat meals with the rest of the family, and except for the time she spent in school, she was behind closed doors in her room.

Even after she was given as clean a bill of health as anyone could following a diagnosis like hers, Hilary kept herself isolated. She was tired most of the time, fell asleep frequently in class, and essentially stopped eating or caring for herself. Most mornings it was all she could do to stick her head in the shower to rinse her hair before going to school. Some days she'd rally and sit up and take notes in class. Between classes, she'd retreat to a bathroom stall and cry. Teachers and school counselors intervened, and her father took her to the family physician, who prescribed antidepressants. Hilary took them for a week or two, felt no effect, and stopped taking them.

That's when I met her. The first reports I read about Hilary indicated that she was not going to be the model student at Spring Creek. She was highly antagonistic toward fellow students and staff, and she refused to abide by the most basic guidelines of the program. In a lot of ways, I thought, who could blame her?

UNDERSTANDING DEPRESSION

While it was plain to see that Hilary was depressed and why, it is not always that easy to identify depression in our teens. One true indicator that a person is depressed is heightened irritability. Unfortunately, "irritable" is often another synonym for "teen." With males, that irritable look may be indistinguishable from their everyday look. A depressed teen often looks sullen and angry, edgy and defiant. I defy any parents of teens to tell me that they've never witnessed "that look" from their teenage son or daughter. Obviously, if your teen wears "that look" as a perma-expression, it's time to investigate what's going on.

One of the worst things about depression is that despite the many advances made in its treatment, being depressed engenders feelings of shame in many teens. Teens, especially males, don't want to appear to be emotionally needy. They don't want to exhibit signs of weakness. To do so would be an admission of powerlessness. They often mask those feelings and walk around looking as if nothing in the world is bothering them. In the case of boys especially, this can be really rough.

The Shame of Depression

Kids are reaching their physical maturity sooner. A twelve-year-old boy of today has reached his physical maturity. In 1850, that degree of physical maturity would be found in a sixteen-year-old. When you consider what we know about emotional maturity and the brain's maturity, you can see that bodies are way out in front of brains and spirits. That's tough for kids to deal with. What's even tougher for kids to deal with than the imbalance of physical maturity and their emotional and cognitive maturity, and is even worse than the shame of being depressed, is the fact that we don't like to be around depressed people. They are no fun. We want to be around fun people, and when people choose to isolate themselves, we tend to let them, or we insist that they "get over" whatever is bugging them.

Serious clinical depression just isn't easy to get over. Teens feel ashamed if they are depressed. Depression causes them to isolate themselves. Many depressed people know that they aren't fun to be around, and they don't want to drag anyone else down, so they isolate themselves even more to prevent loved ones from seeing them suffer. Depressed people can often act like wounded animals and lash out at people who try to get close to them to comfort or help them. They feel guilty for lashing out and don't want to hurt other people, so they isolate themselves even more.

What Is Isolation?

What's really tough about spotting this isolation thing is that many teens who aren't depressed choose to spend time alone. Or we think they're alone, but the way some kids socialize today via the Internet, cell phones, text messaging, and other means can make it look to us as if they aren't socializing and are isolating themselves, but in reality they are fully wired and connected and communicating to a degree we never were able to. A friend of mine with two teenage daughters and one teenage son lamented the fact that he's done well enough financially to afford a cell phone and a home computer for each of them. As he said, "When I was growing up we had one phone line in the house. There was a phone in the kitchen and one in my parents' bedroom. That was it. I lived in mortal fear of receiving a phone call. I'd have to talk in front of everybody, because we spent so much of our time in the kitchen. Or I was afraid that my mother or father would pick up the phone in the bedroom right when I was in the middle of somebody telling me something I would not want my parents to know about. In my parent's house, we always knew when somebody was on the phone."

Today, with a three-thousand-square foot house and three separate phone lines, my buddy John has no idea who's doing what, where, or when. His kids are happier, he assumes, but he'd have to convene a meeting and leave three different voice mails to get it scheduled. That's a bit of an exaggeration, but the point is clear: Given the way things work these days, it's harder to know precisely what is going on and how much communication is taking place. As a parent you have to do your best to be informed about their behavior, but without becoming an all-out spy. Where you must draw the line, however, is when you become worried for their safety. That, more than anything else, is paramount.

SUICIDE: THE WORST DEPRESSION

If you take depression and the shame felt by the victim of depression; add in emotional illiteracy, an inclination to be impulsive, and a nature that is more action oriented than reflective; and combine that with a tendency to lash out violently and the ready availability of weapons, it makes sense that 86% of suicides by older adolescents are committed by males. For younger adolescents that number falls to 80%, but you can see the trend. While girls attempt suicide at a rate twice that of males, boys are simply far more successful at it, using more violently effective means than females.

Suicide rates among teens have risen by a factor of three since the 1950s. One possible explanation for this increase is that the matrix of pain, anger, and confusion we've looked at has some biological component. We also know that kids are reaching their physical maturity sooner, as mentioned above.

If you suspect your child is suicidal, the best course of action is to be direct. When you consider that the third leading cause of death among adolescents is suicide, it also makes sense to be on the lookout for warning signs. Ask your child, "Are you thinking of killing yourself?" Follow that question up with "How would you do it?"

Suicidal ideation (thinking about it) is fairly common among many people. It is also a sign, obviously, in some cases of a person being suicidal. Does that mean that if your child responds yes to your first question, you have to immediately intervene? Yes and no. The reason you ask the follow-up question is that if your child responds with a fairly detailed summation of how he or she would do it, then you need to act swiftly. If you get a "I don't know, a gun maybe," that level of specificity indicates that the child hasn't formulated a plan and is less likely to act on it.

Please know that any talk of suicide should be addressed. Even a flippant remark, a "Oh, I guess I should just go and kill myself since I failed that test," should be remarked upon and noted. You can respond, "Sarah, I know you were joking just then, but I hope you understand how serious that issue is. If that is ever something you think about, even for an instant, I want you to talk to me about those feelings."

That can be the end of it. Obviously, by letting your child know that you've taken note of the statement, you run the risk that he or she will take those feelings underground. Notice, however, that your statements indicated concern but not worry. They were non-judgmental. You may have wanted to say, "I hope you would never do that to yourself" instead of "I hope you understand how serious that issue is." Stating a fact, "Suicide is a serious issue," is always better than rendering a judgment or making an emotional plea. We'll talk more about this kind of communication in the next section.

Teen Suicide Warning Signs

As with teen violence and school shootings, we've learned a lot about teen suicide in the past few decades. While in many cases parents or friends will say they never suspected that a teen was depressed or likely to commit suicide, the truth is that often we apply that salve to our own wounds of feeling guilty about not being able to prevent a loved one's death. It's true that in some cases we won't be able to keep a very determined person from ending his or her own life. In many cases, with teens who are contemplating suicide, we can identify warning signs that they are susceptible to such a rash act.

The following list is from the American Academy of Pediatrics:

- Withdrawal from friends and family members
- Trouble in romantic relationships
- Difficulty getting along with others
- Changes in the quality of schoolwork or lower grades
- Rebellious behaviors
- Unusual gift-giving or giving away possessions
- Appearing bored or distracted
- Writing or drawing pictures about death

- Running away from home
- Changes in eating habits
- Dramatic personality changes
- Changes in appearance (for the worse)
- Sleep disturbances
- Drug or alcohol abuse
- Talk of suicide, even in a joking way
- History of previous suicide attempts

SIGNS OF DEPRESSION

Because depression affects such a huge number of teenagers suffering from lack of fulfillment of all of Glasser's needs, there is a wide range of signs. Many, many lists of these signs circulate on the Internet and through various mental health agencies, so I've tried to narrow them down to a useful number. Some of these lists may be helpful for you, and some are misleading. I like the following from the University of New Hampshire Cooperative Extension Program because it organizes them into categories:

- **Academic signs**
  Student doesn't do well in school and can't explain why. Loses interest in school subjects. Doesn't try as hard or gives up more easily. Turns in unfinished or messy work. May complain of being too tired to finish work.
- **Social/behavioral signs**
  Teen may be very disruptive or show antisocial behavior, such as lying or stealing. Avoids people in general or withdraws from other teens. Behaves in ways that make it difficult to make friends or keep them. Afraid of certain things for no obvious or good reason. May be tired and constantly falling asleep; may act restless, take on appropriate risks.
- **Cognitive signs**
  Teen may have trouble concentrating, remembering things, or making decisions. Has very little or no confidence. Talks about suicidal thoughts or wanting to attempt suicide. Has constant thoughts about death.

- **Emotional signs**
Teen may have low self-esteem, feel guilty, or just seem unhappy in general. May be irritable or complain a lot. Feels hopeless and helpless.
- **Physical signs**
Teen may show change in usual sleeping patterns. Complains about feeling sick, in pain, or tired. Suddenly gains or loses weight or doesn't have the same appetite as before. Looks or acts "slowed down" or "speeded up."
- **Motivational signs**
Teen doesn't care about anything. Can't pay attention to things. Feels bored.

Severe depression is often linked to suicidal behavior. Warning signs for depression and suicide may overlap. However, not all teens who commit suicide are seriously depressed. On the other hand, not all who are seriously depressed attempt suicide.

What Parents Can Do to Help

If your teen is depressed or has expressed to you that he or she has thoughts of suicide, even in the most hypothetical of ways, there are some steps you can take to make sure the situation doesn't evolve into something far worse:

- Listen carefully to what your teen has to say. Don't interrupt. Be supportive and accepting.
- Don't criticize, judge, or downplay his or her feelings or concerns.
- Ask questions about your teenager's feelings. Ask if he or she has thoughts about suicide.
- Try to offer your help without suggesting that your teen is emotionally or mentally disturbed.
- Tell your child that asking for help is not being weak. Stress that asking for help with a problem is a sign of maturity, mental health, and good judgment.
- Try to make your teenager feel comfortable about asking for help. It is best if your teen asks for help on his or her own. Suggest talking to a counselor or doctor, or calling a crisis hotline.

- If you believe your child is suicidal, do not leave him or her alone.
- Call a counselor, doctor, religious leader, or the police for help.

DON'T DESPAIR!

As you can see, the number of possible ways your teenager can act out as a result of unmet needs can feel overwhelming, and I've discussed all of them at the risk of causing you to despair. That's obviously not my intention. Being informed gives you the power that you may feel you lack in the face of so many forces at work on your child. In Appendix C, I've included a host of resources you can consult for information on all the topics we've covered here and elsewhere in the book.

Don't fall victim to your teen's pattern of thinking. You're not alone. There are many people and organizations who can help you out. Asking for help isn't always easy, but there's no shame in it. I grew up in an environment where if you were hurting, you were told to rub some dirt on it, you'll be okay. I agree with the last part of that statement, but as an effective cure-all dirt won't cut it—especially if you stick your head in it and hope your kids' problems will go away. Sure, kids go through phases, and they oftentimes outgrow things— but sometimes those phases are just one step further down, and they may outgrow feeling bad by ending their lives. It's up to us to have the strength they may lack, to model the behaviors we want them to copy. End of sermon. Let's move on.

Part IV

Developing the Right Approach

12

Having the Right Mindset

I've talked to a lot of parents over the years, and many of them tell me that they're at the end of their proverbial rope, the camel's back is broken, their last nerve has been frayed, or whatever other cliché they can come up with to describe the level of frustration and anger they're feeling. We don't ever want to get to that point, but sometimes we wind up there anyway. Whether we've gone down the road and hit a dead end, or whether we anticipate not having to travel that same route and want to get an earlier start through prevention, I can help out. As is often said in therapeutic circles, if you can't start early, you can start now.

In the previous chapters, I've given you the information you need to understand why your child has been acting out and why his or her behaviors have become so extreme. In the pages that follow, we are going to work on the steps you can use to help get your teen back on the right path.

I have to do a lot of work around our place to keep things running smoothly. The other day, my truck started acting up, and the engine was cutting out on acceleration. Not what I needed. After supper, I went out and got my tools and started working on it, figuring it was a clogged fuel filter and hoping it wasn't a bad fuel pump. Cars used to be easy to work on. Today, you need a computerized diagnostic machine more than you need a set of wrenches and the proper application of elbow grease to get something fixed. Well, I'd been having a tough day, and when I got out there, I put a pair of snub-nosed pliers on one of the clamps holding the fuel filter in place, and the darn thing slipped out of my grip, and I barked my knuckles big time on the manifold. That hurt. Worse, I was now more upset than ever, so I figured I'd show that clamp the what for, and I twisted it even harder, and tore a hole right through the fuel line. Gas started dribbling all over, and I had a busted-up hand that was bleeding a bit. I went in the house to get something to wrap around my hand and collect the gas, and in my haste I forget to close the upper cabinet door where I'd taken out a rag. When I stood up after retrieving the rag I'd dropped, I banged my head on the open door.

I went back out to the truck, hand and head throbbing, and I was about to rip the engine right out of it with my bare hands when I heard my daddy's voice reminding me, "There's a time and place for everything, son. You can't keep a steady hand and a clear mind when you've got your dander up."

He was right, of course. I should have never gone out there that night. My mind wasn't right for doing that kind of work.

The thing of it is, and what I want you to remember, is that you can have all the right know-how, and you can have the right tools, but if you don't go into a task with the right mindset, you're likely to do more harm than good.

In working with your teen, it's important to have the correct mindset going in. That means that you have the goal of helping your teen get better, but most of all you have the desire to do what's best for your child and your family as a whole. You need to have not just the best intentions but the purest of intentions. Only with our minds right and focused on the task at hand with pure intention can we succeed. Without those things, when push comes to shove, there's going to be a lot of pushing and shoving going on. That won't benefit anybody.

Part of understanding pure intentions is understanding what they're not. One place not to start is by creating a situation that many of my teen clients found themselves in. When a child engages in any of the behaviors I described in Part III, our natural tendency as a

parent is to tighten the reins and exert more discipline. Unfortunately, as many of us know, that approach may lead to our making
this statement or some variation on it: "I've taken away everything
I could possibly think of—their driving privileges, access to their
friends with a curfew, the cell phone, Internet access, the door to
his/her bedroom—and nothing seems to matter. He/she still finds a
way to _____."

Now that I've given you one key to unlocking what motivates
your child—Glasser's needs—the temptation is to use that information against your child. Our thinking sometimes goes like this:
"My kid isn't behaving the way I want, and if freedom (or fun, power,
belonging, or survival) is so important, then I'll take that need away.
If they want their freedom bad enough, then they'll do what I want
them to do in order to get that freedom back. I'll show 'em who's
the alpha dog in this pack, and only when I get compliance from
them will I reward them with what they want." That sounds good in
theory, but without an underlying foundation of pure intention,
that strategy is likely to succeed in the short term and fail in the
long run.

Think back to the time when your child was happiest with you and
you were happiest with your child. When our kids are young, and
particularly when they are young and able to express their love verbally and in other ways, life for us parents is good. In fact, life is wonderful. I'm sure you can remember the warm feeling of everything
being right in your world when your three- or four-year-olds lit up at
the sight of you, came running to you full speed, and jumped in your
arms and told you how much they loved you. Why do you think they
did that? Was it because of all the things you took away from that
child or because of all the things you gave that child?

And wasn't it great when you could see in your children's eyes the
awe and admiration they felt for you when you did what was to you the
simplest thing, like fixing the track on their Thomas the Tank Engine
railroad set? When my kids were little, I sometimes felt like a combination of Superman, Einstein, and Mother Teresa all rolled into one.
That was wonderful, but of course those perceptions had to change.

I don't know why that all has to change, but it does. I suppose it's
a good thing, but it can also be frustrating for us as parents when

our kids stray from the path we intended them to travel and wander into acting out behaviors. If we spend too much time looking back at those glory days and not enough time figuring out a new strategy to create a relationship with our kids that reflects where we both are in our lives in that moment and acknowledges the developmental changes—physical, emotional, social, and intellectual–that our kids have gone through as they've progressed from toddler to adolescent to teen, then we may never be able to get them back.

In order to develop a mindset of pure intention, you need to abandon your expectations that something will somehow bring back those glory days. Regardless of how much you want your kids to look at you with glazed eyes of wonder, you need to acknowledge that this is an unrealistic expectation. To achieve pure intention, you need to prepare yourself to deal with the present, to put everything—the good and the bad—that your teen has done behind you and focus on that present moment, on righting whatever is wrong.

While I know that this sounds easy enough, the truth is that it is far from easy. Because this is such a difficult step for many parents to take, it helps to understand how and why kids come to view us in the way they do. Before we can have pure intentions, we need to see ourselves through their eyes.

We constantly talk about how kids have changed, and we reflect back on those golden days of yore. Well, one of the things I learned in the military as a firefighter is something that I adopted in my work with young people—the importance of being adaptable and flexible. Our kids are growing up and changing, and we have to accept and actively work to change our approach to them as well.

I know I'm supposed to be a leathery old cowboy type, but the times I enjoyed best with my kids was when I read them bedtime stories or all of us were sitting and watching a movie together. Literature is a great teaching tool, and before we get into some of the specifics of establishing the kind of relationship with your teens that allows them and you to have all your needs met and your teens to meet all of your, and society's, expectations of proper behavior, let's take a look at how our evolving relationship with our kids can be restructured.

We'll use one of the classics of children's literature, *The Wizard of Oz*. We read my kids the book and watched the movie whenever it came on television. We all loved it, and I think I learned a lot from it. I call the lessons I took from that wonderful film, the wisdom from the fourth Oz.

THE FIRST OZ

As you know from the book and the film, Dorothy and her friends travel to the land of Oz because they believe that the Wizard has the power to help Dorothy return home. Metaphorically, of course, Dorothy is all of our children. She has strayed and gotten lost in a world that sometimes frightens and overwhelms her. She wants to return to the warm embrace of her family—needs to, in fact—and so does your teen. Nearly every one of the seriously at-risk kids I've worked with over the years has expressed an intense desire to return home, to have whatever is wrong in his or her family environment be fixed, and to enjoy a harmonious relationship with parents and siblings.

Dorothy and her friends believe that the first Oz can help them. In their minds, this being is a benevolent figure who will grant them their wishes. From what they've heard and imagined, he is all-powerful and uses that power wisely.

This first Oz is you. This is the you that you were when your kids were younger. They looked at you the way Dorothy looked at the Wizard initially—as someone who will provide them with whatever they need. As stated above, that was a great place to be in your relationship with your kids. As adults we have primary needs as well, and power is certainly one of them. In their early childhood and in adolescence, we have nearly total control over our children. We derive a lot of satisfaction from that.

How many of us have sat in a restaurant or other public place feeling a secret sense of satisfaction when we witness another family's child throwing a fit while our kids are sitting there quietly angelic? However, when we're the one with the out-of-control child, our self-esteem takes a blow. Let's not kid ourselves here—a lot of what we think of ourselves and what others think of us is wrapped up in how successful we feel at child rearing. Becoming a parent is a rite of passage for us, and belonging to that club of good and effective parents is important to our self-esteem and sense of empowerment. Being that first all-powerful Oz feels really good, and it's difficult to let go of that role or feel good about ourselves when we don't live up to our own expectations.

Even better than in the story of Oz, your kids aren't just imagining that you are this benevolent being; you are present and active in their lives. That's not to say that you and your toddler or preadolescent enjoyed an always harmonious relationship, but for the most part the two of you enjoyed a solid, close, and loving relationship. We'd all like to remain in the first Oz forever. Unfortunately, that's not possible or good for them or for us.

THE SECOND OZ

As the story goes, Dorothy arrives in the land of Oz, and she is in for a big surprise. The all-powerful benevolent Wizard she'd imagined turns out not to be exactly what she expected. He's mean and tyrannical, and he frightens her and her traveling companions. He's a horrid and apparently wicked man, prone to angry flare-ups and pyrotechnic displays of his almighty power. He seems to rule by fear more than anything else. "Do What I Want or Else" is his motto.

This second Oz is the flip side of the first. Our children, because of their degree of brain development, relative lack of experience, and emotional immaturity, often view us in this way whenever we act in a manner that denies them what they want—notice I said "want" and not "need." This is a critical distinction that we're able to understand but frequently our kids don't. How many times did your child say to you, especially in the cereal aisle or the toy store, "But I NEED it." When we don't comply with the request, we can seem arbitrary, evil, and more of an ogre than a fairy godmother or godfather whose purpose is to grant their every wish.

Teaching our kids at an early age the difference between wants and needs is crucial for their emotional development. In the same way we taught our kids to say please and thank you, we made certain they understood at an early age the distinction between what they wanted and what they needed. It is never too early, nor is it ever too late, to teach and reinforce that message until they know when and how to put their desires and necessities in order. We tried to get our kids to understand that while needs and wants both feel the same emotionally, needs work at a more fundamental level.

Just as children's viewing us as all-powerful and all-knowing and all-wise and kind is a distortion, so is their thinking of us as the embodiment of unfairness, meanness, and indifference. Kids frequently see things as either black or white, and their first recollected experience with our failure to meet what they perceive to be their needs sticks with them for a long time. So does the first time they really encounter our fallibility. Just as Dorothy eventually discovers that the Wizard is really just a man behind a curtain—a silly, weak man—our kids eventually take us down off that pedestal. That can prove to be both healthy and destructive.

But we also have to acknowledge that in terms of our needs, we have to give some of our power over to our children. If we want them to grow and mature, we have to loosen our grip on them. This is especially difficult when our kids are making the transition toward adulthood in their teens. So much of the tension and conflict and power struggle occurs both because of our teens' distorted perceptions of us and because we are reluctant to let go of some of our power over them. It's not all about power either. We're feeling the first tugs of separation anxiety—the sense that our kids don't just belong to us but belong to the world of their peers, classmates, teammates, and all the rest of those "others" out there who are not a part of our immediate family. From behind our curtain, we see the future without their close presence, and not only do we fear for their survival, we have doubts about our own ability to prepare them, and about how we will deal with the freedom that comes when our kids leave the proverbial nest. It's also not easy to let go of the conception of ourselves as the combination of Mother Teresa, Einstein, and Superman that I mentioned earlier.

Letting the Air out of the Bubble Slowly

In some ways, when we display weakness or faults and our children see or hear about it, we've failed to meet one of their needs—survival. Kids need to feel secure and to trust in you and your capabilities. Later in this chapter, I'll talk about how to deal with the crisis of confidence, but for now, I want to remind to you of Danijela. Her swift decline and slip into bulimia, drugs, and alcohol coincided with the discovery that her father had molested her older sister. Sure, there were other factors, including survivor guilt, that contributed to her destructive turn, but a lot of it had to do with seeing her upright father exposed as a fraud. As she told me, "How could I believe anything he was telling me about doing the right things when he was doing the worst thing?"

Danijela's case is an extreme one. We don't have to violate one of our society's most sacred taboos to "fail" in our children's eyes. If we communicate well with our children and use stories of our missteps and weaknesses as a way to help them deal with their own stumbles and failures, then that façade of perfection will fade away instead of crumbling and crashing to the ground all at once. Most of us can deal with gradual change, while sudden catastrophic events can really knock kids off balance. A few words about our own struggles with geometry or a difficulty faced on the job are sufficient. No need to completely bare your soul and your deepest fears and regrets. For one thing, if your children come to you with a problem, you don't want to overshadow or diminish the seriousness of what they are thinking or feeling with "You think you got troubles; did I ever tell you about the time . . . ." Keep the focus on them. Use the stories to illustrate, not dramatize. Always remember which of you is the doctor and which is the patient.

Just as we don't have to be reveal and confess everything to our kids, we don't have to be the sternest taskmaster in order for our kids to think of us as pitiless monsters. Justine, the young woman who struggled with survival needs and turned into a worry wart extraordinaire, had her relationship with her mother deteriorate simply because her mother tried to convince her that many of her fears were groundless. In one session, Justine ranted against her mother, saying, "I would come to her and tell her what I was feeling, which is what she always said to do, and she would listen and tell me not to worry. She'd give me some bullshit reason for why I was wrong about the situation. She wouldn't do anything to fix it. She became such a bitch."

To most of us, what Justine described about her mother would seem to be a pretty reasonable response. But it's always about perception, and until Justine could see for herself that what her mother was doing was not so terrible, her mother became a kind of monster in her eyes. It didn't help that over time Justine's behaviors grew worse and more frustrating and her mother stopped being so reasonable.

I grew up in an era and in an environment in which many of my peers, and to a certain degree me, grew up fearing our parents. They were that Oz-like apparition who loomed large in our lives and imaginations. Some parents have told me that they'd rather be feared than liked if that meant their kids would turn out okay. Fear works for a while, but I've seen the consequences of what happens when the fear ends and the loathing begins. When kids are fearful, it's all about fight-or-flight responses. Neither of those two options results in what parents want most—a healthy teen.

THE THIRD OZ

Eventually, once Dorothy unmasks—well, "un-curtains"—the Wizard, she sees him for what he really is, and he no longer has to put on a display. They both understand their roles and what each of them wants and needs from the other. As a result, he assists her in getting home. Home, of course, is back to a loving relationship with those who matter most to her.

Another way to look at these developments is that Dorothy came to the Wizard and got what she wanted and needed. She didn't really care so much about understanding the Wizard. You may often feel as if that's what you've become as a parent of a teenager—a wish-granting, need-meeting, want-satisfying bank officer. That's not a fun role to play for any parent, and it's easy to see how resentment can build up if you feel that the only communication you have with your teen is when he or she is coming to you looking for what you perceive to be a handout. Whether that handout represents something tangible like a new cell phone or the opportunity to go to a concert, or something less tangible like empathy when something's gone wrong, being the one who gives all the time can take its toll. Maybe that's what frustrated the Wizard and made him so cranky. I don't know how I'd handle having a line out the door of people wanting something from me and giving nothing in return.

It's easy to fall into the trap of thinking about your needs and how they're not being met. I know a lot of parents who have felt deeply the loss of connection they once had with their teens. It's normal and natural to feel that sense of loss, but we can't stay stuck there, fixating on our unmet belongingness need, or the lack of the kind of fun we once had with our kids. We don't want to be stuck with feelings of powerlessness and find our only satisfaction in anxiety over our kids' safety and survival. What kind of life is that?

That's why we need to develop the wisdom of the fourth Oz.

THE FOURTH OZ

Again, when it comes to being the fourth Oz and learning all the lessons from the first three, it's all a matter of perspective. I'm not saying that we should be grateful for every crumb of contact our kids dole out to us. I'm not saying that it's ideal that our kids come to us only when things are going wrong and never share with us their joys and successes. I'm not saying that we should continue to strive to always be the all-powerful, all-knowing, infallible one. I *am* saying that we can hurt our kids by being too benevolent and overindulging them, as well as hurt them when we deprive them too much, too often, and too arbitrarily.

The fourth Oz doesn't exist in the story of Dorothy and the twister that blew through her world and tumbled her life upside down and sideways. We have to use our imagination and intellect to extract the lessons from the experiences and characteristics of the first three Wizards. I know this because parents often come to me hoping that I will be like that first Wizard. They have this look in their eyes and on their hopeful faces that says, "Help me get my family back to where we were when things were so good." It's not that easy, and I can't wave a magic wand like Glinda or just load you all on a hot air balloon.

Besides, our goal isn't to return to the pretwister days of preadolescence when our kids worshipped us and we were in complete control. We can't go back to the circumstances of that time, but we can return to and experience the emotional intimacy and satisfaction of those times. What we have to do is accept that some of the circumstances have changed, and absorb and reapply the lessons from the first three of our Oz incarnations. We have to understand and accept that just as our teens' needs have evolved and are being met in ways apart from us, our needs as parents have to be met in different ways. We have to adapt. We have to grow with our kids as well. How do we learn to do that, and what are some of those lessons we can extract from our experience as the first three incarnations of Oz?

First, we should cherish those moments when our kids are young and view us through a lens that filters out our imperfections. Cherish them because they won't last, and because wanting and believing that your parents are all-good and all-powerful is an expression of love almost beyond measure. Sacrificing that perception and allowing our kids the freedom and power to see us as the fallible human beings we really are is one of the greatest gifts we can bestow on them.

Second, as my daddy and granddaddy used to say all the time, when you lose, don't lose the lesson. We can't hold our kids in suspended animation, and we can't ever go back to having our relationship with our kids be exactly like it was when they were young. We may have lost some of those moments, but that doesn't meant we have to lose the lessons from those years. Keep in mind what I've said all along. Our kids do want us to be parents to them. They do want to be part of a family. They just want and need for some of the elements of that relationship to be on their terms. Change isn't something to fear. Think about your own relationship with your parents for a minute. Didn't it eventually evolve into something more like a friendship, something richer in which the contributions were more equal? Even if it didn't wouldn't you like to have that kind of relationship with your teen?

Third, we have to remember that with power comes responsibility. It is very true that we are responsible for our children and our teens. Sometimes we forget that, and the law sometimes has to step in to remind us—for example, parents may be held financially accountable for the damage their kids inflict on someone else's property through vandalism or accident. But just because you are responsible for someone else's welfare and mistakes, that doesn't mean that you hold absolute power over them. As I said above, fear-based parenting is doomed to failure. Parenting is not an exercise in ego, either. There are limits to the kind of control you can exert on your own kids. Eventually, they are going to have to stand on their own two feet, and that's hard for them to do when they've been wearing shackles their whole life. Instead of standing there and then walking the path to their future, they may just bolt.

I've seen that behavior in horses and cows, and in a lot of kids, too.

Next, it's painful to see the mighty fall, but it's what you do after you pick yourself up and dust yourself off that makes you a hero. Nobody wants to look the fool in their kids' eyes, and I'm not recommending you make a habit of it, but having your kids know you make mistakes and try to learn from them is one of the most important things you can do. Being a role model is important, and showing your kids how to handle adversity is one of the best things you can do for them. The Wizard got found out, but he didn't just take off. He made up for his mistakes when Dorothy called him on his bad behavior. One of the lessons I remember most from my dad is that good judgment comes from experience, and a lot of times the best learning experiences come from making a bad judgment. Share those experiences with your kids.

Finally, and most important, we have to understand that at times our teen's needs and our own are going to come into conflict. I hope by now you understand just how important it is to understand the relationship among your teens' primary needs, their motivations, and their behaviors. Use the same lens through which you examined them to investigate yourself. Understand that in nearly every case, you have to do what's best for your teen even if it means your needs will go unmet or be diminished in some way. That's not all there is to pure intention, but that's a large part of it. In a perfect world, we'd all get what we want and need all the time. In this imperfect world we live in, as parents we should strive to do whatever it takes for as long as it takes to ensure that our kids' needs are met in the most appropriate way possible, no matter the cost to us.

ESTABLISHING PURE INTENTION

What do I mean by pure intention? In many ways, that's being who you are as the fourth Oz. Another term that you may be familiar with is "unconditional love." I like "pure intention" better because I think that love does come with some conditions. One of them is respect. If we operate from a position of pure intention, we are creating an environment in which mutual respect can thrive. To me, unconditional love can sometimes sound a little too pie in the sky: You can go ahead and do anything to me and I'll still love you, so have at it. With pure intention, we make the message plain: I will always love you, and I will always respect your needs and do what I can to help see that they are met, but I won't always respect the actions you take or the choices you make. I also understand that you can say the same of me. But we also have to understand that underlying any of those disagreements and disappointments is a solid foundation of love and respect.

That foundation means that I love you enough to let you fail and to let you see me fail. I love you enough to forgive you and ask for forgiveness. I love you enough to share with you my joys and frustrations, my expectations and the consequences when those expectations are not met. I love you enough to want you to be independent and to know you always have a place by my side. You won't always be given that place; you will have to earn it sometimes, but you'll know exactly what you have to do to get there and stay there. If any of those requirements changes, I'll let you know. You will never be in the dark with me, and I will always be there rooting for you and lending you a hand so that you can get there. That's pure intention.

When you think about pure intention with your own teen, keep in mind Glasser's needs. One way we can establish pure intention is by understanding how those needs operate in our teens' lives and doing whatever we can to ensure that those needs are met in healthy productive ways. We also have to understand that we eventually have to let go.

One of my most satisfying experiences as a parent was teaching my kids to ride a bicycle. Sure, their first steps and words were memorable, but there was something more concrete about seeing them get up on two wheels and ride on their own. I guess it's the first step in their claiming their independence, giving them the chance to enlarge the circle of their experience. I think it's important for parents to remember that bike-riding training, because it wouldn't have been successful if you and your child hadn't trusted each other.

TRUST

Step one in repairing your relationship with your teen or maintaining the good relationship you currently have is to reestablish that trust or keep that trust alive. Keep the image of you assisting your offspring as he or she pedaled that bike while you ran alongside offering guidance and balance. It likely took you a bit of time and effort until the child mastered the skill, but you also likely felt a lot of pride and satisfaction, and so did the child. At some point you had to let go, and part of establishing pure intention is letting your child know from an early age that you will relinquish control gradually as the child is ready and as you are willing. It's also crucial to let your child know that together you will work out the timetable for how that letting go proceeds.

ESTABLISHING CLEAR EXPECTATIONS

We all assume that our children know what our job is as parents. But did your parents ever spell that job out for you, or did you just piece together the job description based on your observations? None of us would be likely to take a job unless we understood its requirements. Would you really trust somebody to be your boss or supervisor if you asked them a question about what you were going to be doing and they said to not worry about it, just let them do the thinking? That's probably an exaggeration, but I've worked with families who needed that kind of reeducation about roles and responsibilities.

Communicating clear expectations about behaviors and roles is one way to build trust. When we do that with our kids, we're in essence telling them, "Hey, you're a smart and reasonable person, and here's what I'm asking you to do." This is the same as being a teacher and walking into class the first day and handing out a sheet that explains the expectations for conduct, the grading and attendance policies, and the core of the curriculum. When we took classes, weren't the best teachers the ones who said, "This is what you are expected to know and be able to do by the time you leave this class." And even better, on a daily basis, they told you what the outcome for that lesson was. "By the end of the period today, you should be able to identify and explain the differences among three types of leadership—laissez-faire, autocratic, and emergent."

Sounds simple, but unless roles are clearly defined and expectations stated, then we find ourselves in a guessing game. There's far too much unpredictability in guessing games. Also, guessing games lend themselves to rules that are far too elastic. When we establish pure intentions, we keep the surprises to the minimum, we let our kids know how the scoring works, we keep them up to date on how they are doing, and we allow them "do-overs" as needed and as earned. At some point, if we have done a good job of parenting, we must trust in what we have taught our children. If they choose not to use what we have taught them, then we must again apply our parenting skills to intervene in their maladaptive behavior and assist them in learning prosocial behaviors.

I remember one of my earliest conversations with Dave, the snowball-throwing good kid who rebelled against being labeled that way. He said to me, "I got blindsided. One minute I'm sitting at home figuring I'm going to have a bunch of hours of community service work to do and worrying about how this is going to look on college applications. The next, I'm on a frickin' plane for Montana and this place."

It's tempting to say that Dave needed to understand the consequences of his actions and that his parents didn't owe him a step-by-step explanation of what steps they would take if he violated the law and got caught. While I don't know this for sure, I can imagine what Dave's parents would say in response: "What did you expect?"

Well, if you operate from a position of pure intentions, your children should always (or to the greatest degree possible) know what to expect. When you operate from pure intentions and communicate clearly with your children, then you shouldn't be the one who is springing surprises on your teen. I know it's tempting to spring one of those "Gotcha!" moments on a misbehaving teen, but our days of playing peekaboo and hide-and-go-seek are over. The game playing has to stop.

CONSISTENCY AND FLEXIBILITY

Boy, if ever there were a tightrope we have to walk as parents, it's between these two points. If the idea is that we shouldn't ever surprise our kids and set clear expectations and all that, how can we ever be flexible? Don't we have to apply these rules and regulations and standards all the time, every time? In a perfect world, maybe we could do that, but in the world of teens, we have to be consistently flexible and flexibly consistent. Okay, that may sound like just a bunch of word play, but it's really not.

When we set up our expectations and consequences, we need to communicate that exceptions will be made. Exceptions, by their nature, are rare occurrences. They are difficult to predict and not something you should count on. If and when an exception is going to be made, you will be made aware of it, probably with the sound of trumpet fanfare or some other means to let you know that something truly wonderful and unique is taking place. Parents face this all the time, especially when it comes to hard and fast rules like curfew. With my kids, if I say curfew is 9:30 and one of them comes home at 9:31, I will consistently say, "You are late. Curfew at 9:30 means 9:30."

If one of our kids comes to us and says, "Mom, Dad, a bunch of us are getting together to watch the video from the homecoming game. We won't start watching it until 8:30, and the thing runs for and hour and a half. Can I stay out until 10:30?" If we feel it's something worthwhile and there's reasonable justification for the video to start at 8:30, we'll likely say okay. We're bending the rule and making an exception for something irregular. That's far better than setting a rule and consistently allowing it to be bent on the teen's terms. That's when you get into trouble. That's when you lose control.

The plots of many television sitcoms about parents and children revolve around a parent doing something that completely surprises the child. The kid wants to go to a concert in another town and will be spending the night rather than driving home. All his friends are going to go, but he's hesitant to ask because he knows his father or mother will freak out and say no. Reluctantly, and goaded into asking by his friends, the young teen asks his mom and dad if he can go, too. They consult and agree. Much joy follows.

That may seem like a fun and happy outcome, but I don't think it's as satisfying a scenario as it could be. Ideally, our teens should know and be able to predict with a great deal of success what's going to be an acceptable exception and what's not going to be. When we've established pure intentions, we've created a filter. Our kids know what requests to bring to us and which ones to discard immediately. If they don't, then we have to step in and offer them some remediation. Let them know what the parameters are, what is truly out of bounds, and what's on the borderline. How do you teach them that concept? Simple: when they ask for an exception, tell them, "Hey, I can't say yes to that. That's way out of bounds, and here's why." Or, "Hey, I'm going to have to think about that one. That's on the borderline, and I'm going to talk it over with your mom and we'll get back to you. When would you like to know our decision?"

POWER

The example above is a good example of how to handle power properly. You've set the rules, established that they are open to reasonable interpretation, and maintained your authority. Your teens don't assume that it's okay to just come home at 10:30 and offer their reason for being late at that time. You've set things up so that they ask first. You are the one who defines the time and the date clearly and specifically. Again, that's a simple common-sense concept but one that often gets overlooked. The message is that even if you let your children get something they want that is different from what you established, they still have to come to you in order to get it. You're still the one who is in control, and you come across as the reasonable, rational, and predictable person you are. Power and control aren't something you wield arbitrarily but exercise consistently—with those predictable exceptions, of course.

THE GOLDEN RULE

No, it isn't whoever has the most gold rules; it's the tried and true "Do unto others as you would have them do unto you." If that rule were put to use more in this world, I think we'd have a far better place to live.

When we establish pure intention, this is probably the one overriding consideration that puts all the others into context. Going back to our example of the curfew exception, think about how you would want to be treated at your place of work when you ask for time off that's outside the normal scope of your vacation days, personal days, sick leave, or whatever other provisions are in your work agreement. You have certain responsibilities in terms of making that request: It has to be specific—when and how much time you will need. It has to placed as soon as is reasonably possible—emergencies come up, but if you know in advance, you give your boss as much fair warning as possible and provide a valid reason. And what are your expectations of your boss? That he or she will evaluate the request fairly, that he or she will understand that sometimes things come up that we can't control, that if the request is granted we won't be made to feel that they are doing us the biggest favor ever, that if it is denied we're given a sound reason for its being handled that way.

When we treat other people the way we want to be treated, we are

- Acknowledging their needs
- Assisting them in meeting those needs
- Respecting the other person
- Receiving respect in return
- Building trust
- Establishing expectations
- Acting consistently
- Allowing for exceptions
- Using power judiciously
- Being empathetic

In addition, we are doing all the things that let people know that we act and choose from a place of pure intention. This is the attitude you need to have with your teens. You need to treat them in the same way that you yourself would like to be treated. You give them the sense that you treat them as equals and not as someone who is superior to them. Condescension is a no-no. You are giving them the same courtesies that you would like them to extend to you. If they fail to reciprocate, the tactics change, but still you need to react as you would like them to react—you cannot allow their behavior to allow you to abandon the Golden Rule.

TIME AND ATTENTION

I've said this before, and I'm saying it again: The most important thing you can do as a parent is spend time with your kids and pay attention to them. This is perhaps the most important thing you can do to establish pure intention. If you do this, then the rest of the steps you need to take to develop a sense of pure intention will fall into place. How do we know when people care about us? When they spend time with us and pay attention to us. We can tell our kids all the time that we love them and support them, but when push comes to shove, if we aren't there with them to share experiences with them, then those words mean very, very little. When we operate from a position of pure intention, we put some of our needs and desires aside to concentrate on our kids.

Nearly every single one of the thousands of teens I've worked with has said to me at one time or another, "Mr. Mike, my parents didn't know or care about what I was doing. I figured if they didn't care what I did, what difference did it make what I did?" Whether that perception is based on facts or is simply the impression those kids got doesn't matter. They believed it and they acted on it. When our kids stop caring about themselves—and many of them do—that's when they really get into deeper trouble with high-risk behaviors like drinking, drugs, promiscuity, and suicide.

Time and attention are the most effective solutions you can apply as a preventive measure or as a therapeutic one after things have gone bad. It is about the most cost effective as well. I'm not saying that every one of the kids who ended up at Spring Creek Lodge Academy, who went through multiple counselors and various alternative programs, wouldn't have ended up with me if their parents had spent more time and paid more attention to them. That's an oversimplification, but I do want to stress how important these two points are. Many of our teens are starving for connection and aching to belong, and the way we can build better connections with them is by spending time with them and paying attention to what they want and need from us.

Pure intention is the starting point in working with your teen, whether you've been doing that from the very beginning or are establishing a new foundation. With the right mindset and by acting from pure intention, you can build on that foundation. It's sturdy. It's level. Using pure intention, the two of you are in the same place, and you're committed to treating your kids the way you would like yourself to be treated. I can't stress enough the importance of cultivating a mindset whereby you're not approaching your teens as a punisher but as someone who is committed to helping them, someone who is on their level.

Once you've accomplished this change in your approach, the next step is to learn how to communicate more effectively with your teen so that your pure intentions are perceived and received correctly.

13

Showing the Right Mindset through Praise

By now, this will sound like a familiar refrain. Growing up is tough. Helping your teen mature is also tough. I'm not going to debate which one is more difficult, but I will point out something that most psychologists and others who work with teens will tell you to be true: The primary key to an adolescent's achieving individuation and going on to being a successful and well-adjusted young adult is self-esteem. If your kid is in pain, becomes confused about the nature of his or her pain, gets frustrated and angry, and then acts out inappropriately, I believe that one of the contributing factors will invariably be a lack of self-esteem.

Teens who lack self-esteem are the ones who are most likely to seek validation from their peers. With a definite need for power and recognition that is much easier to earn from those their age than from authority figures or parents, many of these kids gravitate toward peer groups where they can win easy acceptance. We've already seen the kinds of behaviors that kids will engage in to earn their place in the pack, such as drinking, drug taking, high-risk sexual activity, and violence.

Teens who lack self-esteem also feel threatened more easily than those who have good self-esteem. Their social survival need, much like their need to belong, will also compel them to do things they might not do if they had a stronger foundation of belief in themselves. As I mentioned with gang affiliation, becoming a member of a particular peer group can help allay fears about your place in the pecking order. Having someone you can fall back on for validation and protection is important. While we can do that for our kids in most instances, we can't be with them all the time. They spend more time with their peers at school and in social situations outside of school than they do at home, so when self-esteem is lacking, they seek the backing of other teens.

We've also seen how teens, many of whom lack self-esteem, prey on weaker individuals or groups in order to get the hit of power they can't get elsewhere. If you feel secure in your own position and status, you don't have to go after weaker, less popular, less talented kids—what validation do you really get from dominating someone you have already conquered or who isn't even willing to fight with you? When teens lack self-esteem, when they are insecure about their identity, about their ability to exist with or to create an identity separate from the role they play in the family, they overcompensate for their insecurity by taking broad leaps toward freedom.

Dan is an excellent example of this overcompensation. The middle child of three boys, Dan was uncertain of his identity. His older brother, David, was an extremely bright and studious young man with a real talent for mathematics and science. Sam, the youngest, was a stellar musician and visual artist. Dan was nearly as talented in the same areas as his brothers, but he didn't see that. Because he didn't have the same kind of clear focus on a particular set of skills or interests like David and Sam, he foundered. Dan's parents were fine with his not having settled on a particular path he wanted to follow, but because he wasn't involved in the same kind of structured activities as Sam and David, his parents couldn't attend the science fairs, recitals, and art shows they did in support of the other two sons. As a result, Dan felt less important. Lacking self-esteem and feeling as though he had to somehow separate himself from his siblings, since David was the intellectual and Sam the creative one, David felt he had to become the _____ guy in the family. Then he realized he didn't want to fit neatly into any one slot.

He figured that being the wild child, the black sheep, was the way to distinguish himself from his two brothers and avoid being categorized. That meant being the rule breaker, the one with the fiercely independent streak, the contrarian. If everyone else at school was into hip-hop, he would seek out jazz and blues artists to listen to and to dress like. When longer hair was in, he went with a fifties-look brush cut. The list goes on, but what motivated Dan was his desire to be free of the constraints of his parents' expectations and rules.

Fortunately for Dan, he had very understanding parents who let him explore his freedom—to a point.

Praise has an almost singular ability to counteract problems with self-esteem, and as we'll see shortly, self-esteem problems are often the root of many problems with needs. Having confidence in yourself, truly believing in yourself, truly liking yourself, being comfortable in your own skin—all without building up a façade of false bravado—ain't easy for anybody. Think about your own experiences growing up, and really do an honest and thorough self-assessment. Don't stop there. Think about the kinds of issues you are dealing with today as an adult.

Here's a quick experiment. Take out a sheet of paper and at the top make two columns, one labeled "Likes" and one labeled "Dislikes." Under "Likes" write down everything you like about yourself. Under "Dislikes" write out those attributes you either don't like, feel are somewhat lacking, or need to improve. Don't dwell on this for too long; just take a few minutes to jot down some ideas.

If you're like a lot of people, you probably have a few things in your "Likes" column and many, many more in your "Dislikes." So why the discrepancy? Simple. Most of us are more critical of ourselves than we are willing to praise ourselves or express satisfaction with ourselves. I've already told you how highly self-critical I am, but let's leave me and others like me out of this for a minute. Think about how you were raised at home. Did you grow up in an environment in which you were praised more than criticized? Did your teachers at school provide you with more positive than negative feedback? Were your siblings more likely to compliment you than to make fun of you? Did the proportion of positive to negative feedback change as you got older? Did you experience (or do you remember experiencing) more criticism from parents, teachers, peers, and siblings as you got older? What's your life like today? Do your bosses heap praise on you, lavish you with compliments? Do your kids? Your spouse?

IN PRAISE OF PRAISING

In Chapter Six, we talked about the role of praise with regard to a teen's power needs, but praise is also holds a great deal of influence over the other four primary needs, and it is a crucial component of pure intention. Think about the questions of "Likes" and "Dislikes" in terms of how you have been parenting your children. Sure, when our kids are young and we're fresh and take enjoyment from nearly everything they do, we heap praise on them. "Yay! You made a poo-poo! Good girl!" That's an extreme example, but my point is taken, I hope. As our kids advance in age, skill, and intellectual capacity we tend to treat them more and more like little adults. I'm sure that wherever you work, you seldom get praised and most often get corrected or criticized. That's the way the world is, right? So shouldn't we prepare our kids for that? Aren't we doing them a disservice if we heap mindless praise on them?

I'd have to say yes to that last one. Some educational psychologists spearheaded a movement in educational circles to increase the level and extent of praising that we gave to kids. I knew teachers who bought into that movement and those who didn't. The ones who didn't told me that they couldn't stomach the idea of praising kids for what's expected of them. "You're in your seat on time. Very good. You brought your books, paper, and pencil. Very, very good." Of course, I understand that they were exaggerating (a bit), and I also understand that the notion of praising kids as a way to boost their self-esteem is a good one. When that praise is age appropriate and task appropriate, I'm sure it does wonders for kids.

But remember, our kids are often far more sophisticated and have more highly refined b.s. detectors than we give them credit for. I worked with a lot of teens who told me stories about the "jokes" their schools had become when everybody was being heaped with praise for doing just about anything. The kids knew that this was just a smoke screen, and they resented it. When praise lost its meaning, something they craved was taken from them. Kids want and need rewards, but they need and want to earn them.

There have been reports in the media lately about the current generation of college students being the latest Me Generation. According to some sociologists and psychologists, today's college kids, most of whom are a product of the heap-them-with-mindless-praise school of thought, have an exaggerated sense of their own worth. Their sense of entitlement is all out of whack. I'm sure there's a happy medium to be found somewhere between browbeating the self-esteem out of your kids and pumping them full of hot air. That's the middle ground we're after, and you can do several things to stake your claim to that territory.

TYPES OF INTELLIGENCE

Thanks to a lot of groundbreaking work by educational psychologist Dr. Howard Gardner, we've come to understand that there are many categories and types of childhood intelligence. His book *Frames of Mind: The Theory of Multiple Intelligences* puts forth a theory that has been incredibly useful for me in my work with teens. Rather than thinking of intelligence as a one-dimensional concept that can be measured with one quantity (intelligence quotient), Dr. Gardner identifies eight individual components of intelligence that we all possess to some degree. Those eight intelligences are interpersonal, intrapersonal, logical-mathematical, bodily-kinesthetic, visual-spatial, verbal linguistic, naturalist, and musical. Interpersonal and intrapersonal are, simply put, our people skills. Some people are naturally empathetic and adept at negotiating relationships with others. Other people are extremely introspective and seem to understand a great deal about themselves, their motivation, and their inner emotional lives.

As you would expect, people who have a more highly refined logical-mathematical intelligence work well with numbers and possess the ability to separate reason from emotion in order to solve problems. They can reason from a set of facts to a conclusion extremely well. Athletes and dancers are the most common types of people who have a strong bodily-kinesthetic intelligence. Their degree of physical coordination and control over their bodies exceeds most of ours. If you think you're a klutz or are clumsy, that's another way of saying you're lacking bodily-kinesthetic intelligence. If you're clumsy with words, don't like to read or write, or feel that you're not good at those activities, then your verbal linguistic intelligence isn't on a par with the rest of the eight intelligences.

I have a friend who is severely lacking in visual-spatial intelligence, and he's smart enough to know it. The latest demonstration of this was when he took his oldest daughter to help her move into an off-campus apartment. She'd bought some furniture from Ikea, and he had a devil of a time putting it together. He told me later that when he had to take aptitude tests that required him to look at one image and then select the other image that represents what it would look like if it were turned 180 degrees, he almost fell out of his desk. He had trouble picturing things mentally. I can't tell you the number of times I had to draw a map for him instead of just telling him where something was, and he couldn't orient objects either mentally or physically in space.

Naturalist intelligence characterizes people who have an affinity for the natural sciences and understand how systems work in the physical world. Musical intelligence is fairly obvious, but it extends beyond just being able to play an instrument or sing. Music and math are interrelated, and that same friend who lacks visual-spatial intelligence is also bad at math and can't hear the counts in music to save his life. That's okay—he's brilliant in other areas, and as a fellow therapist I've seen and heard how wonderful he is with people.

Obviously, not everyone possesses the same level of intelligence in each of these areas. As parents we can assist our kids in developing a more powerful sense of self when we recognize their accomplishments in the areas where they are strong, encourage their efforts, and assist them in a nonthreatening and nonjudgmental way in areas where they may be struggling. We all struggle. The key here is that we should recognize the many ways in which our kids excel. In my line of work, I've come across a lot of kids who lack intrapersonal intelligence. They just aren't very self-reflective. Some kids lack interpersonal intelligence. They don't have a grasp on how relationships work and how to manage them. A lack of skill in any one of these areas can lead to frustration. The classic example is the nerdy super-bright kid who is clumsy and is the last one chosen for a team in gym class. His opposite is the talented athlete who struggles to express himself verbally.

Once you start to think about intelligence in a different way, you can start to reward that intelligence in a different way. Some types of intelligence are more conducive to schoolworthy praise than others. Verbal linguistic and logical-mathematical are the two most prevalent types of intelligences kids use in school. Success in English and math mark a student for praise. How well a kid can dance, put on a spin move, turn a table leg on a lathe, and other so-called nonacademic skills aren't recognized and appreciated as much in our schools as the three R's are. Likewise, other types of intelligence lend themselves to other skill sets. Our responsibility as parents is to figure out what types of intelligence our child excels in, and offer specific praise in those areas.

If you operate with pure intention, your teens will sense it, and thus when you offer compliments they will be received not with skepticism but with genuine excitement and pride. Likewise, when you offer constructive feedback on areas of intelligence that are not as strong for them, they will react to your feedback without getting overly defensive.

SPECIFIC IS TERRIFIC

My father was a tough old guy, not prone to physical displays of affection or compliments, but when he gave you one or the other, it really meant something and could turn your bad day into a good one, a good week, or even a good month. So what's the upshot here? Applying praise judiciously and with reasons attached to that praise is the way to go.

For example, after all of my sons' baseball games, the two teams line up and walk past each other to shake or slap hands, and they all mouth a slight variation on the same phrase: "Good game." Half mumbled, half garbled by sunflower seeds or wads of chewing gum, the praise they offer each other would hardly make you faint. Sure, it's a sign of good sportsmanship and all, but when you look at the blank expressions on the faces of 95% of those kids, you know that it doesn't mean a damn thing to them—they're already off thinking about what they're going to do after the game and if Suzy saw them steal that base or whatnot.

I take a different approach, and to those kids who made a meaningful contribution, I point it out specifically. If I know the kid's name, I'll use it: "Hey Jason, you really had that curve ball working tonight. Impressive." You can see the kid's face light up immediately. You mean you noticed what I was doing out there? They look totally surprised at first, and then they look pleased. And get this—they actually look me in the eye and say thank you.

If you can identify a specific behavior and reference it, you'll be more effective in getting your point across. How do you go about doing that? Well, paying attention helps, and so does spending time with your kids.

BOYS WILL BE BOYS—BUT SHOULD THEY?

Why do our kids need significant and precise praise? Mostly because they are under attack from forces working to undermine their self-esteem the rest of the time. These attacks come from within and from without. One of the first areas of conflict kids have is with their physical selves. Body image issues were once thought to be the primary domain of girls. That's not the case. Again, in the book *Raising Cain: Protecting the Emotional Life of Boys*, Dan Kindlon, PhD, and Michael Thompson, PhD, do an amazing job of lifting the veil of secrecy from an area of boys' lives that we seldom look at or talk about. They coined the term "emotional mis-education" to refer to the kind of benign neglect we subject boys to.

When you think about boys and their development, how much time do we really spend encouraging and rewarding them for being sensitive to the needs of others or for being introspective and able to articulate not just their own feelings but their individual points of view about social roles, empathizing with the feelings of others, registering and understanding their own emotional responses to situations and things they read or view, being able to "read" the emotional temperature of a room and situation to respond appropriately, and being respectful of the others' emotional responses that are different from their own? We typically believe that kind of work and that kind of development is what girls are best at. We presume, because boys don't express their fears or anxieties, that they are okay, that they're not needy, that they're confident and self-reliant.

After all, if they aren't openly communicating about what's going on in their world, we assume that they must be okay. If they weren't okay, they'd be saying something to us, right? Here's where we get back to the idea that if we don't teach boys how to communicate about their feelings, and don't make them aware of the importance and nuances of interpersonal and intrapersonal relationships, then they lack the language. Yet, we expect them to understand these concepts, and if they end up feeling hurt, we apply the old "Rub some dirt on it; you'll be okay" bromide. Even worse, we say, "Big boys don't cry" or some variation on that.

So, if a boy gets teased for being too fat, too skinny, having curly hair or straight hair or blonde hair or brown hair or red hair or any one of a thousand other traits or attributes, then he lacks the language to express how he feels about being made fun of. Either that, or he gets discouraged from talking about how he feels because that has been feminized and is therefore discouraged.

If you're the parent of a boy, praise him for expressing these areas that boys so often neglect or are unable to discuss. Encourage him to articulate some of the emotions he is feeling, but also do this with an air of reciprocation. Don't make him feel as though he is the only person contributing to the conversation. These interactions must be met with a willingness to contribute; if he sees that you're willing to share these types of things, he'll be more open to do so himself. This is not to say that you start to lecture him on how things were in your day, but engage him in a discussion, keeping your words about yourself brief, but also contributing useful information that keeps the discussion on an emotional level.

As he displays an ability to talk about himself, reward his articulations with praise. Let him know that he is smart for being able to talk about himself in such a clear manner.

PARENTING REINFORCES ATTITUDES

If you look back at your days raising your kids, you'll probably agree with this statement: Parents spend most of their time talking about emotions by discussing anger with boys and sadness with girls. Parents spend a lot of time talking with girls about emotions and coming up with complex explanations and responses to feelings. Girls tend to express fear, sadness, and anxiety more than boys do. Girls are encouraged and socialized to think about and to ruminate on feelings and the emotional colors of a situation. Boys are more impulsive. Combine that with their propensity toward anger, and you've got acting out.

What do we often do with boys who are impulsive and prone to anger? We don't encourage them to explore their feelings, work with them to help them express themselves better verbally, or otherwise encourage their emotional development. Instead, we play to their strength instead of addressing their weakness. Any coach will tell you that it's easier to get a kid to work on what he's good at than what he's not. That's why a lot of parents resort to what a friend of mine called the "Go blow some stink off" solution. His mother raised three boys, and whenever they got into scuffles with one another, started slinging verbal darts (and sometimes physical ones), or got too testy with their mother, she'd send them outside with the advice to "Go blow some stink off." Her feeling was that getting them out of the house, letting them burn off some of that abundant energy (thus the blow-some-stink-off command), and then returning them to civilization when they had exhausted those fumes was the right approach. Can't blame her for that. Three boys with only two years of age between one another can produce quite a powerful stink of aggression and anger.

Unfortunately, when they got to school, there was only one designated time each day, recess, when they could productively blow some stink off. The rest of the time, they had to abide by a set of rules that seemed very unfamiliar to them. What resulted? Confusion, pain, anger, punishment, more pain, anger, and confusion. Physical activity may have worked for their mother in helping to alleviate the symptoms of their stress, but it did nothing to get to the root cause of it. When the boys acted out at school because of their pain, anger, and confusion, they felt bad about themselves. That caused them pain, and the cycle repeated itself ad infinitum. That's what we call a vicious circle, and we've all likely been sucked into one at some point.

IT'S A WOMAN'S WORLD

So then, because girls are more comfortable with emotion they have it easy, right? As Rosalind Wiseman says in her book *Queen Bees and Wannabes*, which was the basis for the movie *Mean Girls*, young women do start off at a bit of an advantage at school because of their advanced verbal skills. Unfortunately, as they progress through the grade ranks their self-esteem declines from its peak at the age of nine (New York University Child Study Center). Why? According to Wiseman, they get rejected by friends. They get teased for wearing the wrong outfit. They get branded with an undeserved negative reputation. They feel that they have to conform. Over time, insecurity begins to feel normal. Who does most of this tormenting of young girls? Other girls. Sure, boys can say and do mean things, but they sting only for while. What girls do to girls has far more lasting effects on the psyches of adolescents and teens.

Wiseman spends a lot of time talking about and analyzing cliques and the role they play in the lives of young women. What I found most interesting is her belief that not only do they serve to reinforce a norm of conformity, they also cause girls to turn away from their family as the source of comfort, information, and values identification and turn toward the clique itself for most of their validation. How can a young woman feel good about herself if the very group she turns to reinforce her self-esteem and to establish a role outside of the family is mean at best and reinforces the unrealistic standards of physical appearance the media initiate? As a young woman, whether you are or aren't a member of the clique, the popular group, doesn't matter. You are still subjected to these forces.

If you've raised a girl through elementary school and seen her through the difficult transition to middle school and junior high, you know with what terrible swiftness a clique or a friend of your daughter can turn on her. She can come home from school all upset and crying because her best friend, out of the blue and for no apparent reason, has put an end to their friendship. Why? Whim mostly. There's no logic to the forces that move cliques and mean girls to do the things they do, except for the need for power. And what defies logic even more is that our daughters, some of them, still want to be a part of those cliques and seem almost magnetically drawn to those mean girls. So much of our daughters' self-esteem resides in how these fair-weather "friends" (at best) treat them that it is no wonder they struggle with their self-concept.

School also contributes to girls' eroding sense of self. Whereas the early years in school place an emphasis on verbal skills, students in the later grades are expected to think in more abstract terms—particularly in middle school. Simultaneously, girls are also experiencing changes in their bodies, developing breasts and hips, putting on the layers of fat they will need to be mothers. Those additional pounds and inches don't fit in well with the self- and media-constructed image of the ideal body. Another Harvard study showed how the orientation of the boys toward doing and the girls toward feeling actually causes a reversal in self-esteem and rewards. When teenage boys are asked to list their strengths, they offer concrete examples of how they can perform: "I'm good at math." "I can throw a football fifty yards." Girls respond with statements of attributes—not what I can do but what I have or am. For example, "I have nice hair." "I'm a good listener."

In only a few instances did girls mention their intellectual capabilities or their other skills. In school, the emphasis shifts from social skills—cooperation, patience, and politeness—to more rigorous thinking skills. Whereas a girl was once rewarded for being a good reader and writer and being able to express herself well, she now finds that other skills are important. Those who can make the transition thrive, while those who don't suffer. That first C on an assignment or test after a history of all A and B grades can be a real blow—especially when sex, peer pressure, and body image are also ganging up on her. Everyone has expectations that seem out of kilter and pull her in many directions at once.

Because of these negative reinforcements that girls get, it is so important for you as a parent to bring this attitude of specific praise to your teenage daughter's life. Focus on and be aware of the areas of intelligence that she excels in, and be clear that she possesses skills that are both abstract and concrete. Similarly, you must be forthright about areas that she needs to work on. However, don't rush to be critical; always frame the discussion in a tone that reflects the pure intention for progress that you feel she's making.

The important thing to remember, whether your teens are boys or girls, is that once they step outside of your home, they're probably not getting enough positive feedback. Understanding the different types of intelligences can go a long way to making sure that during the time you are at home with them you are giving them the kind of positive reinforcement they don't get when they are at school or with friends.

This is not to say that everything outside the home has an adverse impact on their self-esteem levels, but once they enter the house after a day of school, you have the ability to start making them feel good about the things in their life. Knowing your children and knowing when, where, and what you should praise them for goes a long way toward knowing how to approach their struggles with the five primary needs. In the upcoming chapter, we're going to build on this idea of praise with pure intentions, using it as the foundation for solving your teen's problems—whatever size they may be.

14

Communicating with Your Teen

The other day I walked into the kitchen, where my wife, Janna, and my daughter, Alicia, were having a conversation. They were just catching up on their day, and all was going well. Alicia was also leafing through a catalog. She turned the magazine to my wife and said, "This top is cute."

Janna looked at the photograph and said, "But where could you wear something like that?"

Alicia shrugged her shoulders. "Anywhere. Why?"

Janna pursed her lips and looked away for a moment. "It's just kind of, I don't know . . . . It's not something I'd think you'd wear, that's all."

"And just what do you think I'd be likely to wear? A frumpy sweater? A raincoat?"

"Alicia, honey, all I'm saying . . ."

"Jeez, mom, you don't have to tell me what you're saying, I KNOW what you're saying. You are so critical all the time of every single thing I do, I say, I wear."

"Please don't exaggerate. You always do this. You don't have to be so sensitive about every little thing I say."

"Oh, so that's another one of my faults?"

"That's not what I'm saying. All I'm saying is I don't think that top is cute, that's all. End of story."

"Why didn't you just say so?" Janna flips to another page, "I like it, but it's not anything I would want or wear."

"Have you thought about what you might want to do for your birthday?"

"I have an exam in chemistry, and I haven't had a chance to review a single thing in the last chapter."

Does this scenario sound at all familiar? How did a simple conversation about an article of clothing in a catalog led to a minor dust-up about judgments and sensitivities? Fortunately, the tension between the two of them was short lived, but those comments were likely to be stored in the memory banks of both and will rise again to the surface at some point. Maybe that's just how it is with mothers and daughters and how they communicate. We'll come back to this conversation later on, and I'll talk more specifically about gender and communication in a bit. For now, think about what you've just read and how it is representative of what happens in a lot of communications.

In Chapter Three, I related the story of Justine and her perception that her mother didn't take her worries seriously. I wasn't present for those conversations, so it was difficult for me to assess exactly what was intended, what was said, and what both parties perceived was being communicated. But I can say this with some assurance: what was intended, said, and perceived was different from what the two thought they were intending, saying, and perceiving. Okay, that was confusing, but that's what happens a lot of time when we attempt to make the transition from what we're thinking to what we're communicating to another person. Unfortunately, all the pure intentions and praise in the world won't do a lick of good unless they are communicated in a clear way that doesn't give your teen the chance to mishear, misconstrue, or misrepresent your meaning.

We experience the trials and tribulations of miscommunications all the time. Technological advances have given us nearly unlimited ways to stay in touch with one another, but our skills and abilities as communicators often lag way behind those advances. Maybe it's time to go back to basics.

COMMUNICATION THEORY

As I said, I'm not a big theory kind of guy. When it comes to communication, a lot of what I learned came from my parents. They used to say to my siblings and me, "Talk slowly but think quickly." My all-time favorite was "Remember that silence is sometimes the best answer."

Well, as good as those lessons were, if you find yourself reading this book, then simple pat answers like that aren't what you're looking for. Let's take a quick look at some basic communication theory so that we're all on the same page. We all know how important it is to communicate effectively, and we've all suffered the effects of broken communication and know how frustrating that can be, how angry we can get, and how all that snowballs. What exactly do we mean by effective communication? The definition of that concept is simple:

Effective communication = Shared meaning

Another way to say this is that the person who initiates the communication has an intended message in mind, and the message received by the person at the other end of the communication is the same as the message the sender intended. Keep in mind this idea of intended message and received message. As long as those two are equal, we're in good shape. Unfortunately, it isn't always that easy.

So, who's sharing this message? The person who sent the message (the sender) and the person who received it (the receiver). Simple, right? Well, then, how come so often communication gets all messy, the way it did with my daughter and my wife? Let's take a look at that example again in terms of the simplest components of communication. What was the message my daughter was trying to convey? She thought a top was cute. What was my wife trying to say? She didn't think the top was cute. So what's with all that other stuff that went on? Well, we can say one thing for sure. Originally, this was not effective communication. Why? Because the message wasn't shared. Who do we place the blame on for that? (I do have to go home at night and live with these two women, after all, so I'm not about to step in that one. As a rule, though, it's best not to assign blame when communication breaks down, since that tends to exacerbate the given problem.)

Sending

Well, since we're not going to look at blame, let's examine some of the sources of the breakdown in communication in general terms, starting with sending. What causes a message to not be shared is something communication theorists call interference. There are two types of interference: internal and external. Internal interference has its source in one of the communicators. For example, Alicia may have had a bad day when she wasn't too happy with how she looked because one of her friends at school had commented on her jeans. As a result, she was predisposed to being sensitive about any remark that she perceived to be negative about her appearance. The second type of interference comes from the environment in which the two people are communicating. Typical examples are noise and distracting music. Sometimes external interference can physically prevent the message from being received.

Often the breakdowns occur at the level of the message being created. We call this process encoding. When you're formulating your intended message you have a bunch of choices to make. What means of communication are you going to use? For simplicity's sake, let's confine our discussion to one-on-one verbal communication. When you encode the verbal message, you still have a lot of choices—particularly in terms of which words to use. We all know that words have literal meanings and also carry emotional weight and interpretations. Saying that someone is slim conveys a different meaning than saying someone is skinny. Most of the time, we share similar perceptions of a word's meaning and connotation—the emotional component. When we don't, that's a possible source of a breakdown in effective communication.

Words can have either positive, negative, or neutral connotations. It's not possible and would be really boring if we stuck to words with neutral connotations all the time. We also all know we can use certain words when communicating that will elicit an emotional response from the receiver. In communications with family members, because we know them so well, we know exactly what words, phrases, topics, and past experiences we can call on to get a response out of someone. It's one of the subtle forms of manipulation we use all the time. We use various terms to describe this—pushing someone's buttons, playing the X card, and others. We all learn very early in life how to use language to get what we want. However, we can use those skills for good as well. You've probably been around people who seem to speak a kind of shorthand. Married couples, romantic partners, and siblings seem to be able to share meaning with just a few words that to an outsider seem disconnected and incomplete. The flip side of this efficient and intimate form of communication is that it is based on assumptions and shared perceptions, and those can easily be derailed. If we assume too much and too often, particularly in discussing important issues with our teens, then we may not be sharing the message we think we are sharing.

Receiving

Though interference and encoding are crucial parts of the communication process, they are only one half of the equation. The second half of the communication process is the responsibility of the receiver who has to decode the message. Again, differences in perception regarding the meaning and the connotation of a word can cause real interference in a message being shared. If I had launched into this explanation by talking about the denotative and connotative meanings of words and their influence in conveying a meta-message, we might not have shared meaning because you weren't familiar with what a few of those words meant.

How do we as receivers get around those kinds of problems? With something called feedback. As a receiver of a message, we convey to the sender through subtle and not-so-subtle signals that we either understand or don't understand what the other person is communicating to us. In a conversation, a simultaneous stream of messages and feedback flows between sender and receiver. Most often, we both send and receive signals at the same time. That's why our simple process so often gets messed up. How many times have you been speaking to someone and you know in your heart of hearts that the person isn't really listening to you but instead is thinking of what to say next? So, while you're trying to get your point across, you're distracted because you perceive that the person isn't paying attention, and as a result, you can't be as precise in your word choice as you could be, and that frustrates you, and you say something in a way you hope will convey that you're frustrated with that person as a listener. On and on it goes. Emotions get mixed up in all of this to further complicate the process, and our neat little model of sender and receiver starts to look more like a rat's nest than a smooth and steady flow.

We haven't even included the nonverbal component—the "it's not what you said but how you said it"—that really is subject to interpretation and perception. We'll get to that in a moment, but let's first of all come to some agreement here and share some meaning:

- We all need to work on our communication skills.
- Communicating effectively is the cornerstone of all good relationships.
- Communicating effectively within a family is difficult because familiarity breeds breakdowns.
- "I hear you" is another way of saying "I'm not listening."
- When push comes to shove, there will be a lot of pushing and shoving. Communication isn't about winning; it's about tying the game.

NONVERBAL COMMUNICATION

Theorists believe that 60% to 80% of any interpersonal communication message is conveyed nonverbally—that is, in any manner besides the words themselves. So that means that tone of voice, volume, facial expression, and gestures carry the bulk of the content. We are all masters of saying one thing with our words and meaning another with our tone. When we do that intentionally, we send an intended message we hope will get interpreted correctly. Sarcasm and irony seem to be some of the only ways some teens can communicate. I think that's great.

Notice that when you only look at the words in that last sentence, you get one meaning because you don't have any of the nonverbal cues that let you know I'm being ironic in my remark. That's one reason why I don't like e-mail and think that in certain situations that kind of communication causes more problems than it solves. Sure, you can use the little emoticons :) :(and abbreviations IMHO and other means to get the emotional content of your message across, but that seems really inefficient. I believe that because our kids spend so much time communicating electronically, they are operating at a deficit when it comes to one-on-one interpersonal communication.

Maybe this makes me a Luddite, but I believe that kids and adults need some basic nonverbal guidelines for interpersonal communication. Here are some of the things we all need to learn or be reminded of:

- Making and holding eye contact is essential.
- Speak loud enough to be heard.
- Match your volume to the situation and environment.
- Be aware of your posture and gestures. For example, arms folded across the chest is a blocking move; leaning forward and pointing is aggressive; rolling the eyes is dismissive.
- Don't interrupt the other person.
- Concentrate on what is being said.
- Think before responding.
- Don't rush to fill in a silence.

This last point is important. Communications researchers have determined that for English speakers a pause of about one second is all that lapses between one speaker ending and another beginning. Anything longer than that and we start to get uncomfortable. For us, five seconds can start to feel like an eternity. One of the most effective things I do as a counselor is not to fill in the gaps. I give kids the opportunity to think, to feel, and to come to terms with what they want and need to say. It's very tempting as a parent to want to fill in the blanks for our kids, but that means we're making assumptions and using our perceptions in place of our kids' reality. Those are two of the most common faults I see in how parents and teens communicate.

The Metamessage

In communication theory, the metamessage is that message between, beneath, over, and under what is directly communicated. Metamessages come from the context, the relationship, the timing, and the purpose of the communication. Sometimes those metamessages support the main message being communicated; sometimes they contradict it. We never communicate verbally without also sending a metamessage. The more aware you are of the existence of these metamessages, the better you can communicate effectively and avoid breakdowns. Again, we all usually agree on the meaning of our words, but how we interpret them and their emotional implications vary greatly. That difference in interpretation is the cause of most failures to communicate effectively and share meaning.

For example, you are with a group of your friends and your cell phone rings. You answer it, but before you do, you scan the view screen to see who it is. After your animated phone conversation, during which you share a few laughs with the caller, you say, "I'm sorry. I had to take that call."

The main message, "I'm sorry. I had to take that call," will be interpreted differently by different people. Someone who is not as familiar with you and your phone habits may accept your message at face value, but depending upon experiences with other people in similar situations, he or she may be thinking, "You're not sorry at all." Likewise, a friend who knows that you do this repeatedly and hears the words of your message may then interpret them as "You're not that important to me."

Why? Because your friend has come to understand that is a typical form of your behavior. We bring all kinds of associations and experiences to our communication, and as a result the metamessage can vary from person to person. The better someone knows us and the more history we share with that person, the more complex the metamessages. In the example that opened this chapter, I described the conversation between my wife and daughter. It was loaded, as most conversations are between family members and other intimates, with metamessages that are a result of the history between the two persons engaged in the communication. How do you know when someone is not just responding to what you're saying in the moment but interpreting it in light of all kinds of things, related and unrelated, that have come before it? Notice in both of their statements the times when they used the word "always." That's a definite clue that the person is bringing a lot of history and outside contexts to that communication.

Awareness of the possible metamessages you are sending is only part of the reason to be a more conscious communicator. It's also important, particularly when dealing with people with whom you have a long history and emotional intimacy, to try to turn off your metamessage receptors and take in the message at face value. This is extremely hard to do—especially with your teens. If you become aware of the process of perception and interpretation you filter messages through, you can at least recognize that you're doing it. What you can do next is assess your response, and then discard that perception and replace it with one that is less dependent on all those past associations. You've probably heard the expression "staying present in the moment," and this is one practical application of that more abstract concept.

Metawomen

Deborah Tannen is a professor of linguistics at Georgetown University and a best-selling author of books on interpersonal communication, including *You Just Don't Understand*, which deals with the ways men and women communicate with one another. She spends much of her time researching and writing about how we communicate every day. She's written about communication between men and women and how we communicate at work. In her most recent book, *You're Wearing That? Understanding Mothers and Daughters in Conversation*, she deals with that critical relationship. Even though she considers primarily adult daughters and their mothers, we can learn a lot about communicating with our teens more effectively from her work.

Tannen analyzes how mothers and daughters speak to one another and how metamessages play such a key role in how women interact. I've always wondered why I can say something to Alicia and she will react one way, and Janna can say something nearly identical and Alicia will respond in a nearly opposite—and almost always more negative—way. Tannen points out that mother–daughter communication is highly complex, just as the relationship between the two is. It's beyond the scope of this book to examine this relationship in full, and I highly recommend that you pick up a copy of Tannen's book. As she says of the mother–daughter relationship in her preface, "It is among the most passionate of women's lives, the source of the deepest love and also the deepest anger—even hate—that most women experience. It brings us face-to-face with reflections of ourselves and forces us to confront fundamental questions about who we are, who we want to be, and how to relate to others."

Highly readable and entertaining as well as informative, *You're Wearing That?* can help mothers and daughters avoid falling into the traps that damage communications and relationships.

FROM THEORY TO PRACTICE

Okay, now that you've got a better sense of the sender–receiver conundrum, let's get to some things you can do today to be more a effective communicator. Stephen Covey, the best-selling author of *The Seven Habits of Highly Effective People*, says that we should all "Seek first to understand, then to be understood." I think that's a great place to start in reforming your communication habits with your kids.

Remember that for many years, you were the one who was in a dominant role in your communications with your kids. You knew how to speak and write long before they did, and you got used to being the one who had to interpret what they were saying, clarify their statements, and correct their use of language and syntax. You were the master and they were the apprentice. Well, any good teacher will tell you that it's tough but satisfying when your pupil reaches or exceeds the level of your skills. Old habits die hard, and it's easy to fall into those master dominant routines. You are still wiser, more articulate, and more experienced than your children, but at this stage in their development, they don't need to be reminded of that at every turn. What I have had to remind myself of constantly when establishing a relationship based on pure intention with every one of my clients, with my kids, and with my wife and friends is this:

I am not an expert in the field of them.

In other words, they know more about what they are thinking, feeling, experiencing, and perceiving than I ever will. They are the experts on themselves. Tops in their field, highly regarded and esteemed, and often willing and able to expound on those areas if given the chance. Before every session with the kids I work with, and in dealing with my own kids, I have to take a second and ask my ego to take a walk for a while. As a therapist and as a parent I think that's the trait that has enabled me to be successful (welcome back, Ego) and to enjoy my working and familial relationships.

I know that I don't like it when someone presumes to know me better than I know myself, so I apply the Golden Rule of pure intention here, and doing unto others puts me in a position where I can learn from a master as well as be the master.

It's Not about Who Is Right

It is just about impossible to communicate effectively when you are so busy trying to prove you are right that you lose focus on sharing meaning. Winning isn't about sharing; it's about winning. Let's face it—we all think we're right most of the time, so if we enter into any conversation with another "right-thinking" human who's also intent on proving rightness, we're at a stalemate before we even begin. When parents and teens engage in the right/wrong game, everyone loses. You would not believe how many times I have seen parents tell their children that what they are feeling is wrong. One particular dad was an ex-military "my way or the highway" kind of guy. He was angry most of the time, and so was his kid. As a result, whenever the two of them tried to communicate, you could hear the heads butting all the way in the next county over. Both were so busy trying to prove themselves right that neither ever bothered to listen to what the other had to say. When all you're doing is firing ammo, when you stop shooting words you're too busy reloading to listen. Finally, on one long weekend when the families came to work with their kids, we got them both to listen to each other for the first time. They were both surprised to find out that they shared more of the same views than they had previously thought.

As you think about your own teen, remember that the only "victory" that exists is if your teen is healthy and his or her needs are being met. Any other points that you think you have won in the past or will win in the future need to be checked at the door. There is no score-card for this endeavor, and abandoning this win–lose mentality will go a long way toward making conversations with your teens better.

Pure intention has nothing to do with winning or losing. Pure intention is about trying to make things better. Understanding communication theory will go along way toward easing your interactions with your teens, but communication theory alone is not enough. It needs to be coupled with the right forms of praise and built on a substantial foundation of pure intention to be truly useful.

Once you have all these pieces in the right place, it's time to start talkin'.

15

Talkin' the Right Talk

Despite all that you know about your teen's needs, all that you've learned about behavior, and even with the best of intentions, sometimes it's still hard to take that first plunge and dive into the realm of effective communication. Putting your child at ease and striking the right tone is a delicate balance—an act that seems far more dangerous than anything a tightrope walker has ever tried. But despite this inherent danger, it's a step that you need to take if you are going to start to address the needs that cause your child to act out.

In this chapter we'll focus on specific measures you can incorporate into your everyday life with your teen that not only will make basic interactions easier and less prone to communication mixups but also will assist with the harder conversations about behavior and repercussions. While the scenarios and communication tools that we will discuss here offer specific advice, it's important to remember that these are most effective when they become the ways of all your interactions with your teen. Teens (and all children, for that matter) respond best when they are in a familiar, consistent environment. The more often they can predict and depend on you to react with the right talking, the more successful that talking will be.

GETTING STARTED

I recommend always beginning with a question. Those questions should be open ended—in other words, they don't allow for, or shouldn't encourage, yes or no answers—and they should be focused. For example, "How are things going?" could have served as an icebreaker in the past, but one thing you want to do now is let your teens know that you are paying attention to what is going on in their world. To demonstrate that you care about what's happening and have been paying attention, you could ask instead, "You were saying the other day that you and Jamie were going through a rough patch. How are you feeling about things now?" If you get the one-word response "Better," then it's time to ask for elaboration, examples, impressions.

I realize that on paper, much of this sounds as if you're a journalist interviewing someone, and in some ways that model works here. As the fourth Oz, you are somewhat of a new person in your teen's life. He or she may sense that something is different about you and the approach you're taking, and a little bit of discomfort is normal as you go through this feeling-out process. Don't be discouraged if you feel some unease in your gut. If you don't feel it, it may mean that you're not really doing anything new or different.

A Template for Effective Communication

John Bradshaw is a nationally known therapist and best-selling author of many books. He's probably best known for developing the influential concept of the "inner child" that figured so prominently in a lot of recovery (abuse, alcohol, etc.) literature. He also developed a strategy for communication that I frequently use. It's really effective in situations where emotions might get the best of us.

When you approach your teen, as I suggested above, begin with simple statements of your observations. Step One is "*I* see. . . ." Notice that I've put the emphasis here on "I". Many times we put people on the defensive by putting the other person at the beginning of our statement: "You've been isolating yourself." That is more of an accusation than an observation. You may be saying to yourself, "Whoa, Mr. Mike, how is that an accusation? What if my kid is spending most of her time in her room and comes out only for evening meals? Am I not simply stating a fact?"

Well, in your mind, that statement is as neutral as Switzerland, but your teen will immediately pick up on that emphasis on "You." In communication theory there are concepts called primacy and recency. To put it simply, people remember what you tell them first, and what you tell them last. What's in the middle is often lost. That's good to know, so that when you are organizing a speech, writing a sentence, or communicating in any way, you put the most important stuff at the beginning or the end. As a receiver of communication, we're also aware of this effect and understand that what comes first and last is most important.

If you look at that statement above, it begins and ends with a form of the word "you." As a result of that double emphasis, your teen is going to hear those words something like this, "You have a problem that is yours." If the roles were reversed and your teen said something like that to you, don't you think you'd be back on your heels a bit?

Remember in driver's education when you were taught about how to place your vehicle in traffic? The rule was to give yourself an out. That's what you're doing for your teen here—giving him or her an out. By emphasizing the "I," as in "I see that you're spending a lot of time in your room," you're letting your teen know at the start that this is your opinion, your view. You aren't proclaiming a great truth but just stating something that you've noticed. That's important. In terms of needs, you're giving teens the freedom to respond about your observation, and you're not telling them what you know. In other words, you're not establishing your power over them.

Step Two is to make another "I statement." In this case, you say, "I imagine that something must be bothering you, because you usually don't spend so much time alone." Again, you've given your teen an out and not pinned him or her in with a "There must be something wrong" kind of accusation. You're allowing for the fact that you are interpreting behavior and that your interpretation could be wrong. Not only are you sharing your observation in the hope of sharing meaning, and thus deescalating any power play before it begins, but you're letting your teen know that you are paying attention—

a positive kind of power move that is as nonjudgmental as it is possible to be.

Step Three is to follow up that interpretation with a statement about your own feelings. This is an invitation to sharing and developing emotional intimacy. You might say, "I feel sad because I have the sense that you're unhappy." Sharing feelings and communicating your empathetic reaction are all about cementing a bond of belongingness. We're treading close to the clichéd "I feel your pain here," but as a parent you should be feeling your children's pain. You're not out to win their vote; you just want them to know you care deeply.

You can simply stop there with that statement of feeling and reason, or you can elaborate on it further, but be certain that you don't adopt an accusatory "you should" tone. That's also true of what you say next in Step Four. This is the action-taking step. You tell your teen what you would like him or her to do. "I'd like it if you could tell me if something is bothering you." Notice that in this early stage, you make no offer to do anything but listen. That is important because you want to be able to combat the "There's nothing you can do about it anyway" retort that is likely to come your way.

This formula is highly adaptable, and the example I've just given is useful for the first approach, when you are fact-finding. You can also use it when you want or need to be more directly confrontational. The principles and steps are the same, but your word choice varies. For example, if your teen has started to use objectionable language around you, you might be tempted to say, "I hate it when you talk like that. If you don't have enough respect for yourself to speak nicely, then at least have some respect for me." You can see how that phrasing is loaded with accusations and emotion. You may feel better for getting those emotions out, but in the long run the damage you do may end up causing you more pain and anger. We'll talk more later about deescalating the conflict and having a discussion about the pain and/or anger that may be causing your teen to resort to foul language, but the more immediate concern is extinguishing the behavior and setting boundaries. You can do that and avoid the accusatory tone and emotional layers by following the four steps:

"I hear you using that kind of language. I imagine you either think you're being cute or want to upset me or that something's really bothering you. I feel hurt and angry. I want you to stop swearing when you are speaking to me and when you are in this house."

While Bradshaw's formula doesn't incorporate the additional element of consequences, you could add a consequence to the end of your remarks to more clearly set a boundary. "If I hear you swearing at me again, you will lose your car privileges for a week." Note that the consequence is specific and enforceable.

Finally, the last step is a kind of self-assessment. This final stage doesn't really involve something you say to your teen as much as it is a kind of mental inventory. You think about what you've learned as a result of the conversation and approach you took in speaking with your child. This is important to enable you to put that information to use, either in the future or as the conversation progresses.

Here's a quick recap of what the Bradshaw formula involves:

1. I see/hear . . . (Describe objectively the external behavior that you observe.)
2. I imagine . . . (Give your interpretation of what you assume this behavior means.)
3. I feel . . . (Describe how you feel. Mad, sad, glad, and scared are feelings. "I feel sad" is a feeling statement. "I feel that you are not listening to me" is an interpretation, not a feeling.)
4. I want . . . (Say specifically what different behavior you would like from the other person.)
5. I learned . . . (What I learned from the situation that will assist me in future similar situations.)

While I think that the Bradshaw method offers a good introduction to reshaping your communication with your teen, it does have its limitations. Not every conversation with your teen and the issues you are attempting to resolve will fit neatly into this scheme. Sometimes, perhaps more frequently than you will be comfortable with, the conversation won't be about what you want exclusively. There's going to have to be a lot of give and take and negotiation when you deal with your teen. We'll talk later on about determining what are negotiable and nonnegotiable issues and how to adapt your strategy, but for now, let's assume that everything is subject to debate.

Eliminate Your Internal Interference

You don't always have to be the one to initiate conversations, but you need to be aware of and take advantage of those moments when you have an opening. The other day, for example, I was busy working at home, reading through some files on my laptop computer. I was vaguely aware that Jessy was in the room, and I half heard what he was saying. I was so intent on what I was doing that I didn't respond to him. Out of the corner of my eye, I saw him shrug his shoulders and walk away. I would guess he didn't feel very important. That wasn't the message I intended to send, but send it I did. When I recognized what I'd done, I shut down the laptop and sought out Jessy. The first thing I did was apologize. I told him I was sorry for not listening to him. I left it that—a simple apology. I didn't offer an excuse or rationalization for my behavior, but simply said I was wrong and I'm sorry.

Now, I could have handled that situation a little differently from the outset. I could have gone into my "office space"—a place in the house I can retreat to that signals to the kids, "Do Not Disturb." I could also have said to Jessy, "I see you want to talk with me. I'm in the middle of something right now. If this is really important and needs my immediate attention, let me know. If not, can I find you in five minutes and we can talk then?" Notice again that I would have been specific. I wouldn't have just said "Can we talk later?" but specified what I would do and when. It's important that you don't just set a time and then blow off your child by missing the appointment entirely or arriving late. Apply the same kind of courtesy and respect for your child's time as if you were dealing with a peer or a colleague at work. Doing that communicates a lot, and when you're operating from pure intention, the message you want to send is this: You're important to me. I have other things that are important in my life, but I will set them aside if you need me to.

As I said earlier, in nonverbal communication, very little of what we communicate is based on our words—the denotative (dictionary definition) of those words. Another way to look at the nonverbal component and help cut down on the internal interference we experience as both senders and receivers is to become aware of the other messages we send and receive all the time, seldom being aware they exist.

SUSPENDING JUDGMENT

We all know that it's important to be as nonjudgmental as possible with our teens when working through a decision or negotiating our way through some crisis of acting out. But it feels unnatural. After all, isn't the parent's role to judge the appropriateness or inappropriateness of our children's behavior? That's true—that is our role, but as they get older we have to modify that stance a bit. Let's face it: none of us likes to be judged all the time—especially if we aren't sure what criteria we're being judged on and what the biases of the judge may be.

Modifying our role as judge means using what we've learned about metamessages and communication theory to be the most effective and impartial judge it is possible to be. So what does that mean exactly?

Well, for one thing you can keep your judgments to yourself. You're going to judge your kids' actions, but that doesn't mean that they have to know what you're thinking and feeling. If that strikes you as being dishonest, think of the number of times you—or your teen, for that matter—have played the "not telling something isn't the same as lying" card. In this situation, I'd say that it's all a question of determining proportion and the greater harm. If telling your child exactly what you think of what he or she did in no uncertain terms is going to do more harm than good, then I say keep quiet about it. If you can't keep quiet, be sure to choose the best time, place, and words to convey your message directly.

If your daughter comes home and has been in a fender-bender and you find out that she had six kids crammed in the car and was likely distracted, you can think, "That was incredibly stupid" but say, "I think you exercised poor judgment by allowing all those kids in the car." Another alternative is to ask her a question: "What do you think about your choice to give all those other kids a ride home?" or "What role do you think having all those kids in the car played in the accident you caused?" Notice here that I avoided the closed-end question, "Do you think having . . . ?", which would lead only to a yes or no answer instead of further reflection.

I don't recommend withholding those judgments temporarily and then using them later on to prove a point. That's using past history as an excuse. "Well, remember the last time you got in a car accident; I didn't say anything, but now with this speeding ticket, I've got to say, you are doing some stupid things." It's okay to reference the accident, but it's not really being fair to say, in effect, "I let you off last time, but I can't here." Your teen is going to interpret those words like this: "I've been sitting here for the past six months since that accident thinking you are stupid." That kind of stockpiling of sins isn't going to sit well with your teen, and I'm sure it wouldn't if someone used that tactic on you.

I've already mentioned the importance of staying in the present and noting, but discounting, metamessages about past statements, experiences, and emotional responses will go a long way toward reducing the level of judgment you express when dealing with an issue. Let's return to Janna and Alicia's conversation. If they had both just stuck to the facts of the present situation—Is this blouse cute or not? And suppose Janna hadn't been thinking that the blouse was too low-cut and too revealing, and how much she disliked how some of the girls at the school were dressing, and how Alicia was only going to be in the house for another year, and what was going to go on when she went to college, and Lord knows how those college girls dress, then a lot of the confusion and upset could have been eliminated. And suppose Alicia hadn't been getting the metamessage that Mom's dislike for the top meant that she didn't like my taste in clothes and that was a criticism, and she'd criticized other things about me, and I heard today already from a friend that I dress too preppy and now this, and who's she to criticize me, and I haven't seen a *Vogue* photographer lurking around here taking pictures of *her*.

A note for moms. Deborah Tannen calls them the Big Three: the three topics that mothers tend to criticize (or advise, depending on your interpretation) their daughters about—hair, weight, and clothing. Tread carefully in this territory, and be aware that these are flash-point issues.

OFFERING FEEDBACK

If being nonjudgmental as a rule is difficult, then the really hard part comes when your teen actually calls on you to give feedback about a situation or a behavior. In such instances your teen seems to be asking you to render a judgment on a given situation, and while in many ways this may feel like a catch-22, there is a way to approach this apparent paradox without getting yourself into trouble. You need to know the difference between giving an opinion versus criticizing, and giving advice versus acting as a sounding board.

The best advice I can provide with regard to avoiding the potential advice pitfall is to be up front and ask immediately, "I get the sense that you're looking for advice, but I'm not sure. Do you want me to tell you what I think, or are you just figuring this out for yourself out loud?" At first, that may sound like a long-winded cop-out, but it's really not. We get disappointed when we don't receive from people what we want, need, or expect. So, if it isn't clear from the context of a conversation what your teen wants from you, then ask. How you say it can be as simple as "What are you looking for from me here? Advice or an ear?" I don't expect you to quote word for word, but use the principles in a way that feels natural to you and suits your conversational style.

Opinion versus Criticism

When it comes to the difference between an opinion and criticism, my advice is far less clear cut. We are in tough and troubled waters whenever we enter this sea of sensitivity. Here's where you have to put much of what you've learned about communication into practice. This brief checklist should be helpful:

- Check your own intentions. Do you see this as an opportunity for honest communication or a way to control a behavior, to reward or punish, to teach or be taught, to find common ground or be divisive, to build up or tear down?
- Use the most neutral language possible.
- Check your metamessages, and erase the ones that have caused flareups in the past
- Avoid absolutes—"always, never."
- Say "I notice, I think, I believe, or I feel," not "You are."
- Don't diminish your own importance with "It's just me, and you can take or leave what I say, but. . . ." Your teen will see right through that attempt to cushion a blow.

- Do let your teen know that you're biased—"It's hard for me to be completely direct because . . . ."
- Don't give your teen the "You can't handle the truth" line, in words or in actions.
- Keep your body language in line with the intended message.
- When asked, answer. Don't deflect or delay; your teen will interpret that as dishonesty or fear.

GIVING FEEDBACK AND RESERVING JUDGMENT

Why is it so important, and why do we have to go to such lengths to make sure that our teens don't feel like they're being judged? Isn't it true that we're being judged by others all the time? Our bosses assess our performance formally and informally. Our potential mates and the people we date judge us constantly. So do other friends and family members. That's life. We don't like being judged and criticized, but that's just the way it is. Wouldn't it be better if we just let kids check into the reality hotel and deal with judgments?

I can understand that line of reasoning. I don't agree with it, but I can see how it makes some sense to people. I've told you already that I'm harder on myself that anyone else could ever be. That's who I am, and that's an issue I have to deal with. But there's a big difference between a teen and me, and between your teen and you.

All teens are at a very fragile place in the development of their identity. It's not fully formed, and whether they show it or not, they are very insecure about who they are and who they are becoming. For us to heap even more judgments on top of the judgments that they perceive coming from peers, the media, teachers, coaches, and from us as parents could collapse that fragile identity completely.

One reason why teens dislike being judged so much is that they are afraid that our negative perception of them may be the truth. If they hear often enough that they are untrustworthy, lazy, stupid, or whatever other negative they hear, they will eventually come to believe it. It takes a lot of strength and courage to stand up and fight against the negative things said about you by the people you most trust, believe, and rely on for support. Either your teens will believe it, or they will decide, "Hey, if that's what you think of me, and if that's how you're going to treat me anyway, I may as well just go ahead and be that way." I can't give you exact figures, but I've certainly seen both sides of that coin in my years in working with kids.

A schoolteacher friend of mine gave me some additional insight into this idea of judgment. A teacher constantly has to make assessments about kids in the class. Many of those assessments fall under the heading of grades. My friend told me that when he was a student teacher, he took part in a seminar after school in which all the student teachers got to speak with some kids from the talented and gifted program. The subject of grading came up, and my friend was disturbed by some of the things he heard. He wanted to make sure he was understanding the panel of six kids, so he asked them point blank whether or not what he was assuming he felt was true.

"So what you're saying then is that if you get a B on an assignment, on a test, or in a class as a whole, that means you will think that I believe that you are a B person?"

Four of the six kids nodded their heads. One young woman spoke up. "Absolutely. My grades aren't just a reflection of who I am, they are who I am."

My soon-to-be-teacher friend just sat there in shock. He'd never felt that way. He'd never considered that someone wouldn't be able to separate the product from the person. He said to that young woman, "I have to say, that's kind of scary. I've written lots of papers, but I never thought of them as who I am. They're just something I did."

The young woman smiled and shrugged. "I don't see the separation."

A lot of kids don't understand the distinction between our assessment of their behaviors and who they are as a person. To judge one of those is to judge the other. If you don't like what I do, how can you possibly like me?

To one degree or another, it is likely that your teen feels this way as well. That's why it is important to alter communication to reduce the frequency and intensity of the judgments surrounding who they are and what they do. If you can make that distinction clear to them, and I highly recommend that you teach that lesson early and often and reinforce it regularly, then you will go a long way toward building your teens' self-esteem.

PROBLEM SOLVING—TOGETHER

When your communication is effective and you've proved to your teens that you can offer feedback that is free of criticism, one result is that your teens will feel comfortable confiding in you things that might very well get them into trouble. If you have been dealing with them in a predictable and nonjudgmental manner, then they will feel comfortable coming to you and admitting that they have done something wrong and need your help to fix it. Whereas earlier they wouldn't have told you for fear that you might overreact or become angry, now because they understand your behavior and they know what to expect they are prepared for the kind of help you can offer.

But seeking you out for problem solving presents an additional set of obstacles, and chief among them is this: How do you make your kids understand the significance of their actions while rewarding them for having the courage and the trust to face the music?

When kids came into my office, often they talked about things they knew would get them into trouble and have them drop a level in their program. When they got around to telling me what was going on, that meant they were ready to face the consequences of their actions. One young woman came to me and told me that she had been stealing from her peers. She told me, but she admitted she was afraid of how the staff and her fellow students would react to the news. She was torn. She didn't like the idea of receiving consequences and being dropped a level, but she also didn't like the idea that she'd been deceiving her peers and violating their trust.

We talked about the situation, and I made it clear that *we* were going to decide how *we* were going to handle the situation. I made a point of acknowledging how proud I was of her decision to come to me and to move forward. These were steps in the right direction. I also promised to go with her for support when she told her peers and the staff what she'd been doing. She was more willing to step up and face the consequences of her actions, knowing she wouldn't be going it alone.

While John Bradshaw emphasizes the importance of "I" and "you," when problem solving with your teen it's important to switch to "we" mode. All of your observations and assessments and desires take a backseat to how the two (or more) of you are going to work together to find a solution. In no way does this mean that you're allowing the blame to be shifted from your teen's shoulders. At this stage, it's not about the blame, anyway. If you've been communicating effectively throughout, your teen will understand that her or she is accountable.

RISING EMOTIONS

Even if you follow every aspect of communication theory, reserve your judgment, and offer uncritical, opinion-based feedback, you may still be at a loss to explain some of your teen's responses. While being a more conscious communicator in your words, tone, and approach can pay huge dividends for you, being effective with teens is about knowing when not to talk and when emotions have grown too hot. If it sounds as if it takes more time and effort to use the skills and use the tools of an effective communicator, consider how much time and effort it takes to later rehash a conversation or undo the damage done to a relationship by miscommunication. What are some other skills you need to be a more conscious communicator? When you recognize that you have a gut-level emotional response to words that are in and of themselves neutral, that should be the clue you need to figure out that some metamessage is getting in the way of sharing meaning.

To put it simply, there are times when, for a variety of reasons, it is not right to talk to your teen. Obviously, it's seldom a good idea to confront your teen about some acting out behavior when either of you is in a highly emotional state. No real good can come of it. Does that mean that you should just ignore the situation? Absolutely not, but as much as possible, try to keep the level of emotional fire under control. If you know when you are overreacting, you can put the brakes on and keep yourself in your lane without veering into oncoming traffic or off the side of the road. Don't get so involved in experiencing your emotions that you can't examine the sources of those emotions. Highly charged emotional situations are like car accidents. They may seem to take place in slow motion, but in fact they transpire at a rapid rate. Slow yourself down, Give yourself time to react. The best thing is to communicate clearly and state your position.

Your son has come home and has clearly been drinking. You've sat up waiting, you're tired, you're angry. He's on the defensive and feeling that if you waited up you must not trust him, and he's incapable at that point of understanding that you don't trust him for a good reason, and he's ready to go on the attack at the slightest provocation. The Bradshaw formula is probably the furthest thing from your mind, so you may say something like this: "Look. It's late. I'm upset and disappointed. I want to talk to you about your behavior, but I don't want this to turn into something else. You go to bed, and we will talk about his first thing tomorrow. I'm going to come to your room at 9:30 tomorrow morning. Good night."

When 9:30 a.m. rolls around, you will have had some time to think about what you want to say and to cool off a bit. Resist the temptation to be an arsonist, and don't let your teen be one either. It is very easy to rekindle the smoldering ashes of what you were feeling last night, and for your teen to pour gas on what he senses is a tiny flame. Remember, all the interference generated by those emotions will only make it harder for you to share meaning with your teen. Instead of agreeing on a message that spells out your disappointment, on the steps you both agree to take to remediate the problem, on the consequences for this failure to adhere to the rules, and on the next set of consequences and actions, you run the risk of turning the conversation into one in which your teen tries to communicate the message that you are unfair, unreasonable, argumentative, and judgmental. Don't fall in that trap. If you do, then your teen will remember your emotional response and not the lesson.

When Words Turn Ugly

Nobody wants to get involved in a conversation that turns nasty. We can all be swept up in the moment and say things we may later regret or may struggle to believe came out of our mouths, but it happens. If you find yourself on the receiving end of a verbal attack by your teen, you have to decide where to draw the line. In baseball, it's called the magic word—the one used by players, coaches, and managers that will guarantee they will be kicked out of the game. You have to decide what that word is for you. I don't advocate giving a list of acceptable and unacceptable words to your teens, but you should communicate clearly what level of disrespect you will not tolerate. When they hit that level for the first time, let 'em know.

"I don't like the way you've been speaking to me, but I understand you're upset. What you just said, however, crossed the line. This conversation is over. We'll resume it when you are calmer and can be less disrespectful and when I can respond to you without feeling so hurt."

You're not adding any fuel to the fire, and you're being reasonable in the face of unreason, but you're still communicating clearly your expectations and feelings. When you're done saying those words, or their equivalent, walk away. There's no shame in leaving the field of battle when you've chosen not to engage in it in the first place. You're not trying to ignore your teen, just simply deescalating the situation.

You also want to get the hostages out of the room as well. The kind of conversation that takes place between a parent and a teen who has been acting out and needs to be negotiated with should be a private matter.

STRAIGHT FEEDBACK—THE SPRING CREEK MODEL

With all of these tools and ideas at your disposal, communicating is still no easy task. While these steps are all crucial to understand, not all of them work for every teen, and sometimes it helps to try a different method, one that is rooted in the same ideas but carries a much different structure.

I mentioned very early on in the book how impressed I was with the level of honest communication that went on among the students and staff when I first set foot on the campus of Spring Creek. Staff and students are instructed in a very precise form of communication in which they give each other feedback about their behaviors and attitudes. If the information in the chapter thus far doesn't seem to be working for you, you may want to try using this very specific method of communication with your teen. I don't necessarily see this is a stopgap measure or one that only families in distress should use. When I use the language and format of the Spring Creek model with my kids at home, they think it sounds too much like a "program." I can understand that. Our house isn't a clinical or an institutional setting, and my kids haven't been through the other kinds of programs, therapy settings, and acting out scenarios that the kids at Spring Creek have. However, it can be very useful to understand why this model is put in place and how it works, so that you can modify some of the techniques and principles to suit your individual needs.

The kids at Spring Creek are taught to give each other feedback in one of two ways: "My experience of you is . . ." and "My experience of myself when I am around you is . . . ." This method of giving coaching or feedback removes the perception that I know you better than you know yourself. It allows the sender to inform the receiver of what they have experienced from the other person, rather than saying "You are . . . rude." Instead, they would say something like "My experience of you is that you use attitude as a defense mechanism when someone has hurt your feelings." The first statement is loaded with judgment; the second is more about the sender's perceptions. As I've said from the beginning, perception is individual, changeable, and says less about the person making the statement than about the person being discussed.

The second option, "My experience of myself around you is . . . I feel like I am consistently getting manipulated," uses language that makes the statement even more clearly about your perception as the person giving the feedback. It is even less about the person receiving the feedback, and he or she can choose to take a look at the feedback or simply let it go. This is the "if it doesn't apply, let it fly" mode. Being able to give and receive feedback is very important, as we often don't see our maladaptive coping mechanisms as well as other people do.

At Spring Creek Lodge Academy, when students learn to give feedback, they also learn to receive feedback and are instructed to always say, "Thank you for caring enough about me to be honest." This drives home the point that we are telling you this because we truly care about you and how your life is going. In other words, we're operating from pure intention. These are kids who struggle to make day-to-day life work. Once they can begin to see that the people around them are attempting to assist on the basis of love and compassion, they begin to take a serious look at themselves. The real change comes when they realize they need to make change for themselves. This typically comes after a time when they have heard these messages several times from several people, and the results they create match the feedback they get.

The rules for giving feedback are basic:

- Give honesty with your feedback.
- Use the above-prescribed methods.
- DO NOT give feedback to someone you don't care about.
- Be sensitive.
- Be considerate of the person receiving.
- Do not use feedback as a weapon.
- Do not give feedback when you are angry.
- Come from a place of neutrality.
- Check your timing, and watch the body posture of the person receiving.
- Focus on the behaviors, not personality. Behaviors can change.
- Be direct and specific. Don't stretch it out to hear yourself talk.
- Don't use feedback as a chance to empower yourself.

When receiving:

- Be open to what is being said.
- Be engaged in the feedback process; make eye contact and nod.
- Attempt to understand where the other person is coming from.
- Be sincere and open to making changes if necessary.
- Be respectful. Remember that the sender is giving you his or her experience, not absolute facts about you.
- Be ready to say thank you if you appreciate the feedback.

It's essential that feedback not be used as a weapon. Teens will not be receptive to feedback if someone has used it to hurt them. In the same way that later on we will talk about the difference between a punishment and a consequence, effective feedback and ineffective feedback are differentiated according to the same intention—one is designed to eliminate a behavior, and the other to modify it.

Another reason I like this model of giving feedback is that it reinforces the concept of actions having consequences. When you tell someone, "My experience of you is . . ." you're letting that person know that he or she doesn't exist in a vacuum. What that person does and says has an impact on others. That's not something teens are always aware of. When we talked about teens' cognitive development, one thing I said is that they are frequently not introspective. Another way to say that is that they are self-involved to a degree. Couple that with the feelings of isolation they frequently experience, and you can see why it helps your teens to let them know that you are aware of what they are doing, you have thought about how their behavior influences you, and it has consequences that affect you and others. Letting teens know that they don't live in a bubble is crucial to their developing empathy and connectedness.

My Experience of You in Practice

I began this book with the example of Lauren and the feedback I gave her when I talked about her integrity. I did not use the hard-and-fast format, but she fully understood that my feedback came from a place of pure intention. Several weeks after that session, Lauren gave me feedback one night. "Mr. Mike, my experience is that you work so hard to try to prove to everyone that they can count on you and that you will always be there for them and you do little to take care of yourself." You could have knocked me over with a feather after that. She was keen in her insight, and I was glad to see that she could apply a lot of what she had learned in looking at someone else. I was hoping that she'd turn her sharp eye inward, and eventually she did. She didn't do it alone.

At one group session, Lauren got the feedback from one of her peers: "My experience of you is that you are afraid to go home so you sabotage your success." Nearly every one in the room knew that was true, and I suspected that on some level Lauren did also. It took hearing it multiple times from multiple people before she could fully admit the truth of that statement to herself. That was just Step One, recognition of the problem and its source, before she could take the steps she needed to solve it.

Greg, the young man who was abused and abandoned as a child and struggled so mightily with his survival needs, constantly got this feedback: "My experience of you is that you don't trust me or anyone else." Greg's case was complex, primarily because if he trusted no one, that meant he also didn't trust what was being said to him. That made our individual and group sessions difficult. By hearing the same message over and over, Greg eventually got to the point where he would consider the possibility that a vast conspiracy wasn't out to get him, but his own personality, that was producing some of his problems. If we had said to him, "You are a very suspicious person" or "You are paranoid" or any other kind of "you are" statement, we'd have been simply feeding the machine that he'd created to deal with all the bad things that had happened to him. He couldn't possibly accept, nor should he have, that he was responsible for those bad things, but he had to learn that he was responsible for how he responded to them.

I also remember when Christina got the feedback from one of her peers that she "felt uptight and tense when around Christina because she experienced Christina putting off a 'perfection' vibe." If you recall, Christina was the young Thai-American woman whose parents put enormous pressure on her with high expectations for success. They wanted her to be perfect, and Christina did everything she could to be anything but perfect. Once she got a taste of freedom, she was hooked, and she cultivated a bad-girl image by drinking and smoking pot. Christina was intelligent and perceived that she was resistant to most other kinds of therapy her parents had put her through. When she learned over time that other people felt the same "perfection vibe" coming from her, she really struggled. Learning that we've become what we've tried hardest to avoid is hard. I could have told her that in our sessions, but the message would have just bounced off the armor she'd put on. Christina eventually came to realize that she was trying to be the perfect opposite of what her parents wanted her to be. She was the one who was putting pressure on herself and setting enormous expectations for herself as a "bad girl" that she couldn't possibly live up to.

Christina also would get this feedback from her father: "My experience is, you don't really feel perfect, that it's just a way for you to manipulate and get your way." Christina, and many other teens, have to deal with this one all the time. Parents consistently want to tell their kids how the kid feels. You must first seek to understand, then to be understood. Remember, you may be the boss of your kids, but you're not the expert on them. Our kids are smart, and they typically do not want anyone telling them what to do, let alone how they feel. This will almost always shut them down, and communication stops right there.

What I like about this method is that it is clear, direct, and not subject to the kinds of interpretation that lead to meaning not being shared. Even though it is direct and kids are offering assessments of one another, it is presented in a framework that reduces the level of judgment and acknowledges that these are my perceptions of you, not the absolute truth about you.

Always keep in mind when you're giving feedback that it's important to modify your communication to react to changes that occur. If you sense that your teens are reacting in one way or another, you may have to modify your approach to be more or less direct, depending on how they respond.

I hope your experience with these principles of communication can help you understand better what needs to be done to establish and/or repair your relationship with your teens. Without good communication skills and the ability to share meaning on a regular basis, I can only see you both wandering alone in the darkness, searching for something you can't even name. Effective communication not only helps you name what you're looking for but sheds light on the path you need to take to get it.

16

Making the Right Set of Rules

So far, we've looked at a lot of different pieces of the puzzle. It's time now to combine a lot of these concepts so you can see how they can work together. In other words, it's time to design some rules. Rules are more than just restrictions and guidelines; they articulate a vision of what you want your family life to look like. Rules can help make that vision a reality. They can help create a familiar, consistent environment in which your teens have a firm understanding of what happens when rules are followed and what happens when they are not. They also ensure that all your teen needs are met in positive, productive ways.

As you've probably guessed by now, making rules is a lot harder than breaking them. Making rules requires utilizing every aspect of what we've learned about communication and every element of giving feedback. Discussions about rules and boundaries are the most loaded conversations we have with our teens. These conversations have the most potential to end up with yelling, screaming, hurt feelings, and critical remarks. In short, having a discussion about rules is like walking into a minefield.

Despite these drawbacks, conversations about rules can be easier—especially if you use the pure intentions mindset and communication tools that we've discussed in the previous chapters. Conversations about rules will use all of your understanding about how your teen's mind works, how you should react to your teen, and how to move forward without drowning in the past.

To illustrate how forming rules will pull all of your communication skills together, I'm going to lead you through a scenario that covers the formation of a set of rules about driving with your teen. One reason I chose to use teens and driving as an example is that driving addresses Glasser's structure of needs. While teens don't need to drive to survive, their driving well will contribute to their survival. Driving allows teens to socialize more easily, thus increasing their opportunities for belonging. They also are able to include themselves in the group known as drivers—ask any teen who hasn't yet earned driving privileges how that makes him or her feel. Driving gives teens a much needed and desired feeling of independence or freedom, and that sense of freedom translates into a sense of power. For many teens driving either is a direct source of fun or allows them the opportunity to experience fun.

But driving is also a real danger, and as such it requires rules—rules that you as a parent must set and your child must follow. Sadly, far too many teens don't survive to adulthood because of the poor choices they make when they get behind the wheel of a car or choose to be a passenger in a car driven by another teen. Teens have the highest fatality rate among any age group as drivers and passengers in motor vehicles. Once again, our friends at the Centers for Disease Control and Prevention's National Center for Injury Prevention and Control (NCIPC) provide us with the numbers. Because teens are young and healthy, disease is not one of the leading causes of their deaths. In 2004, the latest year for which statistics are available, unintentional injury, homicide, and suicide were the top three causes of death among teens sixteen to nineteen years old. Of those three, unintentional injury accounted for 6,168 of the 7,636 total teen deaths in that year, while there were 1,765 homicides and 1,523 suicides. As you can see, unintentional injuries far outdistance any other cause of death for our teens. Of those 6,168 deaths, nearly 74% (5,629) were a result of motor vehicle accidents.

In a recent survey, 50% of parents misidentified alcohol as the number one cause of teen automobile accidents. While laws vary from state to state, it is clear that distractions like cell phones are a leading cause of accidents among all drivers. With teens, their inattention and lack of experience only make the problem worse. Most teen fatalities result from single-vehicle accidents, which means that driver error and distraction play a major role. Modeling good driving skills, not using a cell phone while driving, and educating kids about the dangers of driving while distracted will likely produce the kind of results that our "don't drink and drive" campaigns have. I'm particularly sensitive to this idea because while writing this chapter I read about a young man who was killed in an automobile accident while driving and watching a DVD on his laptop. Our kids can make very poor choices sometimes.

So far, we've been talking about teen fatalities, and while the loss of any one teen in a automobile accident is horrific, the temptation may be there to look at the odds and say, it can't happen here. Well, we haven't talked about something else—injuries. More than 300,000 teens were injured in automobile accidents in 2005. With that in mind, the odds are substantially higher when you factor in driver and passenger injuries and fatalities that your kids will be involved in some kind of automobile accident as a teen.

As parents who know all about driving and teens, we have to design a plan that meets our need to keep them safe and alive. So, how do we develop rules that deal with the realities of the facts we know about teens and their driving risks and the realities that driving is an important part of their development into responsible adults? First, we have to lay out the groundwork for them as passengers; then we can move onto a discussion of them as drivers. Let's start with rules for them as passengers.

PASSENGER RULE TALK

Before you have any discussion with your teen about rules to establish, we have to frame the discussion with a rationale for why these rules are necessary. This means providing them with the risk factors of the situation before giving them the actual rules so they can understand and see rationally what evidence you are using to base your decisions on. Keep in mind everything we've learned about effective communication and sharing meaning. It's also important to reinforce the idea that we are basing our decisions not on some arbitrary nebulous set of expectations but on real-world concerns and our observations of our teen's behaviors. This combination of facts and experience-based perception should be the foundation on which you base all your decisions and serve as a starting point for your rules.

In this case, let's assume that our teen hasn't started driving yet but is in the process of earning his or her license. In other words, this isn't a remediation program based on failures to drive safely; it is a baseline set of rules and expectations.

We could begin our discussion by saying something like this:

"We know that you have driver's education this semester, and I've noticed how eager you are to get your license. I can understand that. That said, we're not as eager as you are to see you behind the wheel—we're a little concerned for your safety. Driving is a big step, and we want to do everything we can to support you in making that step successfully. We're going to have to set up some ground rules for you as a driver. We want to do this early on, so there are no surprises for you when you get your license. We've decided to place some limitations on your access to the car and your ability to drive without one of us being present. We thought long and hard about this, and we decided we needed to do this for a couple of reasons. First, we had to consider how responsibly you've behaved in the past. When you first got your mountain bike, you were thrilled. Within a week, that bike was wrecked from a jump that went wrong. We know you like to take risks and love speed, but we also have seen how that has gotten you into trouble when you've been skateboarding, snowboarding, and cycling.

"The last time we went skiing in Colorado, you got cited twice by the ski patrol even after we'd issued a warning to slow down and take it easy. We're glad that things haven't been worse, but thrill-seeking on the slopes or trails is a lot different from being behind the wheel. We have to trust your judgments, and in the past, you haven't always made good choices. We want you to be safe so you can continue to have fun. We also think it's important for you to understand a few things about teens and driving that factored into our decision":

RISK FACTORS

- 61% of teen passenger deaths occurred in vehicles driven by another teenager.
- Seat belt use among fatally injured teen passengers, was only 31%, compared with 41% of teen drivers killed in accidents. In other words, 69% of passengers killed were not wearing seat belts.
- One of every five licensed sixteen-year-old drivers will be in a vehicle crash.
- The first year of unsupervised driving is the most dangerous. In fact, the crash risk drops by more than two thirds after a driver completes his or her first 1,500 miles of independent driving.
- For sixteen- and seventeen-year-olds, carrying just one passenger increases the crash risk by about 50%, according to the Insurance Institute for Highway Safety.
- 33% of all teenage motor vehicle deaths occurred between 9 p.m. and 3 a.m.
- 15% of fatally injured teen drivers had a blood alcohol content of 0.08% or higher. The good news is that this percentage is down 63% since 1982. Our efforts to reduce driving under the influence have been effective for teens. Unfortunately, incidences of DWI-related fatalities among those twenty-one to thirty have decreased by only 21% in that same time. Teen females are less likely to drive and die under the influence of alcohol than are males.
- 77% of all teen accidents (fatal and nonfatal) are due to driver error. One of the largest contributing causes to driver error, in addition to speeding, is distraction. Cell phone use while driving is the number one distraction. Distraction, more than drinking, causes teen driving accidents.

All these statistics are based on 2005 findings, the latest year for which they are available.

"Because of all these risk factors, we've decided to implement these rules":

RULES

- You will wear your seat belt as a passenger at all times in any car under any circumstances.

- Do nothing to distract the driver, and actively discourage your friends from using a cell phone while driving.
- Under no circumstances at any time will you knowingly get into a car driven by someone who has had, or whom you suspect has had, any alcohol to drink at any point in that day. If doing so is what you consider to be your only option, you are to call home, and we will pick you up.
- If a car in which you wish to ride does not have seat belts, you will not be a passenger in that car.
- You will not be a passenger in a car driven by anyone who has had a valid driver's license for less than one full year, unless we have specifically approved that person.
- If you need a ride after 9 p.m. and the only driver available is a teenager and we have not specifically approved that person, you are to call home for a ride, and we will pick you up.*

Yes, but . . .

Depending on your values and what you want to tell your teens, you may choose to mention their possible consumption of alcohol in these passenger rules. Some teens may hesitate to call their parents if they have been drinking. You can handle this a couple of different ways. First, you may opt for a no-fault rule. In other words, if your teen calls for a ride as a matter of safety, all drinking rules are suspended—you won't use any of the usual consequences for drinking if they do the right thing by calling for a ride as a passenger or driver. You may make this a no-fault rule for them as a driver but not as a passenger, depending upon the circumstances.

Second, rather than implementing a no-fault rule, you may offer lesser consequences for their drinking if they call for a ride as either a passenger or a driver. Call this the self-reporting model. For

*Many states now have graduated licensing programs for teens. That means that teenage drivers may not be legally allowed to drive with more than one passenger. It may also mean that they are not legally permitted to drive after a certain time of night—generally 9:00 or 10:00 p.m. Your rules should reflect the laws in your state in order to reinforce the values you've instilled about respecting the law.

example, if your teen calls for a ride and you suspect that he or she has been drinking and confirm that fact, under the self-reporting guidelines you may reduce their grounding period by one half or one third, whatever amount you deem appropriate that will encourage your teen to self-report and call.

A Note on Compliance

Driving behavior is difficult to monitor because a great deal of the time you won't be with your teens when they are engaged in the activity as a driver or as a passenger. However, the same rules need to apply when we are in the car with them. One strategy, which I mentioned earlier, is developing allies. We demand that our kids look out for one another and that they let us know when they think one of their siblings is engaging in behavior that is potentially dangerous or clearly violates the rules.

You can also make your passenger and driver rules clear to all your teen's friends and all of the parents and siblings of your teen's friends. Janna and I have made an effort to get to know most of our kids' friends and their families. Yes, we live in a somewhat small community, but it still takes some time and effort. If our kids don't follow the rules, we've asked that their friends let us know when those violations take place. We also make it clear to other parents and their kids that we are all accountable to and for one another and that the old message that "it takes a village" does apply in our case.

While I don't expect my kids or my kids' friends to "rat them out" every time, I'm sure that a message has been sent and received. Kids generally don't want to get into trouble, and they don't want to get one another into trouble, either. They will help you to enforce the rules, maybe not because they want to do the right thing but because they don't want to be found out later as having aided or abetted a crime.

Later on in this chapter, we'll talk about how to not create a police state. I don't want my kids or their friends acting as a kind of Soviet-era secret police force; I just want them to know and understand our really high-risk, high-priority concerns and our rules are regarding them.

THE PASSENGER CONSEQUENCES

Rules and consequences for violations of those rules go hand in hand. They need to be established at the same time. Deciding the punishment ahead of time not only makes your thought process more transparent and decipherable but enables your kid to know what to expect. Just as we talked about in other parts of this book, immediate, appropriate, clear, and specific consequences need to be established for violations of the vehicle passenger rules. The sequence can begin with denial of privileges or grounding and range all the way up to forbidding your child from riding in cars with anyone other than you, your spouse, or any other designated drivers, depending on the severity of the violations.

Because so many automobile accidents and fatalities also affect teens who are passengers in cars, stricter consequences for driving misbehaviors may be needed. The old ounce of prevention being worth a pound of cure certainly fits here.

DRIVING THE POINT HOME

Now, let's turn our attention to what is probably the more important of the two behaviors—being a driver. In addition to all the points made above about being a passenger, let's add a few more that relate directly to your teen as a driver:

RISK FACTORS
- More than one third of teen driver fatalities involve speeding.
- The rate of crash per miles driven for a teen is four times higher than for older drivers.
- Sixteen-year-olds have a rate of crash per mile twice as high as eighteen- and nineteen-year-olds.
- Approximately two out of three teens killed in automobile accidents were males.
- 54% of teen passenger vehicle occupants killed were drivers.
- 54% of teen motor vehicle crash deaths occur on Friday, Saturday, and Sunday.
- 61% of teen passenger deaths occurred in vehicle driven by another teen.

SOME BASIC PRINCIPLES

- Driving is a privilege that the state grants you. It can be taken away.
- Driving is a privilege that we grant you. It can be taken away.
- You will be driving our property on our insurance, using our money to fuel and maintain it. Have respect for what we've provided you.
- What your friends can and cannot do has little or no bearing on the decisions we make about how, when, and where you drive.
- Until you can demonstrate to our satisfaction that you are a responsible driver, you will not be granted additional driving privileges.
- Your safety and the safety of others on the road is a concern of all of us.

"With those points in mind, here's what we've come up with regarding driving":

The Rules

If your state doesn't have a graduated licensing program, we as parents can institute one on our own. Some of your rules may reflect and reinforce those concepts:

"For six months after passing the state's licensing exam, you will be on a probationary period. That means":

- You will not be allowed to drive without a supervising adult as a passenger (your mother, your father, or another appointed driver).
- You will not operate the vehicle with a passenger other than a supervising adult.
- You will be allowed to drive only during daylight hours and in weather conditions we determine to be good.
- You will wear your seat belt at all times.
- You will obey all traffic laws with specific attention focused on obeying the speed limit.
- You will operate the vehicle without the radio or CD player.
- You will operate the vehicle without the use of your cell phone or MP3 player.

"If, after six months, you have demonstrated the ability to drive responsibly, for the next three months you will be allowed to do the following":

- Drive without a supervising adult.
- Drive during the hours of 6 a.m. to 10 p.m.
- All other rules will remain in force.

"If, after an additional three months, you have demonstrated the ability to drive responsibly on your own, for the next three months you will be allowed to do the following":

- Drive without a supervising adult.
- Drive during the hours of 6 a.m. to 10 p.m.
- Drive with a single passenger, who must wear a seat belt.
- All other rules will remain in force.

"If, after another three months, you have demonstrated the ability to drive responsibly on your own with a single passenger, you will be allowed to do the following":

- Drive without a supervising adult.
- Drive during the hours of 6 a.m. to 10 p.m.
- Drive with multiple passengers—limited to the number of seat belts available in the car.
- All other rules will remain in force.

THE DRIVING CONSEQUENCES

"If during the initial six-month probationary period you fail to put your seat belt on without a reminder, you will lose your driving privileges for a week. The same is true for any violation of traffic laws such as—but not only—speeding, failure to yield, failure to stop, or any other driving conduct we feel is unsafe. This does not mean that you have to be cited by the police for it to be a violation.

"For the second violation of the seat belt or safe driving rules, you will lose your driving privileges for two weeks. For each subsequent seat belt violation, you will lose your driving privileges equal to the number of the violation: third violation = three weeks; fourth violation = four weeks, and so on.

"If during that probationary period you receive a citation from the police for any reason, you will lose your driving privileges until you complete a driver's training program that you will pay for. When you successfully complete that program, you will begin again at day one of your probationary period."

Actual Citations from the Police

"After you have successfully completed the initial six-month probationary period, the rules for seat belt use remain in effect. For any violation resulting in a written warning or a ticket issued, the following consequences will be in place:

"Speeding from five to fifteen miles per hour over the limit: loss of driving privileges for two months, payment of the fine, return to initial probationary rules for two months, restriction to weekday driving only.

"Speeding from fifteen miles per hour and above over the limit: loss of driving privileges for six months, payment of the fine, return to initial probationary rules for four months; restriction to weekday driving only. If there are no additional violations within that first month, you will be allowed to drive on weekends and unsupervised.

"All of these consequences are in addition to whatever the court decides you must do."

Accident

"In case of an accident during any of these phases, you will lose your driving privileges for three months, you will have to take either a basic driver's education class or an advanced safety class at your expense, and you will have to pay for any additional insurance premiums resulting from that accident. If you can't pay for the classes or the premiums, at our sole discretion we will arrange some kind of loan arrangement to enable you to drive again."

Suspicion of Drinking and Driving

"Here we are referring to cases in which there has been no law enforcement involvement. In case we confirm that you have driven under the influence of alcohol or drugs, you will lose your driving privileges for six months. If you violate that no-driving consequence, you will lose your driving privileges for an additional six months and be grounded for two months. A second violation of suspicion of drunk driving will result in revocation of your license, enrollment in a drug/alcohol education program, and grounding for four months. A third violation for suspicion of drunk driving will result in loss of license and enrollment in an outpatient or inpatient substance abuse program. Once you are granted the okay to drive again, you return to the restrictions of the initial probationary period."

Citations for DWI

"Regardless of the court's ruling and in addition to their judgment, you will lose your driving privileges for six months minimum, with a review of the status of that consequence after three months. If at any time you violate that prohibition against driving or don't comply with the ruling of the court, you will lose your driving privileges permanently. Once you are granted the okay to drive again, you return to the restrictions of the initial probationary period."

YOUR RULES HAVE TO BE YOUR OWN

It's important to keep in mind that these rules do not have to be your rules. You may find some of my suggestions too rigid and others not rigid enough, so you will want to modify them according to your own needs. I've provided you with this level of detail and the statistics about teens and driving to reinforce the idea that we have to be specific in dealing with our kids and teach them the facts so they will understand the rationale behind our decisions to make something like driving a high-priority, high-awareness issue for the family. As before, if you have a story to tell about how driving has affected your life, be sure to share it if you feel it is important and reinforces your point. I'm not a big believer in scare tactics, and showing your kids horrific pictures of car wrecks and mangled bodies may not be the best approach to take unless all else has failed. Shock for the sake of shock doesn't do much to modify behavior.

In a sense, I've outlined here just the first steps you could take. As I said before, you don't want to create a police state. But in certain cases of very serious and repeated violations of the rules, and a series of accidents, you sometimes have to step in and take more drastic actions. I know of a family who has had to purchase three cars already for a nineteen-year-old son who keeps getting in wrecks. The kid is a bad driver and likely a danger to other folks on the road, but in the two years that he's been driving and wrecking cars, he hasn't gotten his parents' attention to the degree he ought to have. They keep thinking he just has bad luck. Denial is pretty hard to manufacture in the face of all that evidence, but they somehow manage it.

OTHER MEASURES

In addition to your physical presence, there are always other steps to help monitor your teen's compliance with your rules. As I mentioned earlier, sometimes siblings, friends, and friends' parents can be useful sources of information. That said, the question remains: how far do you need to go to ensure safety?

In regard to the driving scenario, know that one thing running through your mind may be that the state government has all kinds of rules and regulations in place to control our driving behavior, and we still have all kinds of problems with poor and aggressive driving, drinking and driving, and the like. What the heck can I do as a parent with limited resources that a government can't do? Well, you can borrow a trick from the government if you really find your back against the wall and don't want to, can't, or really shouldn't (for extenuating circumstances, such as getting to work or school) deny your child access to a car. For example, on the market today are immobilizers similar to the ones the government uses. They combine a breathalyzer and an ignition immobilizer. These devices can be calibrated to a certain percentage of alcohol, and if the person blowing into it has a blood alcohol level above that specified amount, the device disables the car's ignition system. Sure, these things are costly—upwards of a thousand dollars—but in some cases, that thousand dollars is relatively low compared with court costs, insurance rates, and other dollar figures associated with the consequences of drinking and driving.

Another device is available to help us as parents be more places than we can be physically. Electronic speed monitoring devices and global positioning satellite devices can help you track your teen's driving habits and locations. GPS systems can download information directly to your cell phone, while an ESP, or so-called black box data recorder, can record information and send it in real time to your home computer or record it for download and analysis later. CarChip is one such device, and parents can even set it so that it issues a warning sound when a preset speed limit is exceeded.

Big Brother Is Watching You

I mention these latest technological trends as possible last-resort measures. To use a technological metaphor, they do send mixed messages. First, they let your teens know that you care about them and their safety. I've stressed care, attention, and time as important elements in any parenting plan. It is true that we can't be with our kids all the time watching over them, and for some kids all our efforts to instill proper values, communicate effectively, and establish clear boundaries and consequences will fail. As one parent said to his stepson, as quoted in a March 5, 2005, *Washington Post* article on automobile speed monitoring devices, "It's not that I'm worried about your skills . . . I'm worried about your judgment, which comes as you get older . . . It's a way to prove your ability to be out there on your own."

This parent and I have never spoken, but if we had, I would have told him to approach this subject almost exactly the way he did. His statement is honest and specific, and it doesn't do enough to emphasize what he's observed that leads him to worry about his son's judgment, but he clearly lets his son know that if he performs well, he will earn greater freedom. In fact, the two of them did agree that if the young man is ticket-free by age eighteen, the CarChip will go. All these elements are sound in principle, but without any additional evidence of the teen's abilities as a driver or as a responsible, trustworthy kid, I'm not so sure that this is a needed first step.

GO IN ORDER

As I've made clear before, consequences and rules should be set up sequentially. The same is true when you are working on a remediation program and building steps toward the successful elimination or modifying of an acting out behavior. If your teen has been struggling with an alcohol issue, it makes sense to build in a series of expectations and rewards that are attainable so he or she can experience some success. Often, in our attempts to lay down the law after a major violation of our trust, we err on the side of zero tolerance and come down too hard on our kids. As you saw with the rules and consequences set up for a new driver, there are some baby steps in terms of what the teen is allowed to do and the kinds of consequences meted out for failure to meet those expectations and requirements.

If you've been through several go-rounds with your teen over alcohol consumption, and your zero tolerance plan hasn't brought about the change you've wanted to see, then another approach might be to create a system of rewards for achieving intermediate goals. Programs like Alcoholics Anonymous and their emphasis on one day at a time have some real merit, particularly if your son or daughter is really struggling with an issue. Rewarding our kids who have a demonstrated pattern of abusing alcohol after two drinking-free weekends might make some hard-liners think that rewarding their kids for doing what's expected and not something exceptional is wrong. In my experience, those hard-liners are relatively few and far between. It's more likely that permissive types are going to struggle with the idea of enforcing consequences and staying strong and consistent. Both types—hard-liners and permissives—can learn something from this idea of sequential rewards as well as consequences.

EARNING BACK TRUST

Just as your kids won't perceive you as being too strict if you spell out the consequences of their poor choices ahead of time, they won't think you are too weak if you build in a series of scaled-back consequences as a reward for complying with the rules of a consequence. For example, if your teen spends two weekends unsupervised (not remaining at home as a result of grounding) and demonstrates that he or she has been alcohol free, you can return some previously suspended privilege; you let the teen earn (and notice the emphasis on the teen's earning and not your "giving") back an hour of the reduced curfew. You've found that proverbial win–win. You reduce the acting out behavior, and your teen gets some freedom and fun back.

By using the baby-step consequences and rewards model, you do two additional things. First, by putting those consequences in place for relatively minor infractions, you control just how far your teen can go until your trust has been violated in a major way. For example, in the car driving scenario, if you had consequences set up only for a traffic citation or an accident, that would be a major violation of your trust. You'd be greatly upset, your teen would experience a great deal of pain from having disappointed you (which is a punishment and not a consequence and therefore ineffective) and you would have to initiate a more severe consequence, which would make your teen resentful, and that resentment would trigger either guilt or anger, and the cycle would continue. With these smaller, more incremental exchanges of consequence and reward, your kids know that was lost can be gained back. The sooner they are able to do that, the better off you both will be.

Trust has to be earned, but I do think that most kids have earned the right to some trust initially. It's like the game of Monopoly. You start out the game with a few dollars in hand, and you either increase that amount or lose it after a few rounds of play. Keep in mind also that a zero tolerance stance equates to a zero trust position—whether that's in our mind or our teen's. For a lot of kids, starting out with a zero or having hit that zero point makes them believe that it is easier to just go deeper in the hole than it is to climb out. That old expression about when you find yourself at the bottom of hole you should stop digging comes into play again here. When kids lose hope that they can recover, when they see no way out of the situation they are in, they frequently make the even poorer choice to make matters worse for themselves and consequently for you.

The other problem with a zero tolerance, tough love, I'll-show-'em-who's-boss approach is that our kids don't really learn anything from it. Certainly, putting our kids in a kind of hermetically sealed protective container is effective in one regard—they are kept in line and out of trouble. The problem, besides simply suffocating their spirits and perhaps making them bitter toward us, is that our role as parents is as much to teach *them* how to control themselves as it is for us to keep them in line. By denying them most opportunities to experience struggle and failure, we could prevent them for learning important lessons about accepting consequences, making the connections between their actions and the effects of those actions, and a host of other opportunities.

The idea isn't for them to be blindly obedient automatons but thinking, feeling, rational beings who are prone to err but who learn from their mistakes, accept responsibility for them, deal with the consequences of their actions, and take the right steps necessary to earn our trust and respect. By earning our trust again, they also learn another crucial lesson that we as adults sometimes struggle to master: fortitude and delayed gratification. We all want everything now, and we want our kids to turn around instantly and return immediately to the fold when they stray. Often, it takes more time and positive attention than we would probably like, and it's often far too easy to give up hope or to despair or to grow enormously frustrated at what we perceive to be their lack of progress. Instead of creating a police state to surround them, we want them to police themselves.

FEAR OF RELAPSE

Sometimes those baby steps can seem infinitesimal, and we measure progress in microns instead of miles. Maybe that's because our kids are also our best teachers when they are the worst students. Maybe we will see something in their behavior that makes us examine ourselves, our values, and our actions in a new and stronger light. When our kids make negative choices and act out, we experience an anguish unlike any other. Their actions, whether they make us anxious and doubtful of our own abilities or angry at them for their failures, are ultimately always about their choices. A part of growing up is making bad choices. Your kids will screw up, they will make progress in getting better, and chances are they will backslide a bit.

Living in fear of relapse is probably worse than experiencing those powerful negative emotions and experiences for the first time. Just as it isn't helpful to create a police state initially, it's not good to create one after our kids have messed up. We can create a powerfully toxic environment that actively encourages our kids to fail again when we send off signals of hypervigilance and hyperreactions. If we put a good plan in place, if we make advance preparations for those repeated errors in judgment, then we can rest a little bit easier knowing that we have consequences in place. Part of the burden, the "Oh my God, what am I going to do next?" is lifted from our shoulders. That's not to say that we follow our plan blindly. That would be stupid. We have to pay attention to the feedback we're receiving, look for our kids doing something right, reward and praise them for it, and take a different approach—either relaxing a bit or tightening up as necessary. Kids need boundaries, and they will constantly test those limitations we place on them, so be vigilant and be prepared. I said that we'd talk about fences in this book, so I'll leave you with one more reminder from my daddy: "Build your fences horse high, hog tight, and bull strong." Put 'em up early, put 'em up straight, and ride along 'em every day to make sure they're doing the job they should be doing.

17

Riding Herd on Your Understanding

One thing my daddy used to tell me all the time was if you're riding ahead of the herd, take a look back every now and then to make sure it's still there. With that in mind, I want to take some time to check on you to be sure you're still with me, and I want to do this by sharing some stories with you.

While understanding communication, the five needs, the reasons for acting out, and everything else we've talked about in this book is incredibly important, there's still one crucial step that we haven't addressed: the ability to learn from the past. Now I'm not just talking about your past or your teen's past—I'm talking about everyone's past: yours, mine, some of the parents whose kids we've talked about in this book, and others whose stories offer some cautionary tales about how not to handle situations. I don't know how many of you have seen the bumper sticker that reads "If you think education is expensive, you ought to try ignorance." Well, we try all the time to impress on our kids that it's important to learn from mistakes—their own and ours. It's time now to learn a bit from the experiences of the parents of some of the kids I've worked with over the years. By the time the kids I've told you about got to me, their parents had gone through quite a few steps (in most cases) in order to get their teens' lives back on track. I mention this for a couple of reasons. First, we can all benefit from their mistakes and the missteps they took along the way. Second, I can understand some parents' reactions to what I've been saying about time and attention. I know we all have to work really hard. I know we all feel that we don't get rewarded as much as we could at work—or in some cases that work offers us financial and emotional rewards that our family life doesn't offer—and we don't want to have to come and deal with another feel-bad situation. I know we're all exhausted, stressed, and in need of a little comfort and time and attention ourselves. I understand, I empathize, and I have experienced many of those same feelings myself. Believe me, after spending a whole day working with troubled kids, the last thing I want to do sometimes is endure an evening and night wrangling with more "issues."

Just as I tell it straight with the kids I counsel, I'm going to tell it straight with you: I can give you the hard line and the pragmatic line. First the hard line: This is the deal we all signed up for when we decided to have a family. Maybe you feel that you're getting more than you bargained for, and I know a lot of what I've been saying here has been pretty much putting negative time and attention on parents. I know that some kids, despite good parenting, despite having their parents do their best by paying all kinds of time and attention, can still turn out to be difficult kids. Whether it's because of developmental issues related to their brains, some kind of mental illness, or other physiological reasons, some kids develop antisocial tendencies, and there's nothing a parent can do to prevent that from happening. If that describes your teen, I admire you for the courage you've demonstrated and hope that what I've said in the preceding pages and the ones to come that you'll find something you can hold on to and get your teen back in good shape. I will say this also: You are probably in the minority. That's no comfort for you, but it should serve as a reminder to other parents.

The pragmatic line is this: I can't tell you the cost financially, as well as emotionally and spiritually, of ineffective and inattentive parenting. I've seen parents sell their homes to move into less expensive places, take out a second mortgage, ravage their retirement funds, get buried by credit card debt, work multiple jobs, and lay waste to college funds in order to pay for their disruptive teens' therapy, legal fees, outpatient and inpatient treatment programs, alternative education programs, or prescription drugs, or for programs like Spring Creek Lodge Academy.

So, if you think a little time and attention spent on your kids is costly, then you can't even imagine what not laying out that expenditure can cost you down the line.

Enough said. Let's take a look at a few of the teens you met before, and look more closely at how I came to work with them.

SPENDING TIME

So far, I've been hammering home the point about the importance of spending time with our kids and paying attention to them. As a preventive measure, I can think of nothing else that works as effectively. Now that we've made the turn toward remediation and not prevention, I don't want to leave you with a false impression. It may seem that when we get to the point where we have to enter a kind of rehabilitation program with our kids, all the time and attention we are spending on them is negative. "We're going to be watching you like a hawk." "We're going to sit with you every night to make sure all your homework is done." "We're going to sit down to family dinners whether you like it or not." "We're going to be in touch with every one of your teachers and the parents of your friends." The list could go on, but you get the point.

Spending time and paying positive attention to our kids, even in the remediation phase, is essential. Just as a punishment is meant to inflict pain, time spent with our kids could be viewed as something torturous—for them and for us. We shouldn't let it be that way. Of course, we don't want to send mixed signals and throw the kids a party to celebrate their coming home drunk, but we can and should build rewards and privileges into our plans. Just because we ground our kids, Janna and I don't always prevent them from doing other things that are fun. Grounding doesn't necessarily mean that we put our kids in solitary confinement. We deny them an important component that underlies an acting out behavior—such as unsupervised time or the influence of negative peers—but we don't want to lock them up someplace and ignore them. That would send the wrong signal and reinforce the idea that their need for fun can only be met outside the family. We also don't want to completely deny their freedom or cut them off for too long from the sense of belonging they get from their peers. You get the idea: Being conscious of their needs and that they can be met in the context of the family is important at all times.

Even if you've had to devise a plan to work on a more serious issue like drug abuse, drinking, inappropriate sexual activity, or even an arrest for a crime, resist the temptation to fall into the "We're going to make your life a living hell" trap. Remember, you are trying to make real the ideal vision you had of how your family would function. It's not going to be an Eden-like paradise, but it shouldn't be another one of Dante's circles of hell, either.

I can remember working with Greg, the young man whose father abused him and whose mother abandoned him. He went to live with an aunt and uncle who tried to do their best to undo the damage that had been done to him. Greg's perception was that they didn't care much about him; after all, they weren't his real parents. No matter what they did, Greg would hold them at bay and judge them harshly. Over time, they decided that one thing Greg needed was time and space to himself. He interpreted that as indifference, and when he got into more and more trouble, first at school and later with the law, they stepped back into his life more forcefully than they ever had before.

Here's what Greg had to say: "Most of the time, they didn't give two shits about me and what I did. As soon as I got into any kind of trouble, they were all over me. I couldn't turn around without bumping into one of them and some new order or bullshit rule they'd come up with. Felt like I couldn't even breathe. It was like I'd messed up their perfect little fairy-tale life, and they didn't want me out there ruining their name or whatever."

Greg's comments illustrate the point about negative attention. If the only time you spend time with your kids is when you are dealing with an issue, they'll turn that around in their heads and conclude, "You must think I suck, since the only time you talk to me is when I've disappointed you somehow, so I guess I do suck." Or they will think, "Since you already think I'm a pain in the ass and not good for much, I may as well be the biggest pain in your ass I can be." Obviously, neither of those two responses is all that logical, but it's illogical to expect your teen to be logical.

Positive time and attention can often mean doing something with your teen that is of interest to him or her but may not be of interest to you. If you're worried about your teen's behavior at a concert and believe that while attending one he or she they may engage in acting out behavior, instead of forbidding the teen to go, offer to go along. Your idea may get shot down, but the offer will be remembered. Instead of asking, you can be more proactive. If your teen has been denied access to friends for a while and seems to be cooperating, you may want to get tickets to a concert, a movie, a sporting event, a comic book convention, or any one of hundreds of other things your teen is interested in, and attend the event with him or her.

It doesn't even have to be a scheduled event. You can simply sit and watch a television show your teen is interested in and you aren't. When your teen is in his or room reading or listening to music, check in and ask about the band, the author, the subject of the magazine article. Showing an interest in your teen's life and gaining insight into it through asking questions isn't always easy, and may not always pay off in rich rewards, but it's a start, a crack in the shell, a little bit of thawing of the glacier that has formed between you. I sometimes like to think of dealing with my kids in the same way I did when I was wooing my wife. Instead of thinking about myself and what I wanted and needed and was interested in, I was figuring out ways to discover and then meet her wants and needs and interests. In the middle of a battle, sometimes it's best to step off the field of contention to neutral ground, some place where you both can feel comfortable or even uncomfortable.

Hauling my butt to see Gwen Stefani in concert puts me in my kid's position. As Alicia pointed out to us, "How many times did you drag us to someplace where we felt out of place or had no interest in seeing or doing? We went along 'cause we had to and 'cause we loved you and knew it meant something to you." Turnabout is fair play in this case, and showing our kids that we can be flexible and adapt to new situations is good for them to see.

APPROPRIATE CONSEQUENCES

Danijela was an exception in a lot of ways, and her story serves to re-inforce the point I've made about establishing a plan with your kids that is appropriate and sequential. As a reminder, Danijela was the young Croatian woman whose father had sexually assaulted her older sister. When that horrible truth was revealed, all attention was taken from Danijela and focused on her sister. After Danijela was involved as a passenger in a car accident that involved a peer driving drunk and Danijela's drinking, and after Danijela finally pierced the veil of denial and inattention her parents had put up by con-fessing to her mother all the other misbehaviors she'd committed, her parents immediately looked for other educational settings in which to place their daughter. In part, they wanted her to be out of the toxic environment at home. The furious storm her father's abuse had whipped up had created a place that wasn't good for anyone to be in. Later, when she confessed her transgressions to her mother, Danijela was on her way to Montana from Chicago.

When she arrived, she experienced a lot more than simply culture shock. She was devastated by what she considered her parents' be-trayal. She was wondering why her father was getting all kinds of second chances and was able to remain at home while she had messed up once—in response to what her father had done—and she was sent to what to her was a prison. In a lot of ways, the contrast be-tween Danijela's life one week before her arrival at Spring Creek and in the days after couldn't have left her with any other impression. Her parents, under extraordinary pressure and in the face of diffi-cult circumstances, did what they thought was best. Their first pri-ority was to get Danijela away from the negative influences of her peer group and her family. They had a lot of other options that they could have, and should have, pursued. It is always easy to second-guess with the advantage of hindsight, but what they did was take a young woman who was starving for attention and deny her of it completely and totally.

When she was finally able to discuss her feelings after several months with us, she said, "I remember my parents talking about peo-ple they knew who in World War II and afterward lost family in the Serb Croat conflicts. Some people just disappeared. I felt like I was one of them. It was like my parents just wanted me to go away, didn't want to look at me, didn't want to deal with me. I don't know—maybe in another way I was like a war orphan. There was this other battle going on, and they sent me away. No matter what, I hated what they did and how it made me feel about myself. Out of sight, out of mind—that whole thing."

As parents we jump the gun whenever we create a plan that isn't appropriate and sequential. When the consequences don't seem to match the deed, there is a disconnect that sends a vague communication to the kids. Remember the old joke about the father who swats his son for something he thinks he did wrong? The kid says, "But Dad, I didn't do anything." The father looks at him and says, "You will, though." It's easy to overreact and anticipate. I know that with all the things I've said about what kinds of acting out behaviors kids can engage in, and how many of them are drinking, it's easy to become an alarmist. As a friend of mine used to say, "It's hard to check into the reality hotel and way too easy to check out." Give yourself time to consider all your options. My plan is to give you more to consider in the pages ahead. Also, remember that your plans have to include appropriate and sequential consequences. For major violations, you may have to skip a step or two, but in most cases, when that kind of infraction occurs, we're also talking about legal implications, and those matters are often out of our hands.

UNDERSTAND THE WILD HORSE WITHIN

When I first started in private practice, I worked with a young man who was really struggling with his identity. He was a ranch kid, but you could tell he wanted to be anything but. Instead of the usual jeans and T-shirts or chambray shirts most kids were wearing, all he ever seemed to wear was concert T-shirts and military surplus apparel. He was a mystery to his mother and father, and it seemed that instead of playing sports or riding horses, all he wanted to do was play his guitar. His dad couldn't understand the appeal of all that "noise-making." He hated his son's long hair, and if it wasn't country music, it wasn't worth listening to. Things weren't going so well in family therapy. The young man was sullen and angry most of the time. One evening toward the end of an unproductive session, when I was out of ideas and grasping at straws, I said, "Kelly, why don't you bring in your guitar and play for all of us next time. Pick a song that really means something to you."

For the first time, I could see a bit of light in his eyes. I was also hoping that his parents' eyes would light up, too, getting the idea that maybe if they showed some kind of positive interest in how their son was spending most of his time, they could bridge the gap a bit. Unfortunately, as time would reveal, they didn't get it at all. Kelly came in and played and sang for me a song from the band U2—"Who's Going to Ride Your Wild Horses." He had a really strong and clear voice, and though the music wasn't a match with my usual taste, that song has stuck with me.

In particular I was reminded of it when several years later I met Brian, our snowball-throwing, thrill-seeking honor student gone astray. Brian was doing everything in his power to be a wild horse, though to everyone else he was more of a somber plow horse. Unlike Danjiela's parents, who bounced her out of the house and onto the campus at Spring Creek with a speed that stunned and disoriented her, Brian's parents were the model of patience and the attitude that "It's just a phase; he'll grow out of it." When Brian was first arrested for vandalism, he experienced a real high from breaking free of the expectations that he was a good kid. His parents continued to treat him as that good kid. Brian became a master of the good-at-home, wild-on-the-side dual nature. What his parents failed to realize, and what many of us parents fail to realize, is that our kids are capable of being both tame and untrained.

Brian not only had that inner wild horse nature but also was a bucking bronco just waiting for the opportunity for someone to climb aboard so he could throw the person. When the consequences of his actions didn't really fit the outlaw profile he was hoping to cultivate for himself, Brian had to find other ways to act out. If his parents grounded him, he snuck out of the house. When his mother and father didn't discover his absence, the thrill was reduced, so he took to just blatantly defying them and walking out or not coming home from school.

When they finally upped the level of his consequences, he took that on as an additional challenge. Over the course of a year and a half, he openly defied his parents, taunted and played a game of verbal chess with a therapist, and nearly caused mutiny among the staff and students at a nearby military school, where he was more AWOL than on the ball for his brief stint there. Brian loved to tell me stories about all the "jokers, dweebs, and ass kissers" his parents exposed him to in order to "get me to embrace my angst."

Brian took every move his parents made as a challenge, after he'd rid them of the idea that "boys will be boys and Brian is a good boy." He was essentially daring them to take their best shot, and their hopes of killing that destructive impulse in him with kindness was only inciting him to greater heights and lower depths.

When I talk about making consequences appropriate, I don't just mean that the punishment should fit the crime. It should also fit the unique nature and personality of your teen. Brian's little car vandalism habit cost his parents a lot of money in restitution costs, but they never made him pay for any of it. Lawyer's fees? Easily and quickly absorbed at no cost to Brian. His folks were more concerned about getting his record wiped clean so he could still get into an Ivy League school—and they had the money and resources to do that—than they were in shutting down his operation.

Brian's story is instructive in another way. Some kids get hooked on the cycle of acting out and receiving consequences. They view it all as a game, and sometimes really bright kids, generally good kids, act out in ways similar to Brian's. All kids will test boundaries, but it's the ones who make a sudden transformation who puzzle us the most. We're so used to giving them the benefit of the doubt, like giving a usually mild-mannered horse his lead, that when they bolt, we start out looking for faults in our abilities. When I spoke with Brian's parents, they talked a lot about their own failures. It's true that they didn't recognize at first their son's underlying wild horse nature, but they didn't hold him fully accountable for what he did. They blamed themselves, Brian's peers, society, and television shows like *Jackass,* but they didn't understand that a kid like Brian was itching for a fight, was restless in his pen. Maybe if they'd taken him on a bit earlier, understood better what was motivating him, spent a little more time with him, and focused both positive and negative attention on him, I might never had gotten to know him. Good kids do bad things. Assuming too much about their nature and not being sensitive to changes in behavior and not reacting immediately and appropriately with the right kinds of consequences can come back to haunt us.

DENY THE URGE TO DENY

Brian's parents were clearly in denial at first. They didn't want to admit that his pattern of behavior was leading him to arrive at the destination where his actions seemed to be heading. Well, let me tell you this—a horse will generally go in the direction his head is pointed. That doesn't mean that at the first indication of trouble we have to pull out all the stops. We have to find a balance point somewhere between Danijela's parents' response and Brian's parents' delayed reaction. We also have to face reality even when it's unpleasant.

Some high school teacher friends of mine told me a story that illustrates how parents can sometimes, even in the face of hard truths, look the other way. Spring at American high schools everywhere is notable for two major events—prom and graduation. While we as parents look at these events as rites of passage, the majority of our kids look at these two special days and evenings as excuses to party. Not that they need an excuse, but these events are generally an excuse to Party with a capital P. I don't know about you, but in my day, a spring formal was something that mostly couples went to, and it was a big deal for that night, and maybe you did something together as a group the next day. From what I've heard from kids, the prom is now an extended and expensive long weekend (and sometimes longer) series of extravaganzas.

My teacher friends tell me that one thing they find endearing and frustrating about working with teens is their combination of naiveté and adult-like sophistication. Whenever something major happens at school that causes an uproar, the kids are always surprised when the administration figures out pretty quick who was responsible for the acting out. The kids seem to think that the faculty and staff have some kind of paranormal powers, but the truth is that they usually find out whodunit because some student spills the beans. A lot of the time, the one who spills the beans is the one who "done it." Some kids can't keep their mouths shut. Others are far better at it, and they're the ones to really worry about. A year or so ago, one teacher told me that there was a lot of talk pre-prom about a group of the most popular seniors renting resort cabins and rooms at a lake complex about fifty miles from the city. It was a well-known and popular tourist attraction in the summer, and pretty quiet in the off season. One of the kids used a parent's credit card to book all the rooms and cabins at one site along the lake. He was then selling the spaces to the other kids—many of whom didn't have access to a credit card and were underage.

The owner of the place was a conscientious gentleman, and he was kind of suspicious that someone would rent the whole shooting match sight unseen over the phone and ask to have the rooms held on the credit card but they would be paid for in cash. He must have had teens of his own, since he called the phone number he was given and figured out that the voice on the other line likely belonged to a high school kid. Using the area code, he put the pieces of the puzzle together and called the principal of the high school to let him know what he'd suspected. That information, along with what many of the teachers were hearing, brought the picture into focus. Through a bit of sleuthing, the principal was able to figure out, with a high degree of certainty, who some of the kids were who had planned this weekend excursion. The principal drew up a list of names and called the parents of the kids on the list with the information about what these kids were up to.

Without exception, he was told to mind his own business. None of the parents thanked him for his diligence. The parents of the boy who used their credit card to book all the rooms were probably the angriest at the principal, feeling that somehow their privacy had been violated. What was so strange was that the principal didn't say what he suspected was going to go on at that resort, and most of the angry parents were upset by what he seemed to be insinuating—drinking and sex was going to go on—and yet all the kids ended up spending the weekend and the Monday after the prom as they'd planned.

My friend later learned through some of his close student confidantes that the weekend was essentially what he and the staff feared—

an alcohol-fueled forty-eight hours of uninhibited fun. Many of the students took part in a sex partner swapping game, using a deck of cards to determine who "hooked up" with whom.

PARENTAL DENIAL AND SEX

Many of the most blatant and most dangerous forms of parental denial come from this notion about sexual activity among their teens. While it is very easy to turn a blind eye to much of the behavior, this attitude only breeds problems in the long run. While Lauren's parents were aware of her drinking—they couldn't deny it was a problem after she was found by the campus police passed out in the bathroom of a men's dormitory at the college where they both taught—neither one of them wanted to think about all the possible implications of that location. It was far easier for them to concentrate on the illegal drinking than it was to consider why their daughter was in a men's dormitory and what she might have been doing there.

They didn't want to make the connection between Lauren's mood swings and her radical shifts in identity—from preppy girl to Goth vixen—in any other context than her going through a phase and being negatively influenced by her public school peers. As I've said previously, there's an undeniable connection between alcohol consumption and sexual activity. We're kidding ourselves as parents if we think there isn't. Teenage boys use alcohol to increase their chances of "scoring" with young women. Young women use alcohol to reduce their fears and inhibitions about engaging in sexual activity.

You don't have to watch a spring break "Girls Gone Wild" video to understand the connection between alcohol and promiscuity and high-risk sexual behaviors. Lauren's parents didn't want to see that obvious connection. They—and Lauren—were fortunate.

As Lauren later told me, "I guess in some ways it was a good thing I got shipped out here when I did. A few of my friends got into some really crazy stuff. They were having sex on camera, posing for photographers who put their stuff up on porn sites. I was tempted. It would have been fun. I mean, my body will never look this good, and to think of a bunch of guys getting off on seeing you naked had to make you feel pretty good."

Lauren's revelation of what she might have done is an object lesson for all of us. We do live in a very different world, and our kids' values and beliefs about sex and their bodies are different from ours. The kind of blatant exhibitionism and free-sex attitude that we thought was limited to the sixties and those "dirty hippies" pales in comparison to what our young people are witnessing and participating in today.

I sometimes wonder if it is going to take a father surfing the Web for porn sites and coming across his own daughter's photographs, or a family friend's daughter's photographs, to serve as the kind of wakeup call we may need.

If you do want to set up boundaries and develop a plan with consequences and rewards, short of frequent gynecological exams (which wouldn't be a very effective measure anyway), how do we check for compliance? How do we help our kids develop a healthy attitude toward sex without instilling paranoia and negative feelings about sexuality in our teens?

That's a lot of questions, isn't it? Here are a few points as we consider offsetting the current trends. They may give you some guidance in speaking with your teen and creating a situation you can both be comfortable with. It is important to communicate with your teen how you feel, whether you actively discourage the teen from engaging in sex or give your tacit or expressed "approval."

I know it sounds hard, and it is. This step is going to take all the powers of communication that you've cultivated and then some, but you can do it. Knowing what you know about the increase in incidence in teens' first experience with sex, you can choose a time that's most appropriate, but pick a time BEFORE you get to one of those critical points—whether that's the year in school, the proximity to a big dance or social event or birthday or other marker that may trigger the teen's desire to have intercourse. As is true of most important conversations, make sure to choose the right time and place. If you've thought this through far enough in advance, you can seize a teachable moment—when you're watching a movie or television show that deals with the issues of teens and sex—or, for that matter, adults and sex.

A possible opening would be something like this: "I know that you are getting to the age when sex is something you either think about a lot or are considering doing. I want you to have a good feeling about sex and a good experience with it. I don't think that it's appropriate for you to be sexually active, but statistics tell me that you might be soon. No matter what I say, you will make that decision yourself. I just want you to know as much as you can, so you can make an informed choice. Here are the things I want you to know":

- Vaginal penetration isn't the only means by which STDs can be transmitted.
- Oral sex is a sex act and not a casual interaction.
- It's your body—and you, and not any of your peers, romantic partners, or media personalities should tell you what to do with it.
- There is a double standard: girls who have sex are sluts; boys who do are studs. Don't be surprised when that rears its ugly head.
- You need to have respect for yourself and for your potential partner.
- Women are not here to merely gratify a man's needs.
- Don't pressure someone to have sex, and don't be pressured yourself into doing something you don't want to do.
- Pressuring someone or being pressured to have sex is a form of sexual abuse.
- If you even think you are in an abusive relationship, end it.
- If you know of someone who is an abusive relationship, encourage him or her to end it.
- If you know someone who is abusive, call them on their behavior.
- For any issues of abuse, if you aren't sure or are uncomfortable, talk with a trusted adult, preferably one of us.
- Sex is a natural part of emotionally intimate relationships. Developing a healthy attitude regarding sex is an important part of being an adult and maintaining relationships.
- What you do now may have negative consequences on your well-being—physical, emotional, and spiritual—down the line.

This is a long list, and it makes sense to break these issues down into smaller chunks and have these conversations over time. It's also important that you do your homework and are prepared to not just tell them your thoughts, but to answer any questions they may have. Preparation will also help to reduce some of your anxiety. Remember that if you communicate your discomfort too strongly, you're going to be sending a metamessage to your kids. I don't think that a PowerPoint presentation with charts and graphs and bullet points is appropriate, but do let your teens know that although the subject is important, like most things it can be handled with a light touch. With my own boys, I talk to them frequently about the issue of respect and women. Based on my experience in athletics and the military, I understand the demands of male culture and how it can distort a young man's perspective. Based on what I discussed earlier with regard to gender differences, we have to do whatever we can to get our young men's emotional development and sensitivity on track.

The Talk Continued

Of course, when you have one of these talks you should be open and attentive to the kind of feedback your teen gives you. If they're squirming with discomfort, then you may need to be less explicit. After each statement you make, check to see if your teen seems to be formulating a question. Your kid may be hesitant to ask, but you should be able to pick up on nonverbal cues by reading his or her expression, posture, and manners. Don't assume: Always check for and ask for feedback.

Also notice that you are making the assumption that your teen hasn't had sex yet. That's an expression of trust, and it's important to be prepared for how you will deal with your son or daughter revealing that he or she has already engaged in intercourse. As any good lawyer will tell you, never ask a question for which you haven't already anticipated an answer.

Everything I've said before about effective communication, operating from pure intention, and checking our own reality and values against those we want to transmit to our kids, still applies even though this is probably the most sensitive subject we will have to deal with. The best advice I can give you is to be as honest and open as you are comfortable being. If you approach your teen for one of "those talks" and you are on edge, you'll create all kinds of interference, and that will impede your efforts to communicate effectively. Your metamessage will say much the opposite of your words, and you could do more harm than good. It's difficult for our kids to believe that sex is a normal and natural part of adult life when we're sweating bullets and hemming and hawing like a seized-up tractor motor. If you're struggling with how to approach the subject, then seek help from someone you trust or from an expert in the field.

In raising kids, we often end up having to parent ourselves and confront some of the unresolved issues from our own past. History doesn't have to repeat itself. You can make a difference if you choose to, but you have to do your homework first. Whatever choice you make about dealing with your teen's sexuality, make sure to do it based on what you truly believe and not on your comfort level only. If you want your kids to be responsible, then you have to model that behavior by undertaking your responsibility to make certain that they get the best information and insights possible.

DON'T FORGET ABOUT DRINKING

In talking about drinking among teens, I referred to the connection between self-esteem, drinking, and sexual activity. I just want to remind you of those intertwined issues. When our kids feel good about themselves, have a strong foundation of values, and have parents who serve as strong role models, then it is far easier for them to withstand the pressure from peers and their environment that encourages the kind of acting out we are trying to prevent. Also, keep in mind that you aren't alone; there are other resources you can take advantage of. Don't fall into the trap of denying that you have options available to you. Don't fall into the trap of denying that your kid has self-esteem issues. All teens, to various degrees, have them. It's how well they hide them and how well they manage them that will tell the tale.

DON'T RELY ON THE SCHOOLS,
BUT DON'T AVOID THEM

Today, it's pretty easy to assume that our schools are taking care of educating our kids about sexual matters. As responsible parents we should know what kind of sex education curriculum and materials are being taught in the classroom. First, we need to know this to ensure that the values we hold dear are being reflected in that content and approach. Second, if we learn that those values are different from our own, we need to explain the discrepancies to our kids. Personally, I don't advocate removing your kids from these programs, for a couple of reasons.

Our kids need the information, and if we are aware of the specifics of what's being taught, then we can offer counterpoints to it. For example, if we believe our kids should remain abstinent and that exposing them to ideas like the use of condoms is only going to encourage them to have sex, then we need to offer an explanation for why the information is important while stressing that the value we hold is more important than that information or practice. Also, removing your kids from a sex education program or a portion of it is likely to cause them grief from teasing. This is a tough call, and if you hold a particular value very highly, then go with that and do what you think is right.

I also think we can do right by our kids by supporting and reinforcing what's being taught to them in the schools. We shouldn't just let this all happen in that one context, but bring the message home. Again, I actively encourage you to know what is going on in all of your children's classes. I say this as a mental health professional, as a fellow parent, and as someone who sits on his local school board. Unfortunately, our kids are often likely to be the worst source of that kind of information. Today, with the kind of information technology in many of our schools, teachers are encouraged to post the syllabi and course descriptions and even the daily calendar of assignments on the school's or their own Web sites.

I'm still kind of old fashioned and believe in face-to-face interactions. I always attend parent–teacher nights and make sure that I speak with each of my kids' teachers. I also let them know that if at any time one of my kids' work or behavior is slipping, I expect to be informed. I'm also not afraid to put my kids' teachers on notice that I expect them to help me keep my kids on track and in line. If they haven't posted their policies and procedures and course outline on the Web site or haven't handed them out at the meeting, or, better yet, haven't distributed them to each student and required a parent's signature to indicate that they have been reviewed, then ask for those materials.

DENIAL COMES IN ALL SIZES

Another teacher friend told me a story that illustrates how we as parents are sometimes the last to see because we want to remain blind. His school mainstreams special needs students into the regular classroom. That means that students who have been assessed with behavioral or learning disabilities sit side by side in some classes with other students not in the special education program. Ethan was a student with severe behavioral disabilities, but his parents didn't see it that way. Ethan had zero impulse control and the vulgar vocabulary of the foulest stand-up comedian. He frequently disrupted my friend's class, was prone to fits of rage when asked to leave class, and often had to be restrained from physically attacking fellow students.

Every suspension, every parent conference, every form of discipline wasn't working. He needed to be removed from a regular school environment. His parents fought that option at every turn. They placed the blame on ineffective teachers not willing to do their job. Finally, in order to convince the parents what needed to be done, my friend's classroom was hooked up with surveillance cameras and audio recording equipment. They filmed a series of typical Ethan days and showed the tape to the parents. It was heartbreaking and devastating to witness the parents' reaction. They could make it only through a brief portion before both were in tears.

"I had no idea. I had no idea," they both kept saying. Ethan was in the district's alternative placement program within a week. A month later his parents removed him from that school when nothing improved. My friend had no idea what happened to Ethan after that.

Again, perhaps an extreme case, but another example of how parents struggle to see what is right in front of them. Of course we need to believe the best about our kids, but we have to balance that with nearly constant reality checks. I also know that we sometimes don't pay as close attention as we ought to what the universe is trying to tell us. On at least one occasion I've talked to a parent of a player on my Legion baseball team and given some feedback about the kid: "Hey, I've noticed lately that Jeff seems really down on himself and agitated. He made an error today at short and came in the dugout and whipped his glove off and stomped it. That's not like him. Just thought you'd want to know."

If you as a parent hear something like that and have noticed something yourself or have had a teacher or even one of your other kids report something similar, you need to pay attention to those signs and signals. I know that with so much going on in our busy lives, its sometimes hard to pay attention to everything, but we also shouldn't tune it out purposely. It's not easy to hear bad or troubling things about our kids. They are a reflection of us and of how we treat them. Failing to listen to feedback may delay the inevitable, but it also magnifies it. If we pay attention to the warning signs, then we can intervene early. Reminds me of a saying I used at Spring Creek Lodge Academy: "If one person calls you a duck, probably no big deal, but if a hundred people call you a duck, you better check your butt for feathers."

Epilogue

I've got to be honest with you. I never thought I'd write a book. Mostly, I figured that I probably had something to say that was going to be of value to folks struggling with their teens. But how was I ever going to find the time?

After reading this, you know how important I think it is that we spend time with our kids—positive time. The rewards you'll likely get as a result of doing that one—admittedly not so simple—will likely amaze you. I also freely acknowledge that it is not always easy to find the time to spend with them. Their schedules and our own are often so jam-packed that it's difficult to find moments to even think about one another, let alone spend time in the same place with our loved ones.

Maybe it's easier for me to do because Trout Creek is a pretty simple place, with few of the distractions of a big city. For us, a multiplex theater means that the kids are watching one DVD on the computer while Janna and I watch another on the television in the family room. On the other hand, our lives aren't any less complex than yours probably are. I've got a job to go to every day, and commitments to run the school board, to coach baseball, to volunteer for this or that community project. As understanding as the kids at Spring Creek always were about the times when I couldn't extend my sessions because I had to be with my family, I still felt a strong sense of obligation to be at school with them and with my kids. I confess that I was torn, and only after I stopped banging my head against the proverbial wall did I realize how painful it was to work fifty to sixty hours a week at Spring Creek and at home, as well as carry on a full family life. Some people say that you can't serve two masters, but my daddy had another way of putting it. At some point, he liked to say, you get yourself to where your mouth is writing checks your backside can't cash. I can be in only one place at one time, and I was stretched pretty thin.

Now, I'm not looking for sympathy, just letting you know that I can empathize with you. A lot of what I say about how to help your teens and you develop a better relationship will take time and effort— *lots* of both. That's just how it is. I know we live in a "Hey, Doc, write me up a 'script' so's I can get this thing fixed right away" kind of world. Sometimes I think that may be part of the reason why we find our kids in the mess they're in. Having to give up some of what little free time we have to focus on our children isn't always a lot of fun. It cuts into our freedom, can make us feel a bit powerless, and will make us question our sense of belonging. But it's work we have to do. Maybe we're all paying the piper now for the lack of time and attention we spent on our kids earlier. I can't say for certain that's true in every situation, but it's true in an awful lot of them.

In any case, I just want to let you know that I faced the same dilemma. Not for exactly the same reasons as above, but I did have to question where my priorities were and how I could be best of service to young people and my family. That's why I chose to leave Spring Creek. At first I was doing it to pursue another opportunity—to start up another alternative school, to build something from the ground up. I was flattered to have the opportunity, to have someone place enough faith in me to let me be in charge of the operation. Totally cool. Something I wouldn't or couldn't have dreamed of when I was first in private practice, struggling to get clients to keep their appointments with me.

I changed my mind.

I didn't want to make that kind of time commitment at that juncture in my life. I was eagerly looking forward to a new challenge, but I had several other challenges that needed tending to. First, of course, was my own growing family. My daughter, Alicia, will be going off to college for the first time just about when this book will be published.

Some definite beginnings and endings are associated with the prospect of her enrolling in school and leaving home. Our two boys will be in high school, and if their years are anything like Alicia's were, they will be gone and done in a blink of an eye. I tried as hard as I could, but I'm sure I missed some parts of Alicia's years in high school. I'm sorry if I did, and I don't want to make that mistake again. While I'm going to miss the challenge of starting up a school and working with at-risk kids, I don't regret the choice I made. Family comes first. It's not going to be easy on us financially, but sacrifices need to be made.

Something else happened while I was writing this book and making all these decisions about our collective future. I lost my father to a long bout with respiratory illness. I've quoted my dad pretty frequently and mentioned him a lot. How our relationship shifted from his taking care of me and my siblings to our taking care of him is a long story for another time. What I'm most grateful for, though, is that my dad taught me enough lessons about how to take care of myself. He gave me enough rope—not so I would hang myself but so I would know what it was like to be free and feel the painful tug when I went too far. Because of everything he taught me about duty, responsibility, owning up to and understanding consequences, and having my priorities right, I was prepared to deal with assisting him and my mom at this stage in their lives. I wasn't prepared for losing him, and that's in a lot of ways a good thing and a measure of just how much I loved him and respected him.

My dad was tough; I can't deny that. As I got older I could see both sides of that toughness—the respect among family and peers it earned him and the stubbornness and refusal to accept help that sometimes made the transformation in his relationship with his kids less than smooth. If one of the shifts in our evolving role with our kids is to have them see us for who we are, warts and all, then my relationship with my dad was a pretty good example. Over time I realized he wasn't perfect, and that was okay with me.

I guess what I'm trying to say is that parenting and the relationships (and yes, I do mean for that to be plural) we have with any one of our kids is about the most complex relationship we have with anyone on the planet. We're responsible, literally, for that life existing. I don't want to get all philosophical on you, but please stop sometime and consider that.

I realize now that I'm at or near the end of a lot of things—the relationship with my dad, one phase of my career, one phase of my relationship with my daughter—but I'm also at the beginning of a lot of other things as well. Losing my dad made me want to spend more time with my family. It also made me want to do more, to be of greater service than I have ever been before. That's why I'm back in private practice, still working with kids. Janna and I have given a lot of thought about starting a group home right here at our house in Trout Creek. We've already taken in one young man whose life has been out of control for a while now. He's going to see if he can make a go of it here with us. If he can, then maybe we'll expand our operation. Even if he can't, we may still expand. I'm learning to let go of perfection.

Just because you let go of something or someone doesn't mean that it will leave you. Just before I sat down to write this, I logged onto my computer and checked my e-mail and there were a few messages from former Spring Creek kids. They were checking in on me to see how I was doing, to update me on their lives. I also went to MySpace and checked up on a few I hadn't heard from in a while—looking to see if their lives were shaping up the way we'd expected them to when they left Spring Creek. As long as those kids are out there, I'll still be worrying and wondering about them. That's not just what I do but who I am. I can change one but not the other.

Among the e-mails was a note from Lauren, the young woman you met in Chapter One. She told me to be sure to check my mail in the next few weeks. An invitation to her first child's baptism was on its way to us. Not so long ago, it seems, Janna and I had attended her wedding. I penciled the date into my calendar. It's good to have things like this to look forward to.

I'm hoping that the lessons Lauren learned will make her a good parent, that she'll be able to break the cycle before it gets too deeply ingrained.

I don't have a lot of time to think about that. The shadows are starting to lengthen. I've got some cows to go feed and a mile or so of fence to check on. Then it'll be time to sit down for supper with the kids. It will be good to have them all, plus one, at home. I hope you get to experience that same feeling I do every day.

The Most Painful Choice—When It Is Not Working to Have Your Kid at Home Anymore

The point of this book is to give you the tools and information you need to make sure that you don't end up like the parents of Greg, Justine, Dave, Christina, and Danijela. They all came to the conclusion that it was no longer possible for that child to live at home. I mentioned previously that one of the first steps in any remediation program is to create a vision for how you want your household to function. If the changes and adjustments you make don't bring that vision to life, and you are not comfortable with the revised version of what your life and your family's lives are like, then it is probably time to consider other options.

The first option is to seek help from someone outside the family. This can be a trusted religious person, such as a priest or minister, or a certified mental health care professional. Sometimes the intervention of an agent from outside the family can bring a perspective and detached point of view and insight that we lack when we're caught up in the middle of what seems to be a battle of epic proportions and a test of wills that exhausts us and dominates our lives. If the environment is unhealthy and the teen seems unwilling or incapable of changing, then one option is to change the environment. Notice what I said above: that the child has to be willing to change or be capable of changing. When deciding whether a change of your child's residence is in order, we have to do an honest assessment of our teen. We ask ourselves these questions:

- Does the child recognize that things are spiraling out of control?
- Does the child want help?

Next, assess what steps we've already taken and their effectiveness:

- Has the child attended individual therapy?
- Has the family attended family therapy?
- Does the child have a drug or alcohol problem? If so, have we tried both inpatient and outpatient chemical dependency treatment programs?
- Have we ruled out all possible medical problems?
- Have we consulted with our family physician, school administrators and professionals, and others involved in the child's treatment?
- Have we investigated other possible living arrangements, and are they a real, viable, safe option? (Typically, kids needing this level of care will not do well with Grandma and Grandpa or other relatives and friends.)

Most important, you need to assess the potential threat level your child poses to him or herself and others:

- Is there a danger to other siblings?
- Is the child a danger to self?
- Is the child a danger to parents, grandparents, or others?
- Is this a vague potential threat, an imminent threat (one the child has stated or acted on and then stopped him or herself or been halted by others), or has the child already acted in a way that endangers him or herself or others?

If the answer to that last question is that the threat is imminent or the child has already engaged in dangerous activities, then you need to act sooner rather than later. If you haven't spoken with your teen's school psychologist, you need to do so immediately. If you haven't spoken with a therapist in private practice, you need to do so immediately. If the threat is imminent, or if a repeat of any dangerous behavior (e.g., suicide attempt, running away from home) has occurred, then a trip to a local hospital and its emergency room is in order. Once there, you can be assured that your child will be safe and that either there or at some other health center, your child will undergo a psychiatric evaluation and a more thorough threat assessment will be done.

The safety of our teens, our other children, ourselves, and others is of paramount importance. Once you've done what needs to be done to ensure that no harm will come to your child or to others, you can investigate options for placement outside the home:

Step 1. Ensure your child's safety.

Step 2. Contact an experienced, reliable educational consultant.

Step 3. Ensure that your child is safe.

Step 4. When the educational consultant comes back with recommendations, check out the suggested course of action and narrow your options.

Step 5. Ensure that your child is safe.

Step 6. Visit the residential programs and make your selection.

Step 7. Figure out how to get your child there. This is huge, and I know of many parents who have had to lie and manipulate to make this happen. Some parents have found it necessary to hire professional child escorts to move the child from the home to the new placement. Some people feel this is kidnapping. I have heard that drastic times call for drastic measures.

Step 8. Once your child arrives at the newly chosen program, and you are sure the child is safe, you must stay in close contact while allowing the professionals to do their work. Hold the program accountable, but HOLD YOUR TEEN ACCOUNTABLE FIRST!

Step 9. Take care of yourself. It is time to rejuvenate, engage in therapy, talk to a clergyperson—whatever it takes for you to deal with your guilt and grief. Good parents have children in programs, too!

Step 10. Engage in the program process with your child. You must be a part of the solution. When your child comes home, conditions must be different. This is where we go back through the things we talked about in the book and create a new environment for your teen to function in. Kids do much better when they know what to expect and it remains consistent.

I can't stress the importance of Step 9 enough. You have to take care of yourself. As parents we are caregivers, and women in particular are susceptible to what I call caregiver syndrome. It's become a kind of joke, but the line "I do and I do for you, and this is the thanks I get?" is a reality for a lot of mothers. They work themselves to the point of physical and mental exhaustion and tap out their reserve of patience and nurturing. Above all, be patient with yourself and nurture yourself.

Managing your guilt and grief and anger is essential if the changes that will take place in your child are going to remain in place once the child comes home. You can't work yourself to the point of exhaustion. Taking care of yourself will help you take better care of your other children and your troubled teen when the teen returns.

A NOTE ON ACADEMICS

Therapeutic schools like Spring Creek and others serve best the students who have behavioral problems, histories of chemical dependency, and other serious acting out issues. While a few students have been enrolled because of academic issues, I don't believe that a place like Spring Creek is best for them. The primary reason is that most of these kids, in order to fit in socially, will adapt the behaviors of the more hard-core kids, for lack of a better term. You may send your low-achieving child off to a therapeutic program hoping that the discipline and structure of such a program will help the child get back on track academically, but your child may end up with an education in acting out and exposure to teens the child would likely never encounter back home. Work with your local school district, private tutors, alternative programs, or a private preparatory school before even considering a therapeutic school like Spring Creek.

WHAT QUESTIONS TO ASK AND WHAT TO LOOK FOR
IN A RESIDENTIAL PROGRAM

1. Are you licensed by the state you reside in?
2. Are you a member of the National Association of Therapeutic Schools and Programs?
3. What part in treatment does the family play?
4. How often will I have telephone contact with my child?
5. How often will I be allowed to visit my child?

6. What are the costs of the program?
7. What are the costs that are not listed in your brochure?
8. What does it cost to have my child transported to medical appointments, the airport, and so on?
9. What is your staff-to-student ratio?
10. What is the average tenure of your staff?
11. Who are your staff, and what are their qualifications?
12. Who will be consistently in contact with me to update me on my child's progress?
13. Has your facility ever had allegations of misconduct investigated by your state's DHHS (Department of Health and Human Services) or DCFS (Department of Children and Family Services)?
14. What does the structure of the program look like, and how does my child advance?
15. Will I be a part of treatment planning?
16. How long does the average teen stay in this program?
17. What are your discharge criteria?
18. Do you have a list of references (prior students, prior families, community members who are familiar with the program and its local reputation)?
19. How is the initial treatment planning initiated?
20. Will the program be able to meet the educational needs of my teen?
21. What efforts will be made to promote pro-social behaviors?
22. What methods are used to eliminate maladaptive social behaviors?
23. What behaviors would be considered "zero tolerance" for my teen in your program?
24. What does the daily schedule look like?
25. What will my child's diet consist of?
26. Will my child's weight be monitored? (Many children gain fifteen to twenty pounds a few months after being enrolled in a program.)

By being actively involved in your child's program, you will better understand what you need to do and what your teen needs from you in order to function effectively at home. You will learn strategies, adapt and fine-tune old ones, rid yourself of bad habits, and be better prepared for and more flexible in the face of change.

And positive change is what we all hope for as a result of a child's entrance into a residential program. You may be curious about the outcome of my work with Greg, Justine, Dave, Christina, and Danijela. I keep in contact with many of my former students, sometimes just to keep abreast of what they're up to, other times to assist them as they transition back into their families and others lives. I've been invited to several weddings, and I've seen photos of their babies and new homes.

Sadly, Greg is not one of the success stories. The kind of abuse and abandonment he experienced at such a young age was difficult for him to overcome. He did successfully complete our program, but he never stayed in touch with any of the staff. I only heard about him through a friend he'd made at Spring Creek. He decided to join the military, and even with his checkered past he managed to get in, but he was bounced out during basic training. The last word we had about Greg was that he was working road construction jobs when he could find them, was drinking fairly heavily, and was living alone.

Justine, on the other hand, was able to come to terms with her eating disorder and hyperanxieties. She completed her high school education, enrolled in a junior college back home, and got married. She, her husband, and their baby daughter moved across the country. Justine and her mother managed to work out their differences, and, as Justine told me, "Having 1,500 miles separating us made it a lot easier to be close." Thrill-seeking bad boy Dave didn't manage to fulfill his parents' dream of attending an Ivy League university, but he did graduate from college and now works in the information technology department of a major investment firm in New York. He hasn't turned over a car in years, though he told me that every now and then a cab that splashes him with pothole water has him considering his options.

Christina, the young Thai-American woman with the demanding parents, managed to stay drug and alcohol free during her stay with us. When she returned home, she found it difficult to adjust, and for a while she fell back in with the same crowd, including, as she later described him, "her fucktard" boyfriend. She soon grew tired of all the partying and enrolled herself in a paralegal program, and she now works for a large law firm in Chicago. Her parents still have high hopes that she will attend law school, and she recently took the LSAT but hasn't yet applied to any schools.

Danijela's story was always one of the more heartbreaking ones for me. Her father's violation of trust nearly destroyed the entire family. While at Spring Creek, Danijela was stuck between a rock and a hard place. She knew she really didn't belong there, but she also didn't want to go back home. Finally, she contacted an aunt back home in Serbia, who agreed to let her move in with her. All those hours spent in Serbian school classrooms paid off. She attended university there, just recently graduated, and is now spending the summer traveling through Europe. She has dual citizenship and can't decide whether she wants to work in the United States or her native country or elsewhere. Her postcards are always welcome. I also just learned that her mother and sister are joining her for one leg of the trip. She made no mention of her father.

Those are just a few of the many success stories. Here's to your being able to share yours with me at some point very soon.

Your Rights as a Parent

While it is impossible to specify what rights you have as a taxpayer in your state, be aware that your public schools are obliged to provide for the special needs of your child. That doesn't mean that your child has to be assessed with a learning disability, a behavioral disorder, or a physical disability, or be considered a "special education" student, to qualify for programs outside the bounds of the mainstream classroom or school.

Most states and their departments of education have developed statements of parents' rights and make them available. With Internet access so pervasive today, a quick Google search should enable you to find that statement.

Even better, consult with members of your local school's staff and administration if you feel your child's needs aren't being met. In general, my advice is to not take no for an answer if you are told that nothing additional can be done to help your child succeed. Don't be afraid to climb the ladder and go to the school board if you have additional questions or concerns, or if your questions or concerns haven't been handled satisfactorily. Your local Parent Teacher Association may also be of some use. In Appendix C, I've listed some other parent and education advocacy groups that can help you sort through any issues you might be having.

Appendix C

Resources for Parents

BOOKS

Bradley, Michael J., Ed. *Yes, Your Teen Is Crazy: Loving Your Kid Without Losing Your Mind.* Gig Harbor, Washington: Harbor Press, 2003.

deBecker, Gavin. *Protecting the Gift: Keeping Children and Teenagers Safe (and Parents Sane).* New York: Dial Press, 1999.

Hart, Betsy. *It Takes a Parent: How the Culture of Pushover Parenting Is Hurting Our Kids and What to Do About It.* New York: Penguin Group USA, 2005.

Kindlon, Dan and Michael Thompson. *Raising Cain: Protecting the Emotional Life of Boys.* New York: Ballantine Books, 1999.

Pipher, Mary. *Reviving Ophelia: Saving the Selves of Adolescent Girls.* New York: Ballantine Books, 1994.

Simmons, Rachel. *Odd Girl Out: The Hidden Culture of Girls' Aggression.* Orlando, Florida: Harcourt Brace, 2001.

Tannen, Deborah. *You're Wearing That? Understanding Mothers and Daughters in Conversation.* New York: Random House, 2006.

Wiseman, Rosalind. *Queen Bees and Wannabes: Helping Your Daughter Survive Cliques, Gossip, Boyfriends and Other Realities of Adolescence.* New York: Three Rivers Press, 2002.

Zodkevitch, Ron. *The Tough Love Prescription: How to Create and Enforce Boundaries for Your Teen.* New York: McGraw-Hill, 2006.

ORGANIZATIONS AND WEB SITES

Depression and Suicide

Kids Health
www.kidshealth.org

National Alliance on Mental Illness
Colonial Place Three
2107 Wilson Boulevard, Suite 300
Arlington, VA 22201-3042
(703) 524-7600
www.nami.org

National Institute of Mental Health
www.nimh.nih.gov/healthinformation/depressionmenu.cfm

Youth Suicide Prevention Program
444 NE Ravena Boulevard, #401
Seattle, WA 98115
(206) 297-5922
800-273-TALK (8255)
info@yspp.org
www.yspp.org

Drinking

MADD (Mothers Against Drunk Driving)
511 E. John Carpenter Freeway, Suite 700
Irving, TX 75062
(800) GET-MADD (438-6233)
(877) MADD-HELP (623-3435)
www.madd.org

National Capital Coalition to Prevent Underage Drinking
1616 P Street NW, Suite 430
Washington, DC 20036
(202) 265-8922
info@nccpud.com

Stop Underage Drinking
www.stopalcoholabuse.gov/default.aspx

Drugs

Just Say No Foundation
1777 North California Boulevard
Walnut Creek, CA 94596
(415) 939-6666
www.justsayno.org

National Clearinghouse for Alcohol and Drug Information (NCADI)
P.O. Box 2345
Rockville, MD 20852
(301) 468-2600
www.ncadi.samhsa.gov

National Institute on Drug Abuse (NIDA)
www.nida.gov

NIDA for Teens
www.teens.drugabuse.gov

NIDA for Parents and Teachers
www.nida.nih.gov/parent-teacher.html

Eating Disorders

Kids Health for Parents
www.kidshealth.org/parent/emotions/feelings/eating_disorders.html

National Eating Disorders Association
603 Stewart Street, Suite 803
Seattle, WA 98101
(206) 382-3587
(800) 931-2237
info@NationalEatingDisorders.org

National Institute of Mental Health
www.nimh.nih.gov/publicat/eatingdisorders.cfm
www.nlm.nih.gov/medlineplus/eatingdisorders.html

Sex

Campaign for Our Children
www.cfoc.org/Home

Sexual Information and Education Council
103 West 42nd Street, Suite 350
New York, NY 10036
(212) 819-9770
www.siecus.org

Sexual Violence

Corporate Alliance to End Partner Violence
2416 East Washington, Suite E
Bloomington, IL 61704
(309) 664-0747
www.caepv.org

National Coalition Against Domestic Violence
1532 16th Street NW
Washington, DC 20036
(202) 745-0088
www.ncadv.org

Violence

Center for the Study and Prevention of Violence
Attn: Delbert Elliott, Director
Institute of Behavioral Science, University of Colorado
Campus Box 442, Building #10
Boulder, CO 80309
(303) 492-8465
www.colorado.edu/cspv

Coalition for Juvenile Justice
Attn: David J. Doi, Executive Director
1211 Connecticut Avenue NW, #414
Washington, DC 20036
(202) 467-0864
juvjustice@aol.com
www.nassembly.org/html/mem_cjj.html

Coalition to Stop Gun Violence
1000 16th Street NW, Suite 603
Washington, DC 20002-5625
(202) 530-0340
www.gunfree.org
www.csgv.org

GREAT (Gang Resistance Education and Training)
Attn: Essam Rabazi, Special Agent in Charge
U.S. Department of Treasury
800 K Street NW, Suite 750
Washington, DC 20001

(202) 565-4560
great@atfhq.atf.treas.gov
www.atf.treas.gov/great/great.htm

Office of Juvenile Justice and Delinquency Prevention
Juvenile Justice Clearinghouse
Attn: Shay Bilchik, Administrator
P.O. Box 6000
Rockville, MD 20857
(800) 638-8736
bilchik@ojp.usdoj.gov
www.ojjdp.ncjrs.org

U.S. Department of Education: Safe and Drug Free Schools Program
400 Maryland Avenue SW, Room 1073
Washington, DC 20202
(202) 260-3954

Index

About the Author

Mike Linderman is a licensed counselor who has worked with teens for more than ten years. A veteran of the first Gulf War, he has been married for twenty years and is the proud father of three healthy teens. He lives in Trout Creek, Montana.

Gary Brozek is a former high school teacher turned freelance writer. Based in Evergreen, Colorado he has coauthored or ghostwritten more than ten books on a variety of subjects.